Theory and Practice of Documents for
International Business Bilingual Coursebook (Third Edition)

国际商务单证理论与实务双语教程（第3版）

杨　静　主编

杨鑫坡　刘艳萍　副主编

清华大学出版社
北京

内 容 简 介

本书是为培养涉外经济部门所需的既能熟练掌握外贸专业知识，又能熟练运用专业英语从事进出口业务的复合型人才而专门编写的教材，旨在帮助学习者在熟练掌握专业知识的基础上用英语进行商务活动，并熟练掌握国际贸易相关条款和单证制作。每章有对应的填单、改错练习和案例分析，深入浅出，易于学习掌握。全书中英文对照，兼顾外贸专业和非外贸专业人员的需要，介绍了进出口贸易过程中主要单证缮制的方法和遇到的问题，操作性强。所选案例内容全面、新颖，不仅涵盖了制单的全过程，而且多为近几年来我国对外贸易领域发生的最新案例，实用性强。

本书可作为高等院校国际贸易、国际商务、国际物流、商务英语专业学生的教材，也适合作为外销员、单证员和跟单员的工具书，还可供制单员在资格考试前复习、练习使用。

本书有配套的教学课件和学习网站，满足立体化教材建设的需要，可通过扫描前言中的二维码获取。

本书封面贴有清华大学出版社防伪标签，无标签者不得销售。
版权所有，侵权必究。举报：010-62782989，beiqinquan@tup.tsinghua.edu.cn。

图书在版编目(CIP)数据

国际商务单证理论与实务双语教程 / 杨静主编. —3版. —北京：清华大学出版社，2022.9
ISBN 978-7-302-61606-1

Ⅰ.①国⋯ Ⅱ.①杨⋯ Ⅲ.①国际贸易－票据－双语教学－高等学校－教材 Ⅳ.①F740.44

中国版本图书馆CIP数据核字(2022)第140697号

责任编辑：高 屾
封面设计：常雪影
版式设计：方加青
责任校对：马遥遥
责任印制：宋 林

出版发行：清华大学出版社
网　　址：http://www.tup.com.cn，http://www.wqbook.com
地　　址：北京清华大学学研大厦A座　　邮　编：100084
社 总 机：010-83470000　　邮　购：010-62786544
投稿与读者服务：010-62776969，c-service@tup.tsinghua.edu.cn
质 量 反 馈：010-62772015，zhiliang@tup.tsinghua.edu.cn

印 装 者：三河市金元印装有限公司
经　　销：全国新华书店
开　　本：185mm×260mm　　印　张：18.75　　字　数：422千字
版　　次：2015年8月第1版　2022年9月第3版　印　次：2022年9月第1次印刷
定　　价：68.00元

产品编号：083874-01

编写委员会

主　编 杨　静
副主编 杨鑫坡　刘艳萍
编写成员（按姓氏笔画）
　　　　　刘　婷　陈　英
　　　　　胡维娜　梁玉恒

前 言
Preface

本书是为培养涉外经济部门所需要的既能熟练掌握外贸专业知识，又能熟练运用专业英语从事进出口业务的复合型人才而专门编写的教材，旨在帮助学习者在熟练掌握专业知识的基础上用英语进行商务活动开展全球贸易，并熟练掌握国际贸易相关条款和单证制作。

本书可作为高等院校经济管理类相关专业学生学习国际贸易的辅助教材，也可作为从事国际贸易工作的专业人士的自学参考书，主要有以下几个特色。

(1) 中英文对照，操作性强。本书兼顾外贸专业和非外贸专业人员的需要，全文采用英汉对照方式介绍进出口贸易过程中经常遇到的单证缮制及相关问题，为学习者提供一个在学习专业知识的同时提高英语应用能力的平台。

(2) 所选用的外贸单证案例内容全面、新颖，具有典型性和普遍性，非常适合双语案例教学。

(3) 本书可搭配本课题组编写的《国际商务单证实训教程》(第2版)(清华大学出版社，ISBN：978-7-302-40933-5)使用，方便学习者进行实践操练，实现真正的学做结合。实训深入浅出，易于学习掌握。

(4) 本书有配套的教学课件和学习网站，满足立体化教材建设的需要。

本书经过两次改版，受到众多老师、学生的好评，并被选为区级一流本科课程指定教材。第3版本着精益求精的原则，做了以下改进。

教学资源

(1) 第3版在保持前两版特色的基础上，更新了陈旧的数据，并调整了相关的图表、样例等，同时，对部分文字内容进行了修订。

(2) 第3版加入了大量立体化教学资源，做到一屏三端(电脑屏，纸质端、电脑端、手机端)，方便读者随时随地利用碎片化时间学习。读者可通过扫描右侧二维码，获取配套的慕课学习网站地址和相关教学资源(包括教学课件、习题答案等)。

全书共分11章。前3章主要介绍国际商务单证理论，后8章为国际商务单证实务部分。其中，第4章至第9章分别介绍交易单证、运输单证、出口单证、进口单证、银行单证和特殊单证。第10章主要介绍电子商务和国际贸易单证的发展。第11章主要介绍国际商务单证实用英语，方便读者自学。后8章每章都包括三个方面的主要内容：第一，详细分析制单技巧及常见错误；第二，制单示范；第三，精选单证案例分析，为学习者提供一个解决国际商务单证问题的思路。

编者在编写过程中得到了广西财经学院经贸学院刘婷等多位老师的帮助，也得到了经贸学院的学生们的帮助。美国Shawn Frazier教授为该书英文校对做了大量工作。另外，编者在编写时参阅了多种国内外相关著作和刊物，在此一并表示衷心的感谢！

由于编者水平和学识有限，难免出现差错、疏漏的地方，敬请读者不吝指正。

编者

2022 年 5 月

目录
Contents

Chapter 1　Overview of International Trade Documentation
　　　　　外贸单证概况 ·· 1

　1.1　The Meaning and Role of International Trade Documentation
　　　　外贸单证的定义与作用 ··· 1

　1.2　The Main Kinds of International Trade Documentation
　　　　外贸单证的主要类型 ·· 4

　1.3　The Parties to International Trade Documentation
　　　　外贸单证当事人 ··· 6

　1.4　The Basic Requirements for International Trade Documentation
　　　　外贸单证的基本要求 ·· 14

　1.5　Checklist for Documentation Errors
　　　　单证纠错内容 ·· 15

　1.6　Prerequisites of Documentation
　　　　单证制作的先决条件 ·· 16

　1.7　The Basic Materials of Making out International Trade Documents
　　　　缮制外贸单证的基础材料 ··· 18

　1.8　Development of International Trade Documents
　　　　外贸单证的发展 ··· 18

　1.9　Relevant International Regulations and Practices
　　　　相关国际规则和惯例 ·· 18

Chapter 2　Management and Operation of International Trade Documents
　　　　　外贸单证管理及制作流程 ··· 22

　2.1　Making Documents
　　　　单证的制作 ··· 22

　2.2　The Basis and Operation Process of Making Out Documents
　　　　制单基础与流程 ··· 25

2.3 Examination of Documents
审核单据 ··· 29

2.4 Presentation of Documents
交单 ··· 41

2.5 Management of Documents
单证的管理 ··· 45

Chapter 3 Basic Knowledge
基础知识 ·· 47

3.1 Terms of Payment
付款方式 ··· 47

3.2 Contract for the Sale of Goods
货物销售合同 ··· 55

3.3 Clauses Concerning Documents in the Sales Contract
销售合同中的单证条款 ··· 58

Chapter 4 Transaction Documents
交易单证 ·· 61

4.1 Keys on Transaction Documents
交易单证要点 ··· 61

4.2 The Flow of Transaction Documents
交易单证制作流程 ··· 62

4.3 Kinds of International Transaction Documents
交易单证种类 ··· 63

Chapter 5 Transport Documents
运输单证 ·· 84

5.1 Bill of Lading
提单 ··· 85

5.2 Packing List
装箱单 ··· 102

5.3 Other Certificates
其他证明书 ··· 109

Chapter 6 Export Documentation
出口单证 ·· 110

6.1 Documents Required Before or at Contract Negotiation
合同谈判中或之前所需单证 ··· 111

6.2 Documents Involved in Goods Preparation
备货时涉及的单证 ··· 113

6.3 Documents Concerning Mandatory Inspection
　　与强制检验有关的单证·············113

6.4 Documents Involved in Transportation
　　运输时涉及的单证·················116

6.5 Documents needed for Export Customs Clearance
　　出口清关需要的单证···············117

6.6 Documents Received after Shipment
　　装运后收到的单证·················124

6.7 Insurance Documents
　　保险单证·························126

6.8 Documents for Bank Negotiation
　　银行议付单证·····················134

6.9 Exporter's Instruction Documents
　　出口商指示单证···················152

6.10 Electronic Filling of Documents
　　电子填单·························153

6.11 A Summary of Export Documents
　　出口单证小结·····················153

Chapter 7　Import Documents
　　进口单证·····························157

7.1 Definitions
　　定义·····························157

7.2 Basic Requirement for Making Import Documentation
　　进口制单的基本要求···············157

7.3 Import Licenses, Permits and Declarations
　　进口许可证和进口报关单···········159

7.4 Documents Required by the Import Authority
　　进口国当局需要的单证·············160

7.5 Special Import Transport Documents
　　特殊的进口运输单证···············163

7.6 Banking and International Exchange Documents
　　银行单证和外汇单证···············164

Chapter 8　Banking Documents
　　银行单证·····························166

8.1 Method of Payment
　　支付方式·························166

8.2 International Banking Documents
　　国际银行单证 ··· 168

8.3 Drafts, Bills of Exchange and Acceptances
　　汇票和承兑汇票 ··· 171

8.4 Documentary Letters of Credit
　　跟单信用证 ·· 173

8.5 Document Movement for Issuance of a L/C
　　信用证开立的单证流程 ··· 178

8.6 Document Movement for Amendment to a L/C
　　信用证修改的单证流程 ··· 179

8.7 Opening a Documentary Credit
　　开立跟单信用证 ··· 180

8.8 Document and Goods Movement for Utilization of a L/C
　　信用证下单证和货物的流转 ·· 181

8.9 Discrepancies with Documents
　　单证不符点 ·· 183

8.10 Documentary Collections
　　跟单托收 ··· 184

8.11 Documentary Collections and Documentary Credits
　　跟单托收和跟单信用证 ··· 184

8.12 Documents and Goods Movement in a Documentary Collection
　　跟单托收下单证和货物的流程 ··· 185

Chapter 9　Special Documents
　　特殊单证 ··· 188

9.1 Inspection Documents
　　检验单证 ··· 188

9.2 Insurance
　　保险 ··· 189

9.4 Trade Agreement and Trade Preference Documents
　　贸易协定和贸易优惠单证 ··· 192

9.5 Export Drawback
　　出口退税 ··· 195

Chapter 10　Electronic Commerce and International Trade Documents
　　电子商务和国际贸易单证 ··· 196

10.1 E-Commerce and International Trade
　　电子商务和国际贸易 ·· 196

10.2　E-Documents and E-Payment
　　　电子单证与单证付款 ·· 197

10.3　Electronic Documentation in International Trade
　　　国际贸易中的电子单证 ·· 198

Chapter 11　Practical English of International Business Documents English
　　　　　　　国际商务单证实用英语 ·· 200

11.1　Practical English of Expressions of Documents
　　　实用单证英语表达 ·· 200

11.2　Application of International Trade Documents English
　　　国际商务单证英语应用 ·· 206

Sample 单证样例 ·· 213
Key to Assignment 练习题参考答案 ······································ 245
Appendix 附录 ·· 253

附录1　国际贸易单证业务中的计算 ··· 253
附录2　信用证结算审单准则 ··· 265
附录3　集装箱种类和规格 ·· 266
附录4　币制符号代码表 ··· 268
附录5　报关条件代码表 ··· 268
附录6　贸易方式代码表 ··· 269
附录7　运输方式代码表 ··· 271
附录8　成交方式代码表 ··· 272
附录9　各类商品投保险别参考表 ·· 272
附录10　运输方式代码表 ··· 276
附录11　征免税方式代码表 ·· 276
附录12　报关代码表 ··· 276
附录13　收结汇方式代码表 ·· 282

Resources 参考文献 ·· 284

样例索引
Sample Index

Sample 3-1 Sales Contract
样单 3-1 销售合同··213

Sample 4-1 Purchase Contract
样单 4-1 购货合同··214

Sample 4-2 Proforma Invoice
样单 4-2 形式发票··217

Sample 4-3 Commercial Invoice
样单 4-3 商业发票··218

Sample 5-1 Bill of Lading
样单 5-1 提单··219

Sample 5-2 Ocean Bill of Lading
样单 5-2 海运提单··220

Sample 5-3 Air Waybill
样单 5-3 航空运单··221

Sample 5-4 Combined Transport B/L
样单 5-4 联合运输提单··222

Sample 5-5 Packing List
样单 5-5 装箱单··223

Sample 6-1 Export Licence
样单 6-1 出口货物许可证··224

Sample 6-2 Entry Application Form for Inspection
样单 6-2 入境货物报检单··225

Sample 6-3 Export Application Form for Inspection
样单 6-3 出境货物报检单··226

Sample 6-4 Shipping Note
样单 6-4 出口货物订舱委托书··227

Sample 6-5　Import Shipping Note
样单 6-5　进口订舱委托书··· 228

Sample 6-6　Shipping Order
样单 6-6　托运单·· 228

Sample 6-7　Customs Declaration for Export Commodity
样单 6-7　出口货物报关单·· 229

Sample 6-8　Shipping Advice
样单 6-8　装船通知·· 230

Sample 6-9　Insurance Application Form
样单 6-9　投保单·· 231

Sample 6-10　Insurance Policy
样单 6-10　保险单·· 232

Sample 6-11　Bill of Exchange
样单 6-11　汇票··· 233

Sample 6-12　Certificate of Origin
样单 6-12　原产地证书··· 234

Sample 6-13　Generalized System of Preferences Certificate of Origin
样单 6-13　普惠制原产地证书·· 235

Sample 6-14　Canada Customs Invoice
样单 6-14　加拿大海关发票·· 236

Sample 7-1　Import Licence of the People's Republic of China
样单 7-1　中华人民共和国进口货物许可证·························· 238

Sample 7-2　Customs Import Declaration of China
样单 7-2　中华人民共和国海关进口货物报关单··················· 239

Sample 7-3　Shipper's Letter of Instruction
样单 7-3　国际货物托运书··· 240

Sample 8-1　Irrevocable Documentary Credit Application
样单 8-1　不可撤销跟单信用证申请······································ 241

Sample 9-1　Open Cargo Policies
样单 9-1　进口货物运输预约保险合同·································· 242

Sample 9-2　Verification Form of Export Payment of Exchange
样单 9-2　出口收汇核销单··· 243

Sample 9-3　Beneficiary Certificate
样单 9-3　受益人证明··· 243

Sample 9-4
样单 9-4　贸易进口付汇核销单（代申报单）······················· 244

Chapter 1

Overview of International Trade Documentation
外贸单证概况

1.1 The Meaning and Role of International Trade Documentation
外贸单证的定义与作用

1.1.1 The Meaning of International Trade Documentation
外贸单证的定义

A document is an official paper that serves as proof or evidence of something. Documentation lies at the heart of all international trade transaction. Most international trade is done on the basis of delivery against documents and payment against documents. UCP 600 provides that "Banks deal with documents and not with goods, services or performance to which the documents may relate".

单证是可作为证明或证据的正式的文书。单证是国际贸易交易的核心。单证是国际贸易交货和付款的主要依据。《跟单信用证统一惯例》，即国际商会第 600 号出版物 (简称 UCP 600) 规定："银行处理的是单证，而不是单证可能涉及的货物、服务或履约行为。"

1.1.2 The Role of International Trade Documentation
外贸单证的作用

For different departments (customs, banks, exporter, importer, insurance company, government, and etc.), international trade documents have different roles. However, there is one same point, international trade documents provide proof of ownership of goods at any time and place throughout the transaction and are very important to all the departments.

To the exporter, documents provide an accounting record of a transaction, a receipt for goods shipped, the means for export clearance of the goods, as well as information and instructions to the many individuals, companies and governmental agencies who transport, handle, or inspect the shipment.

To the importer, documents provide an accounting record of a transaction, assurances that the goods ordered are the goods shipped, and the means for clearing goods through customs at the country of destination.

To the shipping company and freight forwarder, documents provide an accounting record of a transaction, instructions on where and how to ship the goods, and a statement giving instructions for handling the shipment.

To the banks, documents provide instructions and accounting tools for collecting and disbursing payments.

To the country of export and its regulatory agencies, documents provide a means of evaluating risks, valuing a shipment and tracing the point of loss in a coverage claim.

To the country of import and its regulatory agencies, documents provide proof of the right to import, statistical and census information regarding the goods imported, evidence that the goods imported will not harm the health and safety of its citizens, and an accounting tool for assessing duties and fees.

国际贸易单证在不同的部门(如海关、银行、出口商、进口商、保险公司、政府等)有不同的作用。然而，相同点是国际贸易单证是贯穿整个交易的物权凭证，并且对所有部门来说都是同等重要的。

对于出口商来说，单证提供了交易的会计记录、装运货物的收据、货物出口清关工具，并为负责运输、处理或检查货物的个人、公司和政府机构提供信息和指示。

对于进口商来说，单证为交易提供结算记录，确保订购的货物是装运货物，并提供目的国海关清关工具。

对于船运公司和货运公司来说，单证为交易提供会计记录，为货物提供装运地点和装运方式说明，并为装运管理提供说明。

对于银行来说，单证可作为收付款的结算工具和说明。

对于出口国及其监管机构来说，单证为评估风险、货运定价和跟踪索赔范围内的损失点提供了一种凭证。

对于进口国及其监管机构来说，单证为货物进口权、与进口货物有关的统计和普查信息提供证明文件，证明进口货物不会伤害公民的健康和安全，是评估税费的会计工具。

1.1.3 Significance of Documentation
单证的意义

Documentation is an indivisible part of international trade. It refers to the preparation and examination of documents involved in a transaction. The major purpose of documentation is to provide a specific and complete description of the goods so that they can be correctly processed for transport, insurance, payment, customs clearance, and etc. For most

Chapter 1 Overview of International Trade Documentation 外贸单证概况

transactions in international trade today, without documentation there will be no possibility of transactions. Considering its importance this chapter is solely devoted to the introduction to the basic requirements and information source of export documentation, and the explanation of the major documents used in export trade.

The importance of documentation, in a sense, can be amplified by saying that in some international transactions the exchange of documents takes priority over the exchange of goods. This is well illustrated in those contracts signed under the trade terms such as FOB/FCA, CFR/CPT and CIF/CIP, where the delivery of goods from the seller to the buyer is symbolized by the handover of title documents, rather than the actual delivery of physical goods. As these types of transactions take a large portion of the total volume of trade, the importance of documentation hence can not be underestimated.

Without proper documents, neither seller could send goods out of their countries and collect payments, nor could buyers release goods without problems. A smooth transaction heavily relies on the correct preparation and presentation of relevant documents at different stages. It is crucial for both the seller and buyer to acquire sufficient documentation skills to be qualified practitioners. In the meantime, compared with importers, exporters are more susceptible to the impact of documentation. It is an essential condition for exportation in the first place. In order to get through the mandatory supervision and control of the customs, presentation of required documents is the prerequisite. Lack of necessary documents or presentation of wrongly made documents is among the most common reasons for delayed release of cargos from the customs.

This also applies to importers when they are handling the import customs formalities. In addition, documents serve as the proof of fulfillment of contract for the seller. Most of the obligations listed on the sales contract could be reflected on the availability of certain documents or the certain contents of a document. A bill of lading, for example, indicates the details of sellers' performance of transportation. Sometimes the buyer requires some documents to ensure that the goods delivered are what he expects. A certificate of quality may be required to guarantee the quality of the product. As a result, by evidence of documents, exporters prove that they have delivered the right goods at the right time to the right place in the right manner. Furthermore, in most cases exporters have to use documents in their collection of payment. If we recall the payment issues, one thing is obvious that most of the popular payment terms ask for the company of documents, especially the title documents as bill of lading. Unable to provide the required documents, the exporter will have trouble in setting payment for his goods delivered.

单证是国际贸易不可分割的一部分。交易单证包括单证的准备和审查。单证的主要目的是具体和完整地描述货物，以便货物在运输、投保、支付和清关时能得到正确的处理。在当今的国际贸易中，大多数的交易不可能在无单的情况下完成。考虑到单证的重要性，本章专门对出口单证的基本要求和信息来源进行介绍，并对出口贸易中的主要单证进行详细的解释。

在某种意义上，单证的重要性可以放大到如此程度：在一些国际贸易中，单证的交换优先于货物的交换。我们可以从以 FOB/FCA、CFR/CPT 和 CIF/CIP 术语成交的合同中看出端倪。在这些合同中，卖方对买方货物的交付以单证的交付为凭据，而不是以实际货物的交付为凭据。这种类型的交易在总贸易量中占了很大一部分，因此单证的重要性是不可低估的。

没有正确的单证，卖方不能将货物送出国门和收到货款，买方也无法正常地提取货物。一笔交易能够顺利进行，极度依赖于每个阶段相关单证的正确制作和提交。对买卖双方来说，具有应有的制单能力是成为一个合格的外贸从业人员的重要因素。同时，相对于买方来说，出口方更容易受到单证的影响。单证是实现出口的基本条件。要通过海关的强制性监管和控制，提交规定的单证是前提条件。必要的单证不齐全或提交的单证有误是通关延误的普遍原因。

对进口商来说，单证也是办理进口清关手续的一个重要内容。另外，单证也是出口商履行合同义务的证据。销售合同上列出的大部分义务可以通过取得某些特定单证或某张单证上的特定内容反映出来，如提单可以说明出口商履行装运货物的细节。有时，进口商要求提供一些单证，从而确保所装运的货物如其所盼。有可能还需要提供品质证书以保证产品质量。通过单证，出口商可以证明其已经在正确的时间、以正确的方式将正确的货物装运至正确的地点。另外，在大多数情况下，出口商需要使用单证来结汇。再回到付款这个主题，我们可以很明显地看到，大多数颇受欢迎的付款方式都以附带单证为条件，尤其是作为物权凭证的提单。如果不能提供规定的单证，出口商就不能为已装运的货物顺利结汇。

1.2 The Main Kinds of International Trade Documentation
外贸单证的主要类型

There are several kinds of documents used in international trade. In many cases, documents issued by one entity (e.g. the bill of lading issued by a shipping or logistics company) may be required by more than one entity (e.g. the importer, customs authority of the country of import, and etc.). The following is a brief summary of the kinds of international trade documentation. Each will be treated in detail in the chapters that followed.

1. Transaction Documents

They are the documents the buyer and seller generate to form the basis of their agreement

Chapter 1 Overview of International Trade Documentation 外贸单证概况

to sell and purchase specific goods under specific terms and conditions. Transaction documents include the letter of inquiry, request for proposal, proposal, letter of intent, purchase order, contract of sale, pro-forma invoice, and commercial invoice. Not all transactions require each of these documents.

2. Transport Documents

They are the documents issued by the logistics company as a receipt and contract for carriage of the goods to the stated destination. These organizations also issue insurance and inspection certificate. All international transactions involving the transport of goods require some form of bill of lading.

3. Import Documents

These documents are required by the customs authority of the country of import and vary greatly from one country to another. The minimum documentation requirement is an entry form and a commercial invoice. However, many other forms may be required, especially if the imported merchandise is sensitive (e.g. animals, weapons, drugs, food), if the importer is requesting special tariff treatment under an import program (e.g. GSP, NAFTA) or if the import comes from certain countries.

Import documents generally include import licenses and permits, a commercial invoice, bill of lading, certificate of origin, import declaration, and inspection certificate. In certain countries consular invoice, insurance certificate, international exchange documentation and bank draft may be required.

4. Banking Documents

These documents are required by the banks especially through a documentary letter of credit or documentary collection procedure. Banking documents include the application for letter of credit or documentary collection, collection order, draft or acceptance, order to open credit, documentary credit, credit advice, order amendment, amendment notification, and order of assignment. Related documents include those which make part of a document package for the importer for the import clearance of the goods in the country of destination.

5. Special Documents

Special Documents are documents required by the importing or exporting country for special commodities. They include export licence for natural resources, import licence for important goods (weapons, ammunition, and etc.), documents relevant with quota. Documents related to specialized goods and trade sensitive countries provide the greatest challenge to traders.

国际贸易主要使用几类单证。多数情况下，一个部门开出的单证（比如由船公司或者物流公司开具的提单）可能被不止一个部门需要（比如进口商、进口国海关等）。以下是国际贸易单证的简单分类。每类单证将在下面章节中做详细介绍。

1. 交易单证

交易单证是买卖双方在特定形式和状况下达成协议卖或者买某些商品的基础。交易单证包括询盘函、报盘函、递盘/报盘、意向书、购货订单、销售合同、形式发票和商业发票。不是所有的交易都需要上述全部交易单证。

2. 运输单证

作为货物装运到目的地的收据和合同，运输单证由物流部门开具。这些物流部门也开具保险和检验证书。所有涉及货物运输的国际贸易都要求某种格式的提单。

3. 进口单证

各进口国海关当局对进口单证的要求截然不同。对单证的最低要求是提供登记表和商业发票。但是在很多情况下，提供其他形式的单证也很必要，特别是当涉及敏感度较高的进口商品（如动物、武器、药品和食物）时；当进口商要求在某个协议下（如一般普惠制或北美自由贸易协定）享受特别关税待遇时；或当进口物品来自某些特定的国家时。

进口单证通常包括进口许可证和批文、商业发票、提单、原产地证明、进口证明和商检证书。在某些国家还要求提供领事发票、保险凭证、外汇单证和银行汇票。

4. 银行单证

通过跟单信用证或跟单托收程序进行贸易时，银行要求必须提供银行单证。银行单证包括信用证申请书或跟单托收申请书、托收单、汇票或承兑汇票、开立信用证通知书、信用证、信用证通知、变更通知、修改通知书和变更安排书。相关单证包括进口商在目的国进口货物通关所需要的单证。

5. 要求的特殊单证

要求的特殊单证是进口国或出口国针对特殊物品而要求提供的单证。其包括自然资源出口许可证、重要物品进口许可证（如武器、军火等），以及与配额相关的单证。对交易者来说，与特殊商品和贸易敏感国家相关的单证挑战最大。

1.3 The Parties to International Trade Documentation 外贸单证当事人

The core of every business transaction is the buyer and the seller, and the involvement of specialized parties are as the followings.

1. The Exporter/Seller

In most transactions the exporters/sellers are responsible for the documentation required by the export authorities, the importers/buyers, or the banks in documentary collection or letter of credit. However, not all the documents listed below are required in all transactions. The exporters/sellers may issue the documents as the followings.

(1) Transaction documents, including proposal, bid or quotation, contract for sale of goods, pro-forma invoice, and commercial invoice.

(2) Export documents, including export license, export declaration, and inspection certificate.

(3) Transport and insurance documents, including packing list, and bill of lading/air waybill.

(4) Banking documents, including documentary collection order and bank draft/bill of exchange, if documentary collection is used. Including bank draft/bill of exchange, if documentary letter of credit is used.

(5) Import documents, including certificate of origin, consular invoice, insurance policy or insurance certificate, inspection certificate, phytosanitary certificate, and specialized inspection certificates.

2. The Importer/Buyer

The importer/buyer has primary responsibility for preparing a number of documents required by the customs authorities of the country of import. Since these documents are easily secured by the exporter in the country of export, the importer is responsible for notifying the exporter of the documents required. The importer/buyer may issue the documents as the followings.

(1) Transaction documents, including request for proposal or request for quotation, proposal, bid or quotation, contract for sale of goods, pro-forma invoice, and commercial invoice.

(2) Transport and insurance documents, including packing list and bill of lading/air waybill.

(3) Banking documents, including letter of credit application, if documentary letter of credit is used.

(4) Specialized documents, including certificate of origin, consular invoice, insurance policy, inspection certificate, phytosanitary certificate and specialized inspection certificates.

(5) Import documents: including import permit, import license, special customs invoice, customs declaration and other specialized documentation.

3. Export Authority

The export authority has three major responsibilities: law enforcement, revenue collection and census. The following is a list of the basic export documentation required by most countries.

(1) The export license/permit.

(2) The export declaration, including destination control or ultimate consignee statement.

(3) The bill of lading.

(4) The commercial invoice.

(5) The certificate of origin.

(6) The inspection certificate.

4. Import Authority

The import authority has three major responsibilities: law enforcement, revenue collection and census. The following is a list of the basic import documentation required by most countries.

(1) The import permit/ license.

(2) The import declaration.

(3) The bill of lading.

(4) The commercial invoice.

(5) The certificate of origin.

(6) The inspection certificate.

5. The Freight Forwarder/Logistics Company

International freight forwarders are in the business of moving goods from one country to another. Logistics companies are in the business of planning and controlling the flow of raw materials, work in progress, or finished products from point of origin to point of destination. Documents issued by the logistics company are as the followings.

(1) The bill of lading.

(2) The insurance certificate.

(3) Inspection certificates.

6. The Customs Broker

The customs broker assists in all aspects of clearing imported goods through customs. They handle the sequence of customs formalities and other details critical to the legal and speedy import and export of goods. Documents issued by the customs broker are as the followings.

(1) The application for import license and import permit.

(2) The import declaration.

(3) The special customs invoice.

(4) Documentation and applications related to refunds, rebates and drawback.

7. The Freight Carrier (shipping line, airline, railroad, barge line, courier)

The freight carriers are in the business of moving goods from one country to another. Carriers range from huge ocean shipping lines that move ship load quantities of crude oil or grain, to courier companies that handle small package shipments of less than one-half kilogram.

It is very important to realize that some carriers are specialists in only one mode of transport. Since international shipments often require more than one mode of transport (sea, air, and land), it may be necessary to use a shipper (or a logistics firm) that can act as a "multi-modal transport operator" and take responsibility for the entire shipping process from point of origin to point of final destination.

Documents issued by freight carriers are as the followings.

(1) The bill of lading.

(2) The insurance certificate.

(3) The air bill.

8. The Government Regulatory Agency

The government regulatory agencies are in the business of enforcing specific laws and regulations designed to protect the economic well-being in addition to the health and safety of their citizens. The government regulatory agencies in US include: Food and Drug Administration, Animal and Plant Health Inspection Service, and Consumer Product Safety Commission.

Documents issued by the government regulatory agencies are as the followings

(1) Certificate of inspection.

(2) Phytosanitary certificate.

(3) Veterinary health certificate.

(4) Safety testing certificate.

(5) Fumigation/sterilization certificate.

(6) Dangerous goods certificate.

9. The International Banks

International banks handle all aspects of international payments from importers to exporters, including the documentary collections and the letter of credit. Documents issued by the international banks are as the followings.

(1) The documentary collection order.

(2) The documentary letter of credit.

(3) The documentary letter of credit amendment.

(4) The documentary letter of credit advice.

(5) The bank draft/bill of exchange.

10. The Insurance Company

The insurance companies provide coverage by contract to indemnity or guarantee another party against risk of losses by stated perils, such as the risk of loss or damage to shipments of cargoes in international trade. Some of the large logistics firms have their own insurance companies as subsidiaries. Documents issued by the insurance companies are the insurance policy or the insurance certificate.

11. The Attorney

Attorneys and law firms are in the business of providing legal advice to clients. The role of attorneys varies greatly from country to country. The contract for sale of goods is issued by the attorney.

12. The Inspection Company

Inspection companies are in the business of providing testing services for exporters, importers, export authorities and import authorities. Inspection companies are often licensed by government agencies or have professional affiliations with recognized industry groups. Some countries require that samples of products be sent in advance of the full shipment for testing by laboratories within the country of import, while others are satisfied with certificates generated in the country of export prior to shipment.

Documents issued by the insurance companies are as the followings.

(1) Certificate of inspection.

(2) Phytosanitary certificates.

(3) Veterinary health certificate.

(4) Safety testing certificate.

(5) Fumigation/sterilization certificate.

(6) Dangerous goods certificate.

(7) Quality certificate.

13. The Notary Public/Document Authenticator

Most countries have appointed or commissioned individuals who are given authority to identify and certify the identity of persons who sign documents with proof of their signature. In some countries, such as England, France and Germany, these individuals often have special legal training, while in other countries they can be qualified after a short course, test and background check. Some countries have no provision for such commissioned persons, in which event consular, judicial or legal professionals will often be used to fulfill authentication requirements.

The key documents "certified" or "notarized" by notaries are as the followings.

(1) Limited power of attorney.

(2) Contract and inspection certificates.

(3) Consular invoice.

14. The Chamber of Commerce

Chambers of commerce provide export education, country market information, assistance with export documentation and trade leads.

Documents issued by the chambers of commerce are as the followings.

(1) Certificate of origin.

(2) Certificate of free sale.

15. The Consular Office

The consular office of country of importation, located in the country of export, is often empowered to "certify" certain documents or forms required for the eventual import of goods.

Documents issued by the consular office are as the followings.

(1) Commercial invoice.

(2) Customs invoice.

(3) Consular invoice.

所有商业交易的核心都是买方、卖方及以下专业当事人的参与。

1. 出口商/卖方

在大多数交易中，出口商/卖方负责向出口国管理当局、进口方/买方，以及跟单托收或者信用证交易下的银行出具其所要求的单证。然而，并不是所有交易都需要下面列出的所有单证。出口商/卖方可能出具的单证如下。

(1) 交易单证，包括询价单、投标或报价单、货物销售合同、形式发票、商业发票。

(2) 出口单证，包括出口许可证、出口报关单、检验证书。

(3) 运输和保险单证，包括装箱单、提单/航空货运单。

(4) 银行单证，如果采用跟单托收，银行单证包括跟单托收通知和银行汇票。如果采用跟单信用证，银行单证包括银行汇票。

(5) 进口单证，包括原产地证明、领事发票、保险单或保险凭证、检验证书、植物检疫证书以及专门的检验证书。

2. 进口商/买方

进口商/买方的主要责任是准备进口国海关当局所要求的单证。由于出口国的出口商很容易获取这些单证，进口商负责通知出口商所需的单证。进口商/买方可能出具的单证包括如下几种。

(1) 交易单证，包括报价函、投标或报价、商品销售合同、形式发票和商业发票。

(2) 运输和保险单证，包括装箱单、提单/航空货运单。

(3) 银行单证，如果使用跟单信用证的话，需提供信用证申请书。

(4) 要求的特殊单证，包括原产地证明、领事发票、保险单、检验证书、植物检疫证明和专门的检验证书。

(5) 进口单证，包括进口许可证、特殊的海关发票、报关单和其他专业的单证。

3. 出口国当局

出口国当局有三个主要职责：执法、征税和普查。下面是大多数国家要求的出口单证。

(1) 出口许可证。

(2) 出口报关单，包括目的地管制声明或者最终收货人声明。

(3) 提单。

(4) 商业发票。

(5) 原产地证明。

(6) 检验检疫证书。

4. 进口国当局

进口国当局有三个主要职责：执法、征税和普查。下面是大多数国家要求的进口单证。

(1) 进口许可证。

(2) 进口报关单。

(3) 提单。

(4) 商业发票。

(5) 原产地证明。

(6) 检验证书。

5. 货运代理／物流公司

国际货运代理公司负责将商品从一个国家运输到另一个国家。物流公司负责计划和控制原材料、在产品或成品的流动，从供应地运输到目的地。物流公司出具的单证如下。

(1) 提单。

(2) 保险证明书。

(3) 检验证明书。

6. 海关经纪人

海关经纪人协助办理所有货物进口清关手续。货物能否合法、快速进出口，他们处理清关手续的顺序和其他的细节至关重要。海关经纪人出具的单证如下。

(1) 进口许可证申请书和进口许可证。

(2) 进口报关单。

(3) 特殊海关发票。

(4) 与退货、退税和退款有关的单证和申请书。

7. 货运承运人（班轮、航空、铁路、驳船、快递）

货运承运人负责将商品从一个国家运输到另一个国家。货运承运人可以是运载批量原油或粮食的海洋班轮大公司，也可以是运送不到半公斤小包裹的快递公司。

有些承运人专业只做一种运输方式，明确这一点非常重要。由于国际货运往往需要不止一种运输方式（海运、空运、陆运），因此可能得用到能做多式联运的托运方（或物流公司），负责将货物从供应地运输到最终目的地。

货运承运人出具的单证如下。

(1) 提单。

(2) 保险证明书。

(3) 空运提单。

8. 政府监管机构

除了保护公民的健康和安全之外，政府监管机构的职责还包括强制执行特定法律法规以保证经济健康运行。在美国，这些政府监管机构包括：食品和药物管理局、动物和植物检验检疫局，以及消费者产品安全委员会。政府监管机构出具的单证如下。

(1) 检验合格证明。

(2) 植物检疫证明书。

(3) 兽医卫生证书。

(4) 安全检测证书。

(5) 熏蒸 / 消毒证书。

(6) 危险品证书。

9. 国际银行

国际银行负责处理进口商对出口商的国际支付，包括跟单托收和信用证。国际银行出具的单证如下。

(1) 跟单托收通知书。

(2) 跟单信用证。

(3) 跟单信用证修改书。

(4) 跟单信用证通知书。

(5) 银行汇票。

10. 保险公司

国际贸易中，保险公司通过合同提供保险，保障合同另一方在遭受约定危险导致的损失时，比如货物运输损失或损坏风险时能够得到赔偿。一些大型物流公司有他们自己的作为其子公司的保险公司。保险公司出具的单证是保险单或保险凭证。

11. 律师

律师和律师事务所给客户提供法律建议。不同的国家，其律师的角色也不同。律师签发货物销售合同。

12. 检验公司

检验公司负责为进出口商、进出口国当局提供商品检测服务。检验公司常常由政府机构或专业公认的行业界组织颁发牌照。一些国家要求商品样本在全部装运前预先寄进口国实验室进行检验，而另外一些国家则要求在发货之前出口国出具证书即可。

检验公司出具的单证如下。

(1) 检验合格证明。

(2) 植物检疫证明。

(3) 兽医卫生证书。

(4) 安全检测证书。

(5) 熏蒸 / 消毒证书。

(6) 危险品证书。

(7) 质量检查证书。

13. 公证人

大多数国家任命或委任个人鉴证单证的签名。在一些国家，如英国、法国和德国，鉴证人通常接受过专门的法律培训；而在另外一些国家，鉴证人可以在短期培训、测试和背景调查后取得资格。一些国家没有委任这些人，在此情况下，领事、司法或法律专业人士往往就是鉴证人。

公证人出具的主要"证书"或"公证"单证如下。

(1) 有限授权委托书。

(2) 合同、检验证明。

(3) 领事发票。

14. 商会

商会提供出口培训、国家市场信息，协助出具出口单证和提供供求信息。

商会签发的单证如下。

(1) 原产地证明。

(2) 自由销售证明。

15. 领事办公室

进口国领事办公室设在出口国，经常被授权为最终进口货物所需的某些单证或表格提供证明。

领事机构出具的单证如下。

(1) 商业发票。

(2) 海关发票。

(3) 领事发票。

1.4 The Basic Requirements for International Trade Documentation
外贸单证的基本要求

So far, there has been no well-established standard for documentation in international trade. In addition, documentary requirements may differ from transaction to transaction and from country to country, largely. The differences mainly lie in areas such as the types needed, content and languages used, and etc. Whatever differences there might be, generally speaking, documentation for every transaction should meet such basic requirements as correctness, completeness, conciseness, cleanness and promptness.

Documents are correct and accurate if the content (including the exact words used) conforms to that in the letter of credit and format of the documents is in line with the requirements. Aside from these, correctness is met when the right types of documents are prepared and the right number of the originals and duplicates are presented.

Documents are considered complete when all necessary documents (including the types and number of originals and duplicates) are prepared and presented in a complete set.

Document should be concise. The seller shall make sure that all documents should avoid redundant, unnecessary or ambiguous words or expressions. Meanwhile, to be clean, documents should bear no marks of correction on the face. When the above "Cs" is all met, the seller should then prepare the documents in time and present them within the time for presentation stipulated in the letter of credit. This lives up to the requirement of promptness.

In brief, exporter should attach great importance to documentation and make sure all documents meet the above requirements in order to ensure the smoothness and success of every single transaction. To achieve this, the seller has to check very carefully so that all documents for a transaction should not only be in strict compliance with the stipulations in the relevant contract and letter of credit but also be in consistency with each other.

迄今为止，还没有任何完善的标准来规范国际贸易单证。而且，每个国家、每笔交易对单证的要求都不同。这些差异主要存在于几个领域，如单证的种类、内容、语言等。不管这些差异是什么，一般来说，每笔交易的单证都应该满足正确、完整、简洁、清洁和迅速等要求。

如果单证的内容（精确到每个词语）和格式与信用证的规定相符，那么单证就是正确和准确的。除此之外，如果单证的种类及所提交的正本和副本的数量是正确的，那么单证就视为正确。

当所有必需的单证（包括正本和副本的种类和数量）都制作完毕而且以全套的形式提交时，单证可视为完整。

单证应简洁。出口商应做到让所有的单证没有任何冗余的、不必要的和模糊的词语或表达。同时，单证应清洁，即单证的表面无纠错的痕迹。当以上要求都满足时，出口商应及时制作单证并在信用证规定的时间内交单。这体现了单证的迅速性。

简而言之，出口商应对单证予以重视，并应做到所提交的单证满足以上所有的要求，以保证每次交易都能够成功和顺利进行。要达到这个目标，出口商不仅要仔细审查所有的单证是否严格符合相关的合同和信用证的规定，还要审查单证之间的一致性。

1.5 Checklist for Documentation Errors 单证纠错内容

(1) Check typing errors in the name of commodity and figures, such as quantity, package number, unit price and total amount, insurance amount, insurance premium, and etc.

(2) Check spelling errors in the names and address of the parties concerned.

(3) Avoid redundant, unnecessary or ambiguous words or expressions in such terms as the name, quality, quantity, time or place of shipment, and etc.

(4) Avoid correction on the face of the documents.

(5) Mark the date of each document clearly.

(6) Check the title of each document to make them the same as the stipulation of the L/C. For instance, an Insurance Certificate is not acceptable when the L/C requires an Insurance Policy.

(7) Make sure some documents' reference numbers required to be mentioned in other documents are correctly presented.

(8) Prepare exactly the same numbers of originals and duplicates as required.

(9) All documents must be properly issued, signed and sealed by the right party.

(10) Arrange the documents according to the order of the issuing date on the documents.

(1) 审查商品的名称和数量，如包装号码、单价、总额、保险金额、保险费等数字是否有打印错误。

(2) 审查有关各方的名称和地址是否有拼写错误。

(3) 避免在名称、质量、数量、装船的时间和地点等条款上出现冗余的、不必要的或模糊的词语或表达。

(4) 避免在单证表面修改。

(5) 每份单证的日期都标示清楚。

(6) 确定每份单证的标题与信用证规定的一致。例如，信用证要求的是保险凭证，那么银行就不接受保险单。

(7) 若要求标示相关单证的参考号码，那么应确保该单证的参考号码在其他单证上被正确标示。

(8) 正本和副本的数量应符合规定。

(9) 所有的单证都应由正确的当事人出具、签署和盖章。

(10) 应根据单证上的签发日期顺序排列单证。

1.6 Prerequisites of Documentation 单证制作的先决条件

Considering the significance of documentation, it is a must for the exporter to present documents correctly and completely. To avoid errors and inconsistency among documents, it is important to be aware of the source of information for producing relevant documents. Usually, documents for an export transaction are to be prepared and examined based on the information from the sales contract, and payment related documents, e.g. a letter of credit,

Chapter 1 Overview of International Trade Documentation 外贸单证概况

and some documents supplied by manufacturers.

The sales contract is the basis of any other documents produced. As mentioned above, a sales contract builds up the foundation of all the transactional activities. It is understandable that all documents must be made out in strict conformity with the contractual terms.

The preparation of documents must refer to the relevant payment instructions as well, especially when a documentary letter of credit is used. If a transaction is made with payment by L/C, the credit will list all the documents demanded as the condition for issuing bank to hold the liability of payment, independent of the importer. Though the issuance of a letter of credit is based on the sales contract, once issued the credit becomes a solely independent document and the guideline for settlement of payment. Beyond all questions, therefore, sellers have to make sure that all documents prepared strictly comply with the stipulations in L/C.

The contents of documents should also be subject to original information obtained from the original documents provided by manufactures. For instance, a packing list provided by the manufactures usually indicates detailed information about the commodity including such details as quantity, specification, gross weight, net weight and measurement. Naturally, they also become the information bases for documentation.

It is also important to note that the above information bases for documentation are not independent of each other. In other words, documents should be made out based on all these criteria simultaneously.

考虑到单证的重要性，出口商必须正确和完整地提交单证。要避免单证错误和出现单证间不一致的问题，出口商应该了解制作相关单证的信息资源。通常来说，出口单证的制作和审查以销售合同及有关的支付单证为基础，如信用证和由供货商提供的单证。

其他单证的制作都是以销售合同为基础。如上所述，销售合同是所有交易活动的基础。这样就可以理解，为什么所有的单证在制作过程中必须与合同条款严格一致。

单证的制作也必须参考相关的付款指示，尤其是在使用信用证付款的情况下。如果一笔交易以信用证为付款方式，那么信用证必须将所有所需的单证明确列出，这是开证行独立于进口商之外履行付款责任的条件。虽然信用证是以销售合同为基础开立的，但是一旦开立，信用证就是一份独立的文件，也是货款结算的标准。毫无疑问，出口商制作的单证必须与信用证规定的严格一致。

单证的内容必须与从供货商处获得的原始单证内容一致。例如，由供货商提供的装箱单往往包含货物的数量、规格、毛重、净重和体积等内容。这些内容自然就成为出口商制作单证的基础。

此外还需注意，以上单证的信息不是相互独立的。也就是说，所有的单证在制作时必须同时参照以上标准。

1.7 The Basic Materials of Making out International Trade Documents
缮制外贸单证的基础材料

The basic materials of making out documents include sales contract, L/C, warehouse order, original materials offered by the delivery department and related materials and requirements of business departments.

制单的基础材料包括销售合同、信用证、出库单、发货部门提供的原始材料,以及业务部门的相关材料和要求。

1.8 Development of International Trade Documents
外贸单证的发展

SWIFT and EDI are widely used in international trade documentation. Now, along with the fast development of computer and internet, more and more companies use computers to make out documents.

在国际贸易单证中,环球同业银行金融电讯系统(SWIFT)和电子数据交换(EDI)已被广泛使用。现在,随着计算机与互联网的快速发展,越来越多的公司使用电子计算机来缮制文件。

1.9 Relevant International Regulations and Practices
相关国际规则和惯例

1. International Regulations and Practices Relevant with Contract

United Nations Convention on Contracts for the International Sales of Goods (CISG) strives to create a uniform international sales law, and to regulate the rights and obligations of buyers and sellers in international transactions for the sale of goods. Until now, a number of countries that account for two-thirds of all world trade have joined the CISG, and the number is on the rise.

2. International Regulations and Practices Relevant with International Payment

(1) International Regulations and Practices for Collection: The Uniform Rules for Collections No. 522 (URC 522).

URC 522 underlines the need for the principal and/or the remitting bank to attach a separate document, the collection instruction, to every collection subject to the Rules-makes it very clear that banks will not examine documents, particularly not to look for instructions addresses problems banks experience in respect of documents against acceptance (D/A) and documents against payment (D/P)-clearly indicates that banks have no obligation to store and insure goods when instructed.

(2) Uniform Customs and Practice for Documentary Credits No. 600 (UCP 600).

The Uniform Customs and Practice for Documentary Credits (UCP) is a set of rules on the issuance and use of letters of credit. This latest version, called the UCP 600, formally commenced on 1 July 2007.

UCP 600 are rules that apply to any documentary credit when the text of the credit expressly indicates that it is subject to these rules. They are binding on all parties to the credit unless expressly modified or excluded by the credit.

3. International Regulations and Practices Relevant with Trade Terms

(1) Warsaw-Oxford Rules 1932.

(2) Revised American International Trade Definitions 1990.

(3) International Rules for the Interpretation of Trade Terms 2010(INCOTERMS 2010).

4. International Regulations and Practices Relevant with Transportation for International Trade

(1) International Regulations and Practices Relevant with Ocean Transportation.

① International Convention for the Unification of Certain Rules of Law Relating to Bill of Lading, 1924(The Hague Rules).

② The Brussels Protocol, 1968(The Visby Rules).

③ United Nations Convention on the Carriage of Goods by Sea, 1978(The Hamburg Rules).

④ CMI Uniform Rules For Sea Waybills, 1990.

(2) International Regulations and Practices Relevant with Carriage of Goods by Road Convention on the Contract for the International Carriage of Goods by Road (CMR).

(3) International Regulations and Practices Relevant with Carriage of Goods by Rail: International Convention Concerning the Carriage of Goods by Rail(CIM), Agreement on International Railroad through Transport of Goods(CMIC).

5. International Regulations and Practices Relevant with International Cargo Transportation Insurance

(1) China Insurance Clause(CIC).

(2) W/W Clause.

(3) Institute Cargo Clause (ICC).

6. International Regulations and Practices Relevant with International Trade Arbitration

(1) Convention on the Recognition and Enforcement of International Arbitral Awards, 1958.

(2) UNCITRAL Arbitration Rules, 1976.

(3) Model Law on International Commercial Arbitration, 1985.

1. 与合同相关的国际规则与惯例

《联合国国际货物销售合同公约》(CISG) 力求建立一个统一的国际销售法，规定国际货物销售交易中买卖双方的权利和义务。到目前为止，世界上 2/3 的国家已经加入了 (CISG)，这个数字还在上升。

2. 与国际支付相关的国际规则与惯例

(1) 托收业务中的国际规则和惯例：《托收统一规则》(国际商会第 522 号出版物，简称 URS 522)。

URC 522 规定托收只是银行帮助委托人代其收取款项，并不保证将委托人托收款项收回；银行对于委托人提交的托收单证不予审查、不核对。托收指示书应该明确注明商业单证究竟是凭付款 (D/P) 还是凭承兑 (D/A) 交给付款人，对于不明确的标注，银行对单证所引起的后果不负责任。

(2)《跟单信用证统一惯例》(国际商会第 600 号出版物)。

《跟单信用证统一惯例》(UCP) 适用于信用证的开立和使用。最新版本为国际商会 2007 年 7 月 1 日颁布的第 600 号出版物，简称 UCP 600。

UCP 600 适用于所有在正文中标明按照该惯例办理的跟单信用证，除非信用证明确修改或排除了该惯例，否则该惯例对一切有关当事人均具有约束力。

3. 与贸易术语相关的国际规则和惯例

(1)《1932 年华沙—牛津规则》。

(2)《1990 年美国对外贸易定义修订本》。

(3)《国际贸易术语解释通则》2010 版本 (INCOTERMS 2010)。

4. 与国际贸易运输相关的国际规则和惯例

(1) 与海洋运输相关的国际规则和惯例。

① 1924 年签署的《统一提单的若干法律规则的国际公约》(简称《海牙规则》)。

② 1968 年签署的《布鲁塞尔协定书》(简称《维斯比规则》)。

③ 1978 年签署的《联合国海上货物运输公约》(简称《汉堡规则》)。

④ 1990 年签署的《签署的国际海事委员会海运单统一规则》。

(2) 与公路货运相关的国际规则和惯例：《国际公路货运合同公约》(CMR)。

(3) 与铁路货运相关的国际规则和惯例：《铁路货物运输国际公约》(CIM) 和《国际铁路货物联合运输协定》(CMIC)。

5. 与国际货物运输保险相关的国际规则和惯例

(1)《中国保险条款》(CIC)。

(2)《仓至仓条款》(W/W)。

(3)《协会货物条款》(ICC)。

6. 与国际贸易仲裁相关的国际规则与惯例

(1) 1958 年签署的《关于承认和执行外国仲裁裁决公约》。

(2) 1976 年签署的《联合国国际贸易法委员会仲裁规则》。

(3) 1985 年签署的《国际商事仲裁法》。

Chapter 2
Management and Operation of International Trade Documents
外贸单证管理及制作流程

2.1 Making Documents
单证的制作

2.1.1 The Basis of Making Documents
制单依据

The main basis of making and reviewing export documents is sales contract, letter of credit, original material of the relevant goods, international common practice and domestic management regulations, and etc. In practice, we should pay attention to the following aspects.

(1) A sales contract is the primary basis for making and examining documents.

(2) In the L/C payment trading, the L/C to replace contract and becomes the main basis of the documents.

(3) Generally, the relevant goods original material are delivery order, packing list, and etc. provided by manufacturers.

(4) In relevant international practices, such as the international chamber of commerce of the UCP 600, as well as the publication No. 522 "collection series", INCOTERMS 2010 and other documents are the basis of some documents problems.

制作和审核出口单据的主要依据是买卖合同、信用证、有关商品的原始资料和国际惯例、国内管理规定等。在实践中，要注意以下几个方面。

(1) 买卖合同是制单和审单的首要依据。

(2) 在信用证支付方式的交易中，信用证取代买卖合同而成为主要的制作单据的依据。

(3) 有关商品的原始资料，一般是生产单位提供的交货单和货物出厂装箱单等单据。

(4) 国际贸易中的有关国际惯例，如国际商会的 UCP 600，以及第 522 号出版物

《托收统一规则》和INCOTERMS 2010等文件，也是正确处理一些单证问题的依据。

2.1.2 Making Steps
制单步骤

Firstly, invoice should be made after understanding the contract, the delivery note and the information such as letter of credit. Some enterprises firstly make a detailed freight list or the warehouse receipt, and then fill in the invoice.

Secondly, the delivery note, letter of credit, trade correspondence, packing list, hold bill, inspection declaration form, customs declaration form, insurance application, certificate of origin, and (passive quotas) license, and etc should be made according to the contract, based on the invoice.

At last, if needed, beneficiary's certificate, shipping advice, certificate of shipping company and draft, and etc., are made and then presented to the related parties.

首先，在了解合同、交货单、信用证等信息后制作发票。有的企业先制作货物明细单或货物出仓单，再填制发票。

其次，以发票为基础，根据合同，制作交货单、信用证、贸易对方来函、包装单据、托运单、报检单、报关单、投保单、产地证、(被动配额)许可证等。

如果有需要，可制作出口商证明、装船通知、船公司证明和汇票等，并分别将单据交给有关方。

2.1.3 Mode of Operation of Making Documents
制单的工作方式

(1) We must grasp the necessary materials and data.

(2) Documents should be checked after material is ready.

(3) Export documents generally based on invoice and packing list. Invoice is the center of all documents. Firstly, invoice should be prepared, then respectively according to the invoice, custom invoice, certificate of origin and insurance policy should be prepared. Shipping order and customs declaration form needed for the consignment are made by reference to the content of the invoice according to the normal operating procedures.

(1) 必须掌握必要的资料和数据。

(2) 资料齐备后必须经过核对。

(3) 出口单证一般以发票、装箱单为基础单据，发票是一切单据的中心，一般先缮制发票，然后按发票内容分别缮制海关发票、产地证、投保单等单证。报运需用的托运单、报关单等按正常的操作程序参照发票内容缮制。

2.1.4 Skills of Making Documents
制单技巧

(1) Payor's identification: Payer, Drawee.

(2) Consignee's identification: Consignee, Cargo Receiver, Receiver.

(3) Identification of the loading port and port of delivery: Loading Port, Port of Loading, Port of Shipment, Port of Unloading, Port of Delivery, Discharging Port, Port of Discharge, Port of Debarkation.

(4) Time sequence of making documents is as follows.

The date of issuing documents should be consistent with logic and international practice. The bill of lading date usually is the key to confirm the date of other documents. Draft date should be later than the date of bill of lading, invoice date and other documents' date, but not later than the validity of the L/C. The relationship of all documents' date is as follows.

① The invoice date should be on the first date of all the documents.

② The bill of lading date should not be earlier than the shipping date stipulated in the L/C.

③ The policy date issued should be earlier than or equal to the date of the bill of lading (generally, 2 days early than the date of the bill of lading), but not earlier than the invoice date.

④ Packing list date should be equal to or later than invoice date, but must be before the date of the bill of lading.

⑤ The date of Certificate of Origin should not be earlier than the invoice date, but not later than the date of bill of lading.

⑥ The date of commodity inspection certificate should not be later than the date of bill of lading, but not too much earlier than the date of bill of lading, especially fresh, easy to bad goods.

⑦ The date of beneficiary's certificate shall be equal to or later than the date of bill of lading.

⑧ The shipping date should be equal to or late than the date of the bill of lading within three days.

⑨ The date of certificate of shipping company should be equal to or early than the date of the bill of lading.

(1) 付款人的表示法:Payer, Drawee。

(2) 收货人的表示方法:Consignee, Cargo Receiver, Receiver。

(3) 装货港和卸货港的表示方法:Loading Port, Port of Loading, Port of Shipment, Port of Unloading, Port of Delivery, Discharging Port, Port of Discharge, Port of Debarkation。

(4) 制作单据的时间顺序如下。

各种单据的签发日期应符合逻辑性和国际惯例，通常提单日期是确定各单据日期的关键，汇票日期应晚于提单、发票等其他单据日期，但不能晚于 L/C 的有效期。各单据日期关系如下。

① 发票日期应在各单据日期之首。

② 提单日不能早于 L/C 规定的装运期。

③ 保单的签发日应早于或等于提单日期（一般早于提单 2 天），不能早于发票日期。

④ 装箱单日期应等于或迟于发票日期，但必须在提单日之前。

⑤ 产地证日期应不早于发票日期，不迟于提单日期。

⑥ 商检证日期不晚于提单日期，但也不能过早于提单日，尤其是鲜货，容易变质的商品。

⑦ 受益人证明日期应等于或晚于提单日。

⑧ 装船通知日期应等于或晚于提单日后三天内。

⑨ 船公司证明日期应等于或早于提单日。

2.2 The Basis and Operation Process of Making Out Documents
制单基础与流程

2.2.1 The Basis of Making Out Documents
制单基础

The Basis of Making out Documents: sales contract, L/C, warehouse order, original materials offered by the delivery department and related materials, and requirements of business departments.

制单基础材料包括销售合同、信用证、库存订单，送货部门提供的原材料和相关材料及商业部门的要求。

2.2.2 The Operation Process of International Trade Documentation
外贸单证缮制流程

There are five operation processes of international trade documentation: verification, calculation, allocation, making and Examination.

外贸单证缮制流程包括核、算、配、制和审 5 个部分。

2.2.3 Main Links of Procedure of Export Documentation
出口单证流程要点

The procedure of export documentation can be shown by Figure 2-1.

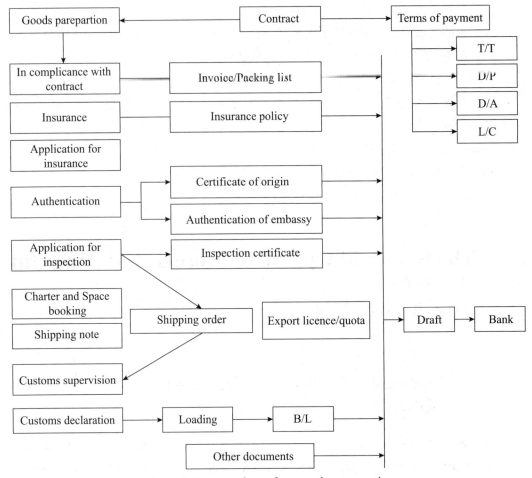

Figure 2-1　procedure of export documentation

1. Order Handling and Goods Preparation

According to requirements of the contract or the L/C, the related person should urge the factory or the warehouse to arrange goods and should check the description, quality, quantity, specification, packing and shipping mark of goods to make sure goods are of good quality and are well packed. Besides, make sure that the quantity of goods meets the need and shipping mark is clear.

2. Urging, Examining and Amending L/C

Try to urge the importer to open the L/C if he fails to open it in due course. After receiving the L/C, the exporter should register and check it and should ask for amendment to it if he finds some problems.

3. Application for Commodity Inspection

When goods are listed in the catalogue of inspection or are required to be inspected by the contract or the L/C, goods must be sent for inspection and quarantine carried out by the inspection authority before getting the customs clearance bill or the inspection certificate.

4. Application of Commodity Insurance

Covering insurance for the contract on CIF basis, the exporter should cover the goods transportation insurance with the insurance company and get insurance documents before shipping goods.

5. Authentication of Diplomatic Missions

The diplomatic missions or other authorized organizations authenticate the identification of the signer of one file to certify the validity of the file.

6. Handling Export Consignment

Filling in export shipping note. Obtaining the shipping order.

7. Export Declaration

After handling the consignment and obtaining the sipping order, the consigner should fill in the export customs declaration form and declare to the Customs within 24 hours before loading. After checking, inspection, levying duties and charges, the Customs can release goods.

8. Obtaining Shipping Documents and Sending Shipping Advice

After the inspection, the Customs will stamp the related documents and release goods. The consigner can ask the carried to load goods with the above documents and obtain the shipping documents. After the shipment, the exporter should inform the buyer of the shipment so that the buyer can cover insurance and be prepared for taking delivery.

9. Comprehensive Making and Examination of Documents

When check documents comprehensively, the exporter should make out other documents accordingly and collect them to make comprehensive checking. After checking documents, the exporter should make out the draft and send it to the bank for the settlement.

10. Presentation of Documents and Exchange Settlement

11. Verification of Export Payment of International Exchange and Drawback

12. Documents Filling Management

出口单证的流程如图 2-1 所示。

1. 收发订单与备货

根据合同或者信用证的要求，相关的人员应该敦促厂方或者仓库备货，与此同时，为了确保货品的质量和包装完好，应该派人员对货品的描述、质量、数量、说明书、包装及唛头进行检查。除此之外，还要确保货品的数量无误及唛头的字迹清晰。

2. 催证、审证与改证

如果进口商到期还未能开证，应该敦促进口商办理开证手续。在收到信用证之后，出口商应该进行登记、核实,发现问题后应该及时修改信用证。

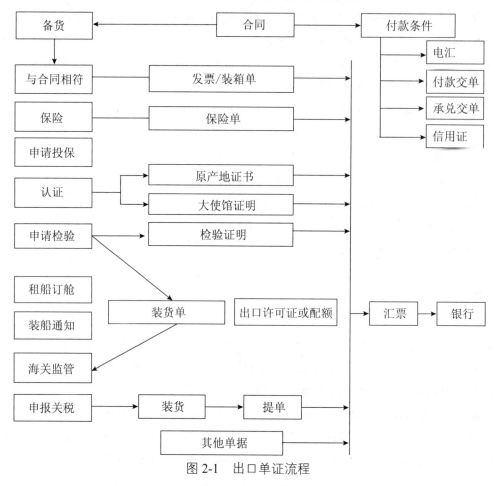

图 2-1　出口单证流程

3. 货物检验申请

当合同或信用证所列货物要接受检查时,必须在检验或检疫之前获得清关单或检验证书。

4. 货物投保申请

以到岸价合同坚持投保,出口商应该向保险公司办理货物运输保险并在货物装运之前取得保险单。

5. 外交使团认证

外交使团或其他授权机构对文件签署者的鉴定,证明文件的有效性。

6. 办理出口托运手续

填写出口装运通知单,获取装运确认书。

7. 办理出口报关手续

在托运和获取装运确认书后,委托人应该填写出口申报书,并在装货前的 24 小时内报关。在审查、检验和缴纳关税后,海关才予以通行。

8. 取得运输单据和发放已装船通知

货物进行商品检验之后,海关将在相关的单据上盖章并给予货物通行。委托人可以根据上述单据要求装载货物并获取装运单证。在装运后，出口商应该通知买方使得买方投保，并做好交接的准备。

9. 综合制单、审单

出口商对单证进行综合的审核时，应该填写相应的其他单证，并逐一进行综合的审核。在审核完单证之后，出口商应该填写汇票，并发送至银行进行结算。

10. 交单结汇

11. 办理出口退税核销

12. 单证归档管理

2.2.4 The General Procedure of Import Documentation 进口单证的一般程序

(1) Application of the quota certificate or the import license.

(2) Application of opening the L/C.

(3) Amendment to the L/C.

(4) Charter and shipping space booking and insurance.

(5) Examination of documents and payment of International exchange.

(6) Application of goods inspection and the customs clearance.

(1) 配额证明或进口许可证申报书。

(2) 申请开立信用证。

(3) 修改信用证。

(4) 租船定舱与投保。

(5) 审查单证与支付外汇。

(6) 货物报检申请和清关。

2.3 Examination of Documents 审核单据

2.3.1 The Purpose of Examining Documents 审单的目的

Documents in conformity with the terms of the L/C are required, but it is not the purpose. The purpose of examination of documents is to ensure "safe and timely collects".

As the L/C is conditional payment commitment of bank payment, this condition is in conformity with the terms. Only on the condition that documents is in conformity with the L/

C, the issuing bank had to accept documents, to fulfill its payment obligations.So conformity condition is the requirement which examination of documents must strictly grasp. Actually, the purpose to master the conformity terms, in which documents should be in conformity with the L/C is "safe and timely collects". Therefore in examination of documents, conformity condition just is a means and the purpose is to ensure safe and timely collects.

单证相符是审单的要求，但它并不是目的。审单的目的是确保"安全、及时收汇"。由于信用证是银行的有条件的付款承诺，而这个条件就是单证相符。只有在单证相符的条件下，开证银行才必须接受单证，履行其付款义务，所以单证相符是审单工作必须严格掌握的要求。但从实际意义来讲，掌握单证相符的目的是安全及时收汇。所以在审单工作中，单证相符只是手段，保证安全及时收汇才是目的。

2.3.2　The Base of Examining Documents
　　　审单的依据

In our country, import and export trade mostly settle by L/C to ensure safe collects. Therefore, in the examination of documents, L/C clauses are the only basis to determine whether documents are in conformity with L/C. And on the conditions of collection, the contract should be considered as the basis. But the other factors, such as the buyer's promise, the contract stipulations, correspondence and goods condition, can only be considered as a reference.They cannot be considered as the basis of conformity. So, L/C clauses must be clear and definite, and the shattered words, ambiguous terms, and mixed rules should be avoided as far as possible, to ensure safe collects.

我国进出口贸易绝大多数采用信用证方式结算，以保证安全收汇。因此，审单工作中，判定单证是否相符的唯一依据是信用证条款。而在托收条件下则应以买卖合同为依据，但其他因素，如买方诺言、合约规定、往来函电、货物情况等，只能作为参考，不能作为单证相符的依据。所以，国外来证条款必须清晰明确，一语双关的字句、模棱两可的条款、含混不清的规定都应尽量避免，以确保安全收汇。

2.3.3　The Method of Examining Documents
　　　审单的方法

The basic ways of document review are the longitudinal auditing method and the transverse audit method.

1. The Longitudinal Auditing Method

On the basis of the L/C and UCP 600, the documents specified in should be checked, the contents of the documents should comply with the provisions of the L/C and UCP 600 and achieve consistent "documents".

2. The Transverse Audit Method

Other provisions of the documents should be reviewed centered with the commercial invoice to make relevant content consistent with each other.

单据审核的基本方法有纵向审核法和横向审核法。

1. 纵向审核法

以信用证和 UCP 600 为基础，对规定的各项单据进行审核，各单据的内容要符合信用证和 UCP 600 的规定，做到"单证相符"。

2. 横向审核法

以商业发票为中心审核其他规定的单据，使有关内容互相一致，做到"单单相符"。

2.3.4 The Key Projects of Examining Documents 审单的重点项目

Drafts, invoice, transportation documents and insurance policy are the the key projects of examining documents.

汇票、发票、运输单据和保险单据等是审单的重点项目。

2.3.5 The Key Points Reviewed and Common Discrepancies of Main Documents 主要单据审核要点及常见不符点

Under the credit, documents presented the document must be audited one by one. The following Table 2-1 includes the main key points and common documents discrepancies audited.

Table 2-1 the main key points and common documents discrepancies audited

Type of Document	The Main Key Points Audited	Discrepancies of Common Documents
Commercial Invoice	(1) The commercial invoice should be issued by the beneficiary.i.e the opener should be consistent with the beneficiary's name and address of the L/C (2) The description of goods such as name of commodity, quantity, unit price, packing, price terms and contract number, must be in strict accordance with the L/C (3) The payee/ bearer of commercial invoice should be the applicant and the payee should be consistent with the applicant and the address of the L/C (4) The invoice date can be earlier than the issuing date and should not be later than the presentation period and the expiry date of L/C	(1) The opener of invoice is not the beneficiary of L/C (2) The name of invoice does not conform to the stipulations of the L/C (3) The payee/ bearer of commercial invoice is not in conformity with the requirements of the L/C (4) The name of importer is different with the applicant of the L/C

(续表)

Type of Document	The Main Key Points Audited	Discrepancies of Common Documents
Commercial Invoice	(5) The invoice amount of invoice should be the same as the draft amount unit price and trade terms of invoice should be consistent with the L/C. The bank is not responsible for checking the detail calculation process or the arithmetic results (6) The signature of the commercial invoice generally is not needed, unless otherwise stated in the L/C (7) The port of shipment, the port of discharge, shipping mark, quantity and weight of invoice should be consistent with other documents listed	(5) The quantity, invoice value and the unit price does not agree with the L/C or are not within the allowed margin of increase or decrease in the L/C (6) The description of goods of invoice is inconsistent with the description of the goods in the L/C (7) The loading port or the port of destination on the invoice does not agree with the bill of lading
Packing List/ Weight List	(1) The name and copies of documents must be consistent with the requirements of the L/C (2) The number and date of packing List must be exactly the same as the invoice's (3) Generally, packing list/weight memo do not show unit price and total amount (4) The size of packages, packing materials, the means of packing, gross/net weight/tare must be consistent with the invoice's	(1) Packing list/weight list does not conform to the stipulations of the L/C (2) Number and date of packing list do not agree with the invoice (3) The consignee and signature of packing list are wrong (4) The contract number and destination of packing list do not agree with the invoice's (5) The specifications and packing of packing list are wrong (6) The name of goods, shipping mark, gross weight are wrong
Bill of Lading	(1) The number of copies of full set of bill of lading must be presented as the requirement stipulated in the L/C (2) The payee/ bearer of bill of lading should be filled in the requirement of the L/C (3) The notify party of bill of lading should be consistent with the provisions of the L/C (4) The consignor of bill of lading should be consistent with the beneficiary of the L/C (5) The bill of lading should indicate the name of the carrier and be signed by the carrier or its agent, the master or his agent (6) Unless there are special provisions, the bill of lading should be clean on board bill of lading	(1) The type of the bill of lading submitted is not consistent with the stipulations of the L/C (2) Fails to submit the full set of effective bill of lading (3) The name of the shipper is inconsistent with the L/C (4) The name of the consignee is inconsistent with the L/C (5) The names of the notify party do not agree with L/C (6) Not properly endorsed (if required) as stipulated in the L/C (7) The bill of lading submitted is not clean

(续表)

Type of Document	The Main Key Points Audited	Discrepancies of Common Documents
Bill of Lading	(7) When price terms is "CFR" or "CIF", Freight column marked should be "Freight Paid" or "Freight Prepaid". When price terms is "FOB", freight column marked should be "Freight Collect" (8) The date of the bill of lading should be not later than the latest shipping date stipulated in the L/C (9) The bill of lading date should be not later than 21 days after the date of shipment.(if L/C has other regulations, it should be according to its provisions) (10) Number, shipping mark, quantity, name of vessel and voyage contained in the bill of lading should be consistent with the invoice. Description of goods is available, but must not conflict with the invoice's	(8) Documents information listed in the shipping such as name, packing and quantity of goods are not in conformity with L/C (9) Freight prepaid or freight collect did not prove as stipulation in the L/C (10) Did not indicate the name of the carrier
Certificate of Origin	(1) Documents should be signed by the letter of credit designated. If there is no regulation, documents issued by beneficiary is also acceptable (2) Name of commodity, marks, quality, quantity and price of the relevant goods records should be consistent with the L/C, invoice and other documents (3) Ensure that the country of origin recorded in the certificate of origin conform to the requirements of the L/C (4) The issuing date should not be later than the date of shipment	(1) The species of certificate of origin submitted do not agree with L/C (2) Agencies of certificate of origin do not conform to the requirements of the L/C (3) The goods information specified in the certificate of origin do not agree with the L/C, invoice and other documents (4) The country of Recorded in the certificate of origin do not match the requirements of the L/C (5) The issuing date of certificate of origin is after the date of shipment
Insurance Policy	(1) Only insurance companies or underwriters or their agents have the right to issue the insurance document (2) Under the CIF and CIP, the insured or the beneficiary is the seller. The insurance policy in negotiable form should be endorsed by the insured (3) Banks accept the insurance document, certificate of insurance and insurance declaration. Insurance policy can replace certificate, but the certificate of insurance does not take the place of the policy	(1) The types of the insurance policy do not conform to the stipulations of the L/C (2) The policy is not issued by the insurance company or underwriter (3) The amount of insurance do not agree with L/C (4) The description of the goods on the policy do not agree with L/C (5) The insurance amount in lowercase or uppercase is inconsistent with each other

(续表)

Type of Document	The Main Key Points Audited	Discrepancies of Common Documents
Insurance Policy	(4) The same money must be used to issue the insurance document as to open the L/C. The minimum amount of insurance amount shall be the CIF or CIP value plus 10%, or 110% of total amount of the L/C for payment, acceptance or negotiation with 110% of the invoice value, with strong one in amount (5) Original copies of Insurance policy should conform to the requirements of the L/C (6) The date of the insurance policy should not be later than the issuing date of B/L (7) Coverage should comply with the stipulations of the L/C (8) Compensation place should comply with the stipulations of the L/C, usually in the importing country (9) Name of vessel, route, port, date of shipment listed on the insurance policy should be consistent with the bill of lading (10) Description of goods should list the name of commodity, marks, quantity and so on, and should be consistent with the invoice, bill of lading and other shipping documents	(6) Port of shipment or port of discharge does not agree with the stipulation of the L/C (7) Coverage doesn't agree with the stipulation of the L/C. For example, make a mistake non-delivery risks as TPND (8) Do not provide a full range of insurance document (9) Insurance policy without endorsement or endorsement is not correct (10) The date of insurance policy is later than the date of bill of lading
Inspection Certificate	(1) It should be issued by the issuing agency stipulated by the L/C (2) Inspection items and contents should accord with the requirement of the L/C. If inspection results are not in conformity with the requirement of the L/C, the buyer can refuse to pay (3) The date of inspection should not be later than the date of shipment, but not too early, otherwise it will lead to the failure test	(1) The types of inspection certificate submitted do not agree with L/C (2) The issuing institutions of inspection certificate do not conform to the requirements of the L/C (3) Inspection items and contents do not conform to the requirements of the L/C. Inspection results is not in conformity with the requirements of L/C (4) The inspection date is later than the date of bill of lading, or fresh, perishable commodities is inspected too early

（续表）

Type of Document	The Main Key Points Audited	Discrepancies of Common Documents
Bill of Exchange	(1) Under L/C, draft should list drawn clause including the issuing bank, L/C number and the issuing date which should be consistent with the L/C (2) Currency should conform to the stipulations of the L/C, the amount should be in conformity with the stipulations of the L/C. Draft amount in general should be 100% of the invoice value, and no more than the credit amount (3) The payer of a draft should be the issuing bank or the paying bank specified. If the paying bank is not provided by L/C, it should be the issuing bank and the applicant should not pay (4) The issuer of the draft should be the beneficiary, usually exporters, and should be consistent with the beneficiary's name and place of the L/C (5) The payment deadline of bill should be consistent with the L/C (6) The issuing date of drafts must be within the validity of the L/C. It should not be earlier than the invoice date (7) Usually, the payee of draft is the negotiating bank (8) The issuer of draft must sign and seal. Draft without the signature and seal of the issuer is invalid	(1) The issuing date of the bill is later than the validity of the L/C (2) The sum is greater than the amount of the L/C (3) Uppercase and lowercase of the amount of draft is not conformity with each other. The amount of draft in words is not accurate, or fail to fill "ONLY" (4) The currency do not agree with the invoice or the L/C (5) The bill does not conform to the stipulation of the L/C, or the date of payment is not clear (6) The contents of the draft has been changed (7) The number of copies of the draft submitted is not correct (8) Draft clause is not listed according to the stipulation of the L/C (9) Fail to or being wrong to list the L/C number (10) The issuer fail to sign and seal

在信用证项下，所提交的单据必须进行单证、单单的逐一审核。表2-1为主要单据审核要点及常见不符点的说明。

表2-1 主要单据审核要点及常见不符点

单据种类	审核要点	常见不符点
商业发票	(1) 发票应由信用证受益人开立，即开立人应与受益人名称、地址一致 (2) 商品的名称、数量、单价、包装、价格条件、合同号码等描述，必须与信用证严格一致 (3) 发票的抬头应为开证申请人，即抬头人应与信用证开证申请人名称、地址一致 (4) 发票日期可以早于开证日期，不得迟于最迟交单期和信用证到期日 (5) 发票金额应与汇票金额相同，发票单价、贸易条件应与信用证相符，银行不负责核对详细核算过程或计算结果	(1) 发票的开立人不是信用证受益人 (2) 发票名称不符合信用证规定 (3) 发票的抬头人与信用证要求不符 (4) 进口商名称与信用证上的开证申请人不同 (5) 货物数量、发票金额及单价与信用证不一致或不在信用证允许的增减幅度之内

(续表)

单据种类	审核要点	常见不符点
商业发票	(6) 商业发票一般不需要签字，除非信用证另有规定。 (7) 发票上的装运港、卸货港、唛头、数量、重量应与其他单据所列一致	(6) 发票对货物的描述与信用证中货物的描述不相符 (7) 发票上的装运港或目的港与提单不一致
装箱单/重量单	(1) 单据的名称和份数必须和信用证要求相符 (2) 号码、日期与发票完全相同 (3) 装箱单/重量单一般不显示单价和总金额 (4) 货物包装大小、包装材料、包装方式、毛重/净重/皮重等需与发票一致	(1) 装箱单/重量单不符合信用证规定 (2) 号码、日期与发票不一致 (3) 收货人、签发人有误 (4) 合同号、目的地与发票不一致 (5) 规格、包装有误 (6) 货名、唛头、毛重有误
提单	(1) 提单必须按信用证规定的份数全套提交 (2) 提单的抬头人应按信用证要求进行填写 (3) 被通知人的名称、地址应与信用证的规定相符 (4) 提单上的发货人应与信用证的受益人一致 (5) 提单应标明承运人名称，并经承运人或其代理人签名或船长或其代理人签名 (6) 提单上的批注。除非信用证有特别规定，提单应为清洁已装船提单 (7) 当价格条件为"CFR"或"CIF"时，运费栏应注明"Freight Prepaid"或"Freight Paid"。当价格条件为"FOB"时，运费栏应注明"Freight Collect" (8) 提单的日期不得迟于信用证所规定的最迟装运日期 (9) 提单的交单日期不得迟于装船日期后21天(信用证有其他规定者按其规定) (10) 提单所载件数、唛头、数量、船名、航次等应和发票相一致，货物描述可用总称，但不得与发票货名相抵触	(1) 提交的提单种类与信用证规定不相符 (2) 未提交全套有效的提单 (3) 托运人的名称与信用证不相符 (4) 收货人的名称与信用证不相符 (5) 被通知人的名称与信用证规定不一致 (6) 未按信用证规定正确背书(如果需要的话) (7) 提交了不清洁的提单 (8) 运输单据中所列货物的名称、包装、数量等信息与信用证规定不相符 (9) 未按信用证规定证明运费已付或运费到付 (10) 未注明承运人的名称
产地证	(1) 文件应由信用证指定机构签署，如果没有规定，则受益人出具的单据也可以接受 (2) 货物名称、唛头、品质、数量及价格等有关商品的记载应与信用证、发票以及其他单据一致 (3) 确保产地证记载的产地国家符合信用证要求 (4) 签发日期不迟于装船日期	(1) 提交的产地证种类与信用证规定不一致 (2) 产地证的出证机构不符合信用证要求 (3) 产地证上记载的货物信息与信用证、发票及其他单据不一致 (4) 产地证记载的国家与信用证要求不一致 (5) 产地证签发时间在装船日期后

(续表)

单据种类	审核要点	常见不符点
保险单	(1) 必须是保险公司或保险商或其代理方才有权签发保险单据 (2) 在 CIF、CIP 贸易条件下，被保险人是卖方或受益人，应由被保险人背书 (3) 银行接受的是保险单据、保险凭证、保险声明。保险单可以代替保险凭证，但保险凭证不能代替保险单 (4) 保险单据必须使用与信用证相同的货币开立，最低保险金额应为 CIF 或 CIP 价格的金额加 10%，或者信用证要求付款、承兑、议付金额的 110% 与发票金额的 110%，两者中取金额较大者 (5) 保险单正本份数应符合信用证要求 (6) 保险单的日期不应晚于提单签发日 (7) 承保险别应符合信用证规定。 (8) 赔偿地点应符合信用证规定，一般是在进口国 (9) 保险单上所列船名、航线、港口、起运日期应与提单一致 (10) 货物描述应列明货物名称、唛头、数量等，并应与发票、提单及其他货运单据一致	(1) 保险单的种类不符合信用证规定 (2) 保险单不是由规定的保险公司或保险商出具 (3) 保险金额与信用证规定不一致 (4) 保险单上对货物的描述与信用证规定不一致 (5) 保险金额大小写不一致 (6) 起运港或卸货港与信用证规定不一致 (7) 保险单的投保险别与信用证规定不一致，如误把交货不到险当成偷窃、提货不着险 (8) 未提供全套保险单据 (9) 保险单未经背书或背书不正确 (10) 保险日期迟于提单日期
检验证书	(1) 检验证书应由信用证规定机构签发 (2) 检验项目及内容应符合信用证的要求，检验结果如与信用证要求不符，买家可拒付 (3) 检验日期不得迟于装运日期，但也不得过早，否则会导致检验失效	(1) 提交的检验证书种类与信用证规定不一致 (2) 检验证书的出证机构不符合信用证要求 (3) 检验项目及内容不符合信用证要求，检验结果与信用证要求不符 (4) 检验日期晚于提单日期，或鲜活、易腐烂商品检验过早
汇票	(1) 信用证名下汇票，应列出出票条款，其中开证行、信用证号码及开证日期应与信用证相符 (2) 货币名称符合信用证规定，金额应与信用证规定相符，且大小一致。汇票金额一般应为 100% 的发票金额，且不超过信用证金额 (3) 汇票付款人应为开证行或指定的付款行。若信用证未规定，应为开证行，不应以申请人为付款人 (4) 汇票出票人应为受益人，通常为出口商，且应与信用证受益人名称、地点相符 (5) 汇票付款期限应与信用证规定相符 (6) 汇票出票日期必须在信用证有效期内，不应早于发票日期 (7) 汇票收款人通常为议付行 (8) 汇票的出票人必须签字盖章，无出票人签字盖章的汇票视为无效汇票	(1) 汇票的出票日期迟于信用证有效期 (2) 汇票金额大于信用证金额 (3) 汇票金额大小写不一致或汇票大写金额不准确，大写金额最后漏填 "ONLY" (4) 货币名称与发票或信用证不一致 (5) 汇票付款期限与信用证规定不符，或未明确付款日期 (6) 汇票的内容被更改 (7) 汇票提交的份数不正确 (8) 未按规定列明 "出票条款" (9) 漏列或错列了信用证号码 (10) 出票人未签字盖章

2.3.6 Processing Method of a Problem Documents
有问题单据的处理方法

When auditing, importers (the applicant) focus on whether documents conform to L/C and whether the goods are consistent with documents. After audit if any problem found, they should be recorded in the audit form and report to business department and finance department. If the exporter (the applicant) decided to refuse to pay after the audit, they should state discrepancies stipulated in documents and L/C clauses on the documents arrival notice under the import L/C, and build a special seal for finance within the time returned to the bank.

In accordance with the relevant provisions of the UCP 600 and ISBP, the issuing bank must review these documents within a reasonable time the next day up to five working days after receipt of the relevant documents, and make the decision of the payment or refuse to pay. If the issuing bank audit documents, there are substantial discrepancies in the surface of the negotiating documents and decide to refuse to pay, they shall promptly notify the sender in telecommunications not later than fifth banking days since the second day of the receipt of documents.If the issuing bank audit documents, there are no substantial discrepancies and agree to pay, they shall immediately give the applicant (importer) to audit the relevant documents copy under L/C the documents arrival notice and confirmation and limit its reply three days so that the issuing bank can notice in five working days.

进口商(开证申请人)审单的重点主要是根据行业做法与商品特性审查单据的真实性，审查单证是否相符及单、货是否相符。审查后如发现单据有问题，要记录在审单记录表上，并及时上报业务部门和财务部门。若出口商(开证申请人)审查后决定拒付，应在进口信用证下的到单通知书上列明单据与信用证条款规定的不符点，并加盖财务专用章在银行规定的时间内返还银行。

按照 UCP 600 和 ISBP 的有关规定，开证银行必须在收到有关单据次日起至 5 个工作日的合理时间内审核这些单据，并做出付款或者拒付的决定。若开证银行审核议付单据表面与信用证条款有实质性不符点而决定拒付，应立即以电讯方式通知寄单人，不得迟于收到议付单据的第二天起第五个银行工作日。若开证银行审核议付单据表面与信用证条款无实质性不符点并同意付款，应立即将有关单据复印件和进口信用证项下到单通知书和确认书一并交给开证申请人(进口商)审单，限其在三天内答复，以使开证行能在五个工作日内对外通知。

2.3.7 Sample of L/C Examination
审证范例

DOCUMETNATRY CREDIT

BENEFICIARY: SHANGHAI IMPORT& EXPORT TRADE CORPORATION

1321，ZHONGSHAN ROAD SHANGHAI，CHINA

DATE Of ISSUE：01 / 04 / 04

1SUING BANK：NATIONAL AUSTRALIA BANKL IMITED SYDNEY (TRADE AND INTERNATIONAL—PAYMENTS)

FORM OF DOCUMENTARY CREDIT: IRREVOCABLE

DATE AND PLACE OF EXPIRY：17 / 05 / 04IN COUNTRY OF BENEFICIARY

APPLICANT: THE CLOTHING COMPANY AUSTRALIA PTY LTD

101BURWOOD HIGHWAY BURWOOD VIC 3125

KNITTED GARMENTS OF 92PERCENT COTTON AND 8PERCENT SPANDEX AS PER ORDE NO.1354MULTISTICH CREW 400 PCS USD 5.20 USD2080.00 CFR MELBOURNE AUSTRAUA

DOCUMENTS REQUIRED (1N DUFLICATE UNLESS OTHERWISE STATED)

+FULL SET OF CLEAN ON BOABD MARINE BILL OF LADING MADR OUT TO THE ORDEROF SHIPPER BLANK ENDORSED AND MARKED FREIGHT PREPAID

+COMMERCIAL INVOICE

+PACKKING LIST

+CERTIFICATE OF ORIGIN

+PACKING DECLARATION

ADDITIONAL CONDITIONS

+ALL DOCUMENTS IN DUPLICATE UNLESS OTHERWISE STIPULATED.

+DOCUMENTS NEGOTIATED WITH OR SUBJECT TO ACCEPTANCE ANY DISCREPANCY WILL ATTRACT A HANDLING FEE OF USD 40. THIS FEE WII BE DEDUCTED FROM PPROCEEDS REMITTED BY OUR SELVES.

+CONTACT AT SUNTOR AND BLOOMING IS JIMMY ON TELEPHONE 216399001.

+ALL DOCUMENTS MUST BE IN THE NAME OF：

MAGGIET CORPORATION PTY．LTD

10l BURWOOD HIGHWAY BURWOOD VIC 3125

+INSTRUCTIONS FOR NEGOTIATING BANK ON PRESENTATION OF DOCUMENTS UNDER THIS L/C. THE NEGOTIATING BANK'S PRESENTATION SCHEDULE MUSTINDICATE THE NUMBER AND DATE OF ANY AMNENTS THAT HAVE BEEN AVAILED / REJECTED UNDER THEIR NEGOTIATION.

The process of examining documentary credit is as follows.

(1) Examining L/C.

① Examining what type the L/C belongs to，revocable L/C or irrevocable L/C?

② Examining whether the name and address of applicants or beneficiaries are correct.

③ Examining whether the dates of L/C (issuing date, shipment date, delivery date, expiry date, etc) are reasonable or not.

④ Examining whether the descriptions of shipping goods or amount of L/C is correct, including name, specification, packing, quantity and unit price.

(2) Grasping Main Items of L/C.

Exporting of <u>KNITTED GARMENTS OF 92PERCENT COTTON AND 8PERCENT SPANDEX AS PER ORDER No. 1354MULTISTICH CREW 400 PCS   USD 5.20   USD 2 080.00 CFR MELBOURNE AUSTRALIA</u>

(3) Deciding Which Document We Should Complete.

① Commercial Invoice

② Packing List

③ CERTIFICATE OF ORIGIN

④ PACKING DECLARATION

⑤ DRAFT

⑥ BILL OF LADING

(4) Making Out Documents Required.

审核信用证的步骤如下。

(1) 审核信用证。

① 审核信用证种类是可撤销信用证还是不可撤销信用证。

② 审核申请人或受益人的名字和地址是否正确。

③ 审核信用证上的日期是否合理(开证日期、装运期、交货期和有效期等)。

④ 审核信用证中货物的描述和金额是否正确，包括名称、规格、包装、数量和单价。

(2) 掌握信用证中商品的要点。

出口各类针织服装92%的棉和8%氨纶

订单号 No.1354 MULTISTICH CREW

400件　单价5.2美元　总价2 080.00美元

价格术语CFR　墨尔本　澳大利亚

(3) 决定应该完成什么单证。

① 商业发票。

② 装箱单。

③ 原产地证。

④ 包装声明。

⑤ 汇票。

⑥ 提单。

(4) 缮制所需的单证。

2.4 Presentation of Documents
交单

2.4.1 Presentation under L/C
信用证下的交单

1. Normal Presentation of Documents

There are three requirements of presentation: the first is that the document is all ready. The second is that the content must be correct. The third is to submit documents timely.

2. Discrepant Documents

UCP 600 Article 15 b: When an issuing bank determines that a presentation does not comply, it may in its sole judgment approach the applicant for a waiver of the discrepancies. This does not, however, extend the period mentioned in sub-article 14 b.

For discrepant documents, common international rules provide that exporters should guarantee to negotiating bank and ask for guarantees negotiation. If the negotiating bank agree to negotiate the documents, that exporters should make a statement to the issuing bank.

1. 正常单据交单

交单的要求有三条：第一是单据齐备；第二是内容正确；第三是提交及时。

2. 有不符点单据的交单

按照 UCP 600 第十五条 b 款的规定，当开证行确定交单不符时，可以自行决定联系申请人放弃不符点，然而这并不能延长第十四条 b 款所指的期限。

对于不符点单据的交单，国际上普遍规定出口商提供担保书给议付行，要求担保议付，如议付行同意议付单据，并向开证行声明。

2.4.2 Presentation under non L/C
非信用证结算方式下的交单

1. Presentation under T/T

If payment by T/T before shipment, exporters have all received the contract value T/T by importers before shipment. After shipment, all documents including ocean bills of lading will be directly sent to the importer, or order the shipping company to Telex release the bill of lading to the importer.

If payment by T/T after shipment sent by the bill of lading fax, exporters will fax marine bill of lading to the importer and will send all documents including the ocean bill of lading to the importer when importers T/T all the contract value to exporters' bank account.

2. Presentation under Collection

Presentation under Collection is more flexible. Types and content of documents and date of presentation of documents are decided according to the contract and the situation of importer. When presentation, the exporter should also provide the clear collection instructions to banks. Some Banks provide fixed format for exporters to fill in. The collection instructions mainly include: means of collection, conditions of presentation, the detail address of payer, the specific name and address of collecting bank, a notarial protest certificate on the condition of refusing to pay(If not, to choose by the remitting bank), the expenses of the collection item and other special conditions.

1. 电汇项下交单

如果装运前采用电汇结算方式，出口商在装运前已全部收到进口商电汇的合同金额。在装运后，就直接把包括海运提单在内的所有单据寄给进口商，或指示船公司把提单电传给进口商。

如果装运后凭提单传真件电汇结算，出口商在装运后，把海运提单传真给进口商，等进口商把合同金额电汇到出口商银行账户后，才把海运提单在内的所有单据寄给进口商。

2. 托收项下交单

托收交单较灵活，单据种类、单据内容、交单时间由出口商根据合同和进口商的情况决定。交单时，出口商还应向银行提供明确的托收指示书，有的银行提供固定格式供出口商填写。托收指示书的主要内容包括：托收方式；交单条件；付款人的详细地址；代收行的具体名称及地址；在拒付情况下，是否要做成拒付证书(如无，则由托收行代为选择)；托收项下的费用；其他特殊条件。

2.4.3 The Procedure of Bank after Presentation by Exporter under L/C
信用证下出口商交单后银行的工作流程

Negotiation bank examine documents → negotiation bank forward documents and ask for payment → issuing bank honor and pay → applicant purchase documents → negotiation bank pay beneficiary.

在信用证下，出口商交单后银行的工作流程为：议付行审单→议付行寄单索偿→开证行承兑并付款→申请人付款赎单→议付行向受益人付款。

2.4.4 The Processing of Discrepant Documents under the L/C with Relief
信用证项下不符单据的处理与补救措施

The issuing bank to contain the discrepant documents shall have the right to refuse to pay. Some inexperienced company upon receiving notice from the issuing bank dishonored often panic and accept the price requirements of their clients in a hurry, which led to the economic losses directly. In fact, documents dishonored under a credit, does not mean that the payment for goods under export was sentenced to death penalty, the price also is not the only way to solve the problem. Facing the discrepancies put forward by the issuing bank, the exporter shall take the following measures.

1. Review whether the Premise Condition of the Discrepancies Put Forward by the Issuing Bank is established

The premise condition of the discrepancies put forward by the issuing bank include:

(1) Within a reasonable time discrepancies are put forward to the documents reminder by the issuing bank, i.e. commenced from the date following the receipt of documents within five working days.

(2) Without delay in telecommunications way the discrepancies will be informed to the reminder.

(3) Discrepancies must be one-time put forward, that is, such as first mentioned discrepancies, even if there are substantial discrepancies of documents, the issuing bank has no right to put forward again.

(4) When discrepancies are noticed, safekeeping disposal or refund of documents must be shown.

The above conditions must meet at the same time, otherwise, the issuing bank is not entitled to claim documents discrepancies and refuse to pay.

2. Whether Audit Discrepancies from the Issuing Bank is Established

Trade documents member should examine and verify the issuing bank of discrepancies carefully according to the terms of the L/C, the UCP and ISBP to judge whether it was set up. If not, should argued with the issuing bank by the negotiating bank until the issuing bank make payment.

(1) If discrepancies are set up and conditions allow, documents can be resubmitted. Relief of discrepant documents under the L/C is when documents are refused to be payed by the issuing bank due to discrepancies, the beneficiary may resubmit the documents replaced or corrected back to the bank within the prescribed period of time in a timely manner.

According to the regulation of UCP 600, the bank decides to refuse to pay when there are discrepancies after audit, and then the issuing bank can be exempt from responsibility to make payment of the L/C. But when the beneficiary fills the documents that conform to the stipulations of the L/C within the allotted time, the issuing bank must be liable for the payment. If the beneficiary wastes a lot of time in the early stage of the operation, he/ she will lose time to resubmit the documents.

(2) If discrepancies are set up and documents cannot be resubmitted, positive negotiation with the applicant should be made. The issuing bank dishonored does not mean that the applicant refuse to pay, if the applicant give up the discrepancies in the end, in spite of the issuing bank is not bound by decision of the applicant, but he/she will cooperate with the applicant to make payment typically. So after the issuing bank refuse to pay, if discrepancies do set up, and the consistent documents can't be resumitted, the relationship between the applicant and the actual situation of the deal should be analyzed to determine how to negotiate with and persuade the applicant to accept discrepancies and make payment. As long as the quality of goods pass and commodity market price is better, generally the applicant does not refuse to accept the documents as an excuse. Additional, the way of reducing the price also can be taken to enable the applicant to pay payment.

(3) If discrepancies are established, and the applicant refuses to accept the documents, another buyer can be found in the country of import. If the applicant refuses to accept discrepant documents, importer of beneficiary may try to find another buyer. After all, the beneficiary has the discretion of the documents. But the premise is that the L/C requires to submit a full set of original bill of lading. If 1/3 original bill of lading has been sent to the applicant, 2/3 original bill of lading is submitted to the bank. This is likely to face the lost plight of goods and money.

(4) If the beneficiary fails to find the buyer, he/she can only return the documents and goods. Before making this decision, however, whether the cost of the goods and the value is profitable must be closely calculated.

开证行对于包含不符点的单据有权拒付。一些经验不足的公司在接到开证行的拒付通知时往往惊慌失措，匆匆忙忙接受客户的降价要求，直接导致经济损失。其实，信用证项下的单据被拒付时，并不意味着出口项下的货款被判了死刑，降价也不是解决问题的唯一办法。面对开证行提出的不符点，出口商应当采取以下措施。

1. 审核开证行提出不符点的前提条件是否成立

开证行提出不符点的前提条件包括以下几个。

(1) 在合理的时间内提出不符点，即在开证行收到单据次日起算的5个工作日之内向单据的提示者提出不符点。

(2) 无延迟地以电讯方式将不符点通知提示者。

(3) 不符点必须一次性提出，如第一次所提不符点不成立，即使单据还存在实质性的不符点，开证行也无权再次提出。

(4) 通知不符点的同时，必须说明单据代为保管听候处理，或退交单者。

以上条件必须同时满足，否则，开证行便无权声称单据存在不符点而拒付。

2. 审核开证行所提的不符点是否成立

外贸单证员应根据信用证条款、UCP 和 ISBP 认真审核开证行所提的不符点，判断其是否成立。若不成立，应通过议付行与开证行据理力争，直至开证行付款。

(1) 若不符点成立，条件允许，可补交相符单据。信用证项下不符点单据的救济是指当单据由于不符而遭开证行拒付之后，受益人可在规定的时间内及时将替代或更正后的相符单据补交给银行。

根据 UCP 600 的规定，单据经审核存在不符点，且银行决定拒付时，则开证行所承担的信用证项下的付款责任得以免除；但当受益人在规定时间内补交了符合信用证规定的单据，开证行必须承担其付款责任。如果受益人在前期操作过程中浪费了大量时间，就会丧失补交单据的时间。

(2) 若不符点成立，且无法补交相符单据，此时要积极与开证申请人洽谈。开证行拒付并不意味着开证申请人拒付，如果开证申请人最终放弃不符点，尽管开证行并不受开证申请人决定的约束，但一般会配合开证申请人付款。所以开证行拒付后，如果不符点确实成立，且无法补交相符单据，应分析开证申请人之间的关系及此笔交易的实际情况，以决定怎样与其交涉，说服开证申请人接受不符点并付款。只要货物质量过关，商品市场价格较好，开证申请人一般不会以此为借口拒绝接受单据。另外，也可以采取降价的方式，使开证申请人能付款赎单。

(3) 若不符点成立，且开证申请人拒绝接受单据，则可在进口国另寻买主。若开证申请人拒绝接受不符点单据，受益人可以设法在进口国另寻买主，毕竟受益人拥有对单据的处理权。但其前提是信用证要求递交全套正本提单，若 1/3 正本提单已寄给开证申请人，2/3 正本提单提交给银行，则可能会面临钱货两失的困境。

(4) 如果受益人无法在进口国另寻买主，就只有退单退货了。不过在做出此决定之前，一定要仔细核算运回货物所需的费用和货值，看看是否有利可图。

2.5 Management of Documents
单证的管理

Banks deal with documents but not with goods, services or performance to which the documents may relate. So management of documents is very important. It is the basis of international trade.

1. Personnel Organization Settings

To ensure international trade documents made correctly, and promptly circulated, performed its functions, each trade enterprise is required to arrange related personnel, and set up corresponding organization. There are two types of organization, functional and simple types.

2. Significance of Management of Documents

(1) To provide guarantee for completing an agreement.

(2) To provide raw materials for statistical analysis in order to improve the management level of International trade.

(3) To provide information for inquiry and processing accident of business mistakes.

3. Requirements of Management of Documents

(1) To establish a complete documents file management system.

(2) To analyze the quality and efficiency of the documents frequently.

银行处理的是单证，而不是单证可能涉及的货物、服务或履约行为。因此，单证管理相当重要，它是国际贸易的基础。

1. 人员机构设置

为保证国际商务单证正确地制作，并及时流转，发挥其作用，各贸易企业都需安排相关人员，设置相应的组织机构。组织机构有职能型和简单型两种。

2. 单证管理意义

(1) 为完成履约提供保证。

(2) 为统计分析提供原始资料，提高外贸工作管理水平。

(3) 为查询和处理业务差错事故提供资料。

3. 单证管理要求

(1) 要建立完备的单证档案管理制度。

(2) 要经常分析提高单证工作的质量和效率。

Chapter 3

Basic Knowledge
基础知识

3.1 Terms of Payment
付款方式

3.1.1 Collection
托收

1. Definition

In simple terms, a collection means that the creditor (the exporter) entrusts the bank to collect payment from the debtor (the importer). The bank acts as the intermediary.

2. Types of Collections

(1) Clean collection: A collection in which the demand for payment (such as a draft) is presented without additional documents.

(2) Documentary collection: A collection in which the demand for payment (such as a draft) is presented with additional documents. It is a method of effecting payment whereby the exporter/seller ships goods to the imports/buyer, but instructs a bank to collect a certain sum from the importer/buyer in exchange for the transfer of title, shipping documents and other documentation, enabling the importer/buyer to take possession of the goods. Documentary collection includes documents against payment(D/P)and documents against acceptance(D/A).

(3) Documents against payment (D/P): If the collecting bank presents a sight draft, the payer will pay at sight. The bank will send the documents to the drawee so that he can pick up the goods. We called this process D/P.

(4) D/P at sight: It refers to the documents sent to the collecting bank located in the import country and the collecting bank presents to the importers. After examining the documents without any mistakes, the importers will make payment for the documents immediately.

(5) D/P after sight: It refers that the importer will honor the draft immediately after examining the documents without any mistakes. And he will make payment for the documents

on the maturity. Before the expiry of the draft, the draft and the shipping documents will be taken care of by the collecting bank.

(6) Documents against acceptance (D/A): It means that the seller will send the documents to the buyer as the condition that the buyer accepts draft(s). That is, the buyer can obtain shipping documents from the collecting bank and make extraction of the goods after he accept the draft(s). The buyer will pay until the maturity date.

1. 定义

简单来说，托收是指债权人（出口商）出具汇票委托银行向债务人（进口商）收取货款的一种结算方式。银行扮演的是中介的角色。

2. 托收种类

(1) 光票托收：付款凭证（如汇票）不附带其他额外单据的托收。

(2) 跟单托收：付款凭证（如汇票）附带有其他额外单据的托收。跟单托收是一种付款方式，出口商/卖方将货物发运给买方，并指示银行向进口商/买方收取一定金额，以换取货物和其他文件使进口商/买方拥有货物。跟单托收分为付款交单 (D/P) 和承兑交单 (D/A)。

(3) 付款交单：如果代收行提示的是即期汇票，付款人见票即付，银行就将货物单据交给付款人，付款人可凭单提货，这一过程叫作付款交单。

(4) 即期付款交单：单据寄到进口方所在地的代收行后，由代收行向进口商提示，进口商审单无误后立即付款赎单。

(5) 远期付款交单：进口商见票并审单无误后，立即承兑汇票，于汇票到期日付款赎单。在汇票到期前，汇票和货运单据由代收行保管。

(6) 承兑交单：卖方的交单以买方承兑汇票为条件，也就是说，买方在汇票上履行承兑手续后，即可从代收行取得货运单据，凭此提取货物。等到汇票到期日，买方再付款。

3.1.2 L/C 信用证

1. Definition

A letter of credit or L/C is a conditional undertaking of payments by a bank.

2. Features

(1) L/C is a letter issued by a bank, and it is also banker's credit.

(2) L/C is a self-sufficient instrument.

(3) Banks deal with documents.

3. Parties of Letter of Credit

(1) Applicant: Applicant means the party on whose request the credit is issued.

(2) Issuing Bank: Issuing bank means the bank that issues a credit at the request of an

applicant or on its own behalf.

(3) Beneficiary: Beneficiary means the party in whose favour a credit is issued.

(4) Confirming bank: Confirming bank means the bank that adds its confirmation to a credit upon the issuing bank's authorization or request.

(5) Nominated Bank: Nominated bank means the bank with which the credit is available or the bank nominated by any bank in the case of a credit.

(6) Presenter: Presenter means a beneficiary, bank or other parties that make a presentation of documents.

4. The Content of L/C

(1) Name and address of the issuing bank.

(2) Type of the credit.

(3) Name and address of the beneficiary.

(4) Amount of the credit and its currency.

(5) Expiry date of the credit and its place to be expired.

(6) Name and address of the applicant.

(7) L/C number and date of issue.

(8) Drawer and drawee, tenor.

(9) Full details of the goods.

(10) Full details of documents to be presented.

(11) Partial shipment permitted/not permitted.

(12) Transshipment allowed/not allowed.

(13) Port of shipment and port of discharge.

(14) Latest date for shipment, and the latest date for presentation of documents.

(15) Instructions of the advising bank, negotiating bank or paying bank and other special terms and conditions.

(16) The undertaking clause of the issuing bank.

1. 定义

信用证是由银行开立的有条件承诺付款的书面文件。

2. 特点

(1) 信用证是一种由银行开立的书面文件，也是一种银行信用。

(2) 信用证是一种独立自主的文件。

(3) 信用证处理的是单证。

3. 信用证有关各方

(1) 申请人：向银行申请开立信用证的人。

(2) 开证银行：接受开证人的申请，开立信用证的银行。

(3) 受益人：信用证上所指定的有权使用该证的人。

(4) 保兑行：受开证行授权或委托对信用证以自己名义保证付款的银行。

(5) 指定银行：信用证可以承付或议付的银行，以及由信用证涉及的银行所指定的银行。

(6) 交单人：提交单据的受益人、银行或其他相关方。

4. 信用证的内容

(1) 开户行的名称和地址。

(2) 信用证的种类。

(3) 受益人的名称和地址。

(4) 信用证金额及货币。

(5) 有效期和地点。

(6) 申请人的名称和地址。

(7) 信用证号码和开证日期。

(8) 出票人和付款人、汇票期限。

(9) 货物的详细资料。

(10) 提交单证的详细资料。

(11) 是否允许分批装船。

(12) 是否允许转船。

(13) 装运港口和卸货港口。

(14) 最迟装船期和最迟交单期。

(15) 通知行、议付行或支付行的说明及其他特殊条款和条件。

(16) 开证行的承诺条款。

5. Sample of Letter of Credit 信用证范例

APPLICATION HEADER 0700 1840 07130 MRMDUSADXBXXX. 1561 893704 070514 1549 N *HSB BANK USA,N.A *NEW YORK，NY	银行间互对的密押 开证行为汇丰银行纽约分行
SEQUENCE OF TOTAL *27: 1/2	页次，本信用证电文有两页，这是第一页
FROM OF DOC. CREDIT *40 A: IRREVOCABLE	信用证种类是不可撤销信用证
DOC. CREDIT NUMBER *23395	信用证号码是 23395
DATE OF ISSUE 31C: 140130	信用证开证日期是 2021 年 1 月 30 日
APPLICABLE RULES*40E: UCP LATEST VERSION	使用规则：《跟单信用证统一惯例》最新版
EXPIRY *31D: DATE 140515 PLACE CHINA	信用证到期日为 2021 年 5 月 6 日，到期地点为中国

（续表）

APPLICANT *50 PORT ROYAL SALES, LTD 95 FROEHLICH FARM BLVD WOODBURY, NY 11797 USA	开证申请人为 PORT ROYAL SALES 有限公司，佛勒利希农场大道 95 号，伍德波里，纽约州 11797 美国
BENEFICIARY *59: TIDER INDU STRIAL CO., LTD NO.310 XINYANG ROAD, GUANGZHOU CHINA	受益人，即合同卖方，广州市金泰尔工贸有限责任公司
AMOUNT: *32B CURRENCY USD AMOUNT 31 200	信用证总金额为 31 200 美元
POS./NEG. TOL(%) 39A: 5/5	信用证金额加减 5%
AVAILABLE WITH/BY *41D: ANY BANK BY NEGOTIATION	本信用证为自由议付信用证
DRAFT AT.. 42C: SIGHT	开立即期汇票
DRAWEE 42 D: APPLICANT BANK	汇票的受票人为开证行
PARTIAL SHIPMENTS 43P: PERMITTED	允许部分发运
TRANSHIPMENT 43 T: PERMITTED	允许转船
PORTT OF LAODING/AIRPORT OF DEPARTRURE 44E: GUANGZHOU, CHINA	装运港是广州
PORT OF DISCHARGE/ AIRPORT OF DEPARTRURE 44F: NEW YORK/USA	卸货港是纽约港
LATEST DATE OF SHIP. 44C: 210430	最迟装运日期是 2021 年 4 月 30 日
DESCRIPT. OF GOODS 45 A: 24/454 PINEAPPLE BROKEN SLICED IN LIGHT SYRUP, 4 800 CARTONS, ALL OTHER DETAILS ARE AS PER BENEFICIARY'S P/I NO. TDF 270102 DATED 18 JANUARY 2021 PRICE TERMS : FOB GUANGZHOU, CHINA	货物描述：24/454G 糖水菠萝片罐头，4 800 箱额，其他细节按照受益人 2021 年 1 月 18 日号码为 TDF270102 的形式发票的内容 价格条件：FOB 广州，中国
SEQUENCE OF TOTAL: *27: 2/2	本信用证有两页
DOCUMENTS REQUIRED 46A: 1) SIGNED COMMERCIAL INVOICE, 3-FOLD 2) FULL SET OF CLEAN ON BOARD ORIGINAL MARINE/OCEAN BILL OF LADING, MADE OUT TO ORDER AND BLANK ENDORSED MARKED: FREIGHT COLLECT TTIFY: APPLICANT, INDICATING NAME, ADDRESS, TELEPHONE AND FAX NO. OF THE CARRYING VESSEL'S OF AGENT AT THE PORT DISCHARGE 3) PACKING LIST IN 3 COPIES STATING: QUANTITY, DESCRIPTION, MEASUREMENTS, GROSS AND NET WEIGHT, BUYERS PURCHASE ORDER NUMBER AND L/C NO. 4) ORGINAL CERTIFICATE OF ORIGIN 5) BENEFICIARY'S STATEMENT CERTIFYING THAT THE SHIPMENT UNDER THIS LETTER OF CREDIT CONTAINS NO WOOD PACKAGING	应提交的单据： (1) 已签署商业发票一式三份 (2) 全套清洁已装船正本海运提单，做成空白抬头空白背书，标明运费到付，通知开证申请人，标明在目的地的承运人的代理人名称、地址、电话号码和传真号码 (3) 装箱单一式三份，标明数量、货物描述、体积、毛净重、买方订单号和信用证号码 (4) 原产地证正本 (5) 受益人证明：本信用证项下货物没有使用木质包装

(续表)

ADDITIONAL CON. 47 A: 1) ALL DOCUMENTS MUST BEAR OUR CREDIT NUMBER 2) UNLESS OTHERWISE SPECIFIED HEREIN, DOCUMENTS ISSUED PRIOR TO THE DATE OF THIS DOCUMENTRARY CREDIT ARE NOT ACCEPTABLE 3) GOODS MUST BE SHIPPED IN 3X20' FCL CONTAINER(S) AND BILL(S) OF LADING MUST EVIDENCE THE SAME BILL(S) OF LADING MUST INDICATING THE ONTIANER NUMBER(S) AND SEAL NUMBER(S) 4) 5 PERCENT MORE OR LESS IN QUANTITY AND AMOUNT ARE ACCEPTABLE 5) EACH CAN INTED WITH NET SHOULD HAVE LABLES PRINTED WITH NET WEIGHT, DATE OF PACKING AND EXPIR DATE 2 YARS FROM THE DATE OFPRODUCTION IN ENGLISH LANGUAGE	附加条款： 1) 所有单据标明本信用证号码 2) 除非另有规定，早于信用证开证的单据不接受 3) 货物必须用 3 个 20' 整箱包装，提单对此要做出证明，并且要标明集装箱号和集装箱封号 4) 数量和金额允许 5% 增减 5) 每个罐头要用英文标注的标签，内容为净重、包装日期和从生产日期起保质期为两年的到期日
DETAILS OF CHARGES 71 B: ALL BANKING CHAR GES OUTSIDE COUNTRY OF ISSUE FOR ACCOUNT OF BENEFICIARY	费用细节：进口国以外的所有银行费用由受益人承担
PRESENTATION PERIOD 48: 15 DAYS AFTER TRANSPORT DATE, BUT WITHIN VALIDITY	交单期：在装运日后 15 天内并在信用证有效期内
CONFIRMATION *49: WITHOUT	不保兑
SE ND TO REC. INFO. 72: AFTER RECEIPT OF CREDIT CONFORM DOCUMENTS WE SHALL COVER ACCORDING TO YOUR INSTRUCTIONS AND AS PER L/C TERMS	银行间的通知：一收到与信用证条款相符的单据，我们将按照信用证和你方指示贷记你方账户

6. Kinds of Letter of Credit

(1) Irrevocable L/C.

(2) Honorable and Negotiable L/C.

(3) Confirmed L/C.

(4) Banker's Usance L/C.

(5) Transferable L/C.

(6) Back-to-Back L/C.

(7) Revolving L/C.

(8) Reciprocal L/C.

6. 信用证的种类

(1) 不可撤销信用证。

(2) 议付信用证。

(3) 保兑信用证。

(4) 银行远期信用证。

(5) 可转让信用证。

(6) 背对背信用证。

(7) 循环信用证。

(8) 对开信用证。

3.1.3 Remittance
汇付

Remittance refers to the transfer of funds from one party to another among different countries, that is, a bank (the remitting bank) at the request of its overseas branch or correspondent bank (the paying bank) instructing them to pay a named person or corporation (the payee or beneficiary) domiciled in that country.

1. Telegraphic Transfer(T/T)

Remitting by cable/telex/SWIFT (T/T) is exactly the same as a mail transfer, except that instruction from the remitting bank to the paying bank are transmitted by cable instead of by airmail.

2. Mail Transfer(M/T)

Remittance by airmail is more generally known as mail transfer, i.e. M/T. A mail transfer is to transfer funds by means of a payment order or a mail advice, or sometimes a debit advice issued by a remitting bank, at the request of the remitter. A payment order, mail advice or debit advice is an authenticated order in writing addressed by one bank to another instructing the latter to pay a sum certain in money to a specified person or a beneficiary named thereon.

3. Remittance by Banker's Demand Draft (D/D)

Remittance by banker's demand draft is often referred to as D/D. A banker's draft is a negotiable instrument drawn by a bank on its overseas bank.

汇付指的是国与国之间资金的转移，即汇出行委托汇出行海外分行或代理行将货款支付给定居在海外分行或代理行所在地的指定收款人。

1. 电汇

加押电报、电传或 SWIFT 汇付与信汇几乎相同，唯一不同的是，电汇是汇出行通过电传的方式将委托书传给付款行而不是通过航空邮件形式。

2. 信汇

以航空邮件形式进行汇付被大多数人认为是信汇。信汇是汇出行应汇款人的申请，将付款委托书、信汇通知书或借记通知书寄给汇入行实现资金的转移。付款委托书、信汇通知书和借记通知书是一份由一家银行向另一家银行开立的，指示解付行支付一定金额给指定收款人或受益人的凭证。

3. 票汇

票汇通常是指通过银行汇票进行汇款的汇付。银行汇票是银行在其海外分行开立的可兑现的票据。

3.1.4 Remittance and Collection 汇付和托收

Telegraphic transfer and mail transfer are expressed in bold line, and draft transfer in dotted line(see Figure 3-1).

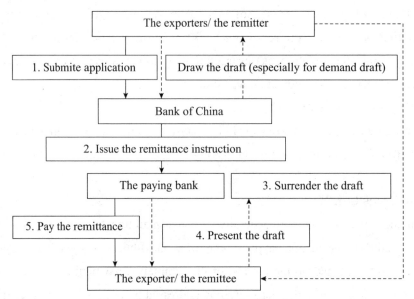

Figure 3-1　The flow chart of remittance

电汇和信汇用实线表示，票汇用虚线表示(见图 3-1)。

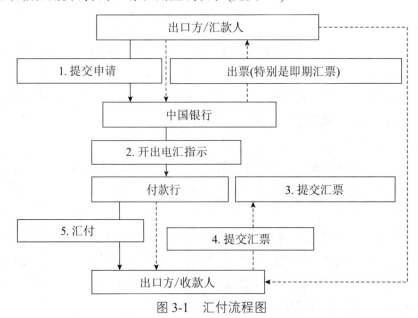

图 3-1　汇付流程图

3.2 Contract for the Sale of Goods
货物销售合同

3.2.1 Definition
定义

Sales contract (see Sample 3-1) is the formal written agreement between buyer and seller naming the parties to the transaction, products and prices, responsibilities and rights, and terms and conditions. The drafter has the advantage to claim greater influence on contract terms, but the disadvantage is subject to strict interpretation of the terms.

销售合同(见样单3-1)是买方和卖方之间的正式书面协议,确定了交易各方、产品、价格、职责和权利、条款和条件。起草者的优势是可以对合同条款施加更多影响力,劣势是受条款严格解释的约束。

3.2.2 Provisions for a Complete International Contract
完整国际贸易合同条款

Not every provision as the following is applicable to every transaction, Regardless of whether you draft the terms of the contract by yourself, or hire an attorney, you need to be aware of key contract provisions.

(1) Contract date.

(2) Identification of parties.

(3) Goods-description.

(4) Goods-quantity.

(5) Goods-price.

(6) Payment-method of payment.

(7) Payment-medium of exchange.

(8) Payment-exchange rate.

(9) Cost and charges-duties and taxes.

(10) Costs and charges-insurance.

(11) Costs and charges-handling and transport.

(12) Packaging arrangements.

(13) Delivery-date.

(14) Delivery-place.

(15) Delivery-transfer of title.

(16) Transportation-carrier.

(17) Transportation-storage.

(18) Transportation-notice provisions.

(19) Transportation-shipping time.

(20) Transportation-insurance.

(21) Import/export documentation.

(22) Invoice preparation and delivery.

(23) Re-exportation prohibition.

(24) Inspection rights.

(25) Indemnities.

(26) Intellectual property rights.

(27) Warranties.

(28) Enforcement and remedies.

(29) Arbitration provisions.

(30) Time is of the essence.

(31) Modification of contract.

(32) Cancellation.

(33) Liquidated damages.

(34) Attorneys' fees.

(35) Force majeure.

(36) Inurement and assignment.

(37) Conditions precedent.

(38) Governing law.

(39) Choice of forum.

(40) Severability of provisions.

(41) Integration of provisions.

(42) Notices.

(43) Authority to bind.

(44) Independent counsel.

(45) Acceptance and execution.

接下来的每一项条款并不适用于所有交易，但无论是你自己还是请律师起草的合同条款，都需要注意这些关键的合同条款。

(1) 合同日期。

(2) 合同当事人。

(3) 货物—描述。

(4) 货物—数量。

(5) 货物—价格。

(6) 付款—方式。

(7) 付款—货币币种。

(8) 付款—外汇率。

(9) 成本和费用—税费。

(10) 成本和费用—保险费。

(11) 成本和费用—搬运费。

(12) 包装安排。

(13) 交货—日期。

(14) 交货—地点。

(15) 交货—所有权转移。

(16) 运输—承运人。

(17) 运输—储存。

(18) 运输—通知条款。

(19) 运输—装运时间。

(20) 运输—保险。

(21) 进口/出口单证。

(22) 发票准备和交付。

(23) 再出口禁止条款。

(24) 检验权。

(25) 赔偿。

(26) 知识产权。

(27) 保证。

(28) 执行和补救措施。

(29) 仲裁条款。

(30) 时间是至关重要的。

(31) 合同的修改。

(32) 取消。

(33) 违约赔偿金。

(34) 律师费。

(35) 不可抗力。

(36) 生效条款。

(37) 先决条件。

(38) 适用的法律。

(39) 法院的选择。

(40) 终止条款。

(41) 完整的协议条款。

(42) 注意事项。

(43) 约束力。

(44) 独立检察官。

(45) 接受和执行。

3.3 Clauses Concerning Documents in the Sales Contract 销售合同中的单证条款

In trade practice, stipulations concerning documents may not be necessary to appear in every contract. In some cases, documents required are stipulated in the contract. They may constitute part or whole of the contents under the column "Remarks" or they may be mentioned in the attachment to a contract. And it is not uncommon, however, that there are no such stipulations in the contract at all. In that case, the agreement concerning documents remains an oral one between the buyer and the seller and is binding upon the parties concerned. Still, it is advisable that the relevant stipulations be laid down in the contract in terms of the types, issuing authorities, number of originals or copies, and etc.

While it may not appear in a sales contract, the stipulation "Documents required' is always a necessary part of a documentary L/C. Under an L/C transaction, sellers are paid, against documents presented; buyers pay and receive goods against documents released; and the banks deal in the documents instead of the goods. Documents play such an essential role in L/C transaction that documents to be presented (or to be required) should be clearly stipulated in the relevant letter of credit.

Examples of Clauses of a Sales Contract:

(1) Signed commercial invoice in triplicate indicating the contract number.

(2) Full set (3/3) plus two copies of clean "on board" marine bill of lading made out to order of ×××company.

(3) Packing list in duplicate, indicating gross weight and net weight, measurements and quantity of the packages.

(4) Insurance Policy or Certificate in triplicate covering War Risk and All Risks irrespective of percentage for 110% of the invoice value.

(5) Weight and quality certificate in triplicate indicating the number of bags shipped, total gross and net weight, packing, actual quality analysis result issued by CIQ.

(6) GSP certificate of origin Form A in duplicate issued by CIQ.

(7) Fumigation/disinfection certificate in triplicate issued by CIQ.

(8) Phytosanitary certificate in triplicate issued by CIQ.

(9) Health certificate in triplicate issued by CIQ for the information into the European Community of peanuts and certain products derived from peanuts originating in or consigned from China.

(10) Beneficiary's statement certifying that...

(11) Shipment details including number of bags shipped, total gross and net weight, packing, B/L date and number, container and seal number, ETD Qingdao and ETA Lisbon Portugal has been sent to applicant by fax (Fax No. ×××××××××) within 4 days of the shipment date.

(12) One complete set of non-negotiable shipping documents has been sent to the applicant by fax (Fax No. ××××××) within 4 days of the shipment date.

在贸易实践中，不是每一份合同都必须标示出与单证相关的条款。在某些情况下，对所需单证在合同中做了明确的规定。这些要求可能是"备注"中的部分或全部内容，也可能是合同附件中的说明。然而，合同中完全没有规定所需单证的情况也很常见。这时，关于单证的规定就是买卖双方之间的口头规定，且这对双方当事人都有约束力。尽管如此，仍建议在合同中明确规定单证的种类、签发机构、正副本数量等。

即使销售合同中无要求，"单证要求"条款仍然是跟单信用证的一个必要组成部分。在信用证交易方式下，卖方凭提交的单证得到付款；买方凭收到的单证付款和提货；银行在办理业务时处理的是单证而不是货物本身。单证在信用证交易中很重要，因此需提交（或要求）的单证必须在相关信用证中清楚说明。

销售合同条款的样例如下：

(1) 一式三份已签名、标示合同号码的商业发票。

(2) 一整套(3/3)正本及两份副本的"凭×××公司指示"为抬头的"清洁已装船"的海运提单。

(3) 一式两份标示毛重、净重、体积、包装和数量的装箱单。

(4) 一式三份的保险单或保险凭证，投保一切险和战争险，投保金额是发票金额的110%。

(5) 一式三份标示装运的包裹数量、总毛重、总净重、包装的重量和质量证书及由中国出入境检验检疫局签发的实际质量分析结果单。

(6) 一式两份由中国出入境检验检疫局签发的普惠制原产地证明。

(7) 一式三份由中国出入境检验检疫局签发的熏蒸/清毒证书。

(8) 一式三份由中国出入境检验检疫局签发的植物检疫证明。

(9) 一式三份出口至欧盟的原产于或托运自中国的核桃和核桃产品的由中国出入境检验检疫局签发的健康证书。

(10) 受益人证明书证明……

(11) 装运量、总毛重、总净重、包装、提单日期和号码、集装箱号码和封号、预计交货时间(青岛)和预计到港时间(葡萄牙里斯本)等装运细节已经在装运后 4 天内通过传真(传真号码××××××××)发送给开证申请人。

(12) 在装运后 4 天内,一整套不可转让海运单已经通过传真(传真号码××××××××)发送给开证申请人。

Chapter 4
Transaction Documents
交易单证

Transaction documents are issued by the buyer and seller to define their business relationship and provide an accounting record of individual transactions. These documents range from a simple letter of inquiry to a contract for the sale of goods and a commercial invoice. This category does not include specific export, transport, import, or bank documentation.

In the most straightforward sale, the buyer might call or fax the seller and order a quantity of goods, and the seller simply issues an invoice. At the other end of the spectrum, the process can be much more formal with an importer/buyer submitting an RFP (request for proposal) for bids on a product with 100 pages of detailed specifications, engineering charts and the like.

Fortunately, most businesspeople are already familiar with basic transaction documents because these are virtually the same as the ones used in domestic business.

交易单证是确定买卖双方业务关系的个人交易结算凭证，包括简单的询盘、销售合同和商业发票，但并不包括特殊出口单证、运输单证、进口单证和银行单证。

最简单销售方式是，买方通过电话或传真告知卖方需要订购一定量的货物，卖方开具发票。较正式的是进口商 / 买家需提交长达 100 页关于产品的详细说明和设计图表等的递盘。

事实上，由于外贸单证与国内业务的大部分流程相似，因此大部分的业务人员都熟悉基本交易单证。

4.1 Keys on Transaction Documents
交易单证要点

The quantity and formality of transaction documentation is influenced by the relationship of the buyer and seller, the countries of export and import, as well as the goods sold. For example, if the buyer and seller know each other, the preliminaries may be handled by telephone and the only transaction document issued will be the commercial invoice.

The key documents in this category are the commercial invoice. Copies of this document will be retained by the exporter and presented to the export authorities, the freight carrier, the import authorities, the importer and the bank (if a documentary collection or letter of credit is used).

Transaction documents may need to have additional information and be in the language of the country of export or import.

交易单证的数量和形式受到买方和卖方之间的关系、进口国和出口国,以及所销售货物的影响。例如,如果买方和卖方相互认识,首先可通过电话进行沟通,唯一需要开具的交易单证是商业发票。

交易单证中最重要的单证是商业发票。商业发票的副本由出口商保存,呈递给出口国当局、货运公司、进口商当局、进口商和银行(如果使用跟单托收和信用证)。

交易单证可能还需要以进口国或出口国语言表示的其他信息。

4.2 The Flow of Transaction Documents
交易单证制作流程

A typical exchange of documents between buyer and seller proceeds in the following pattern.

(1) The prospective importer/buyer sends a LETTER OF INQUIRY to the proposed exporter/seller asking if the company either has certain products available or would like to bid on a project.

(2) The seller sends a REPLY LETTER stating an interest in bidding and perhaps includes a CAPABILITIES STATEMENT.

(3) The buyer sends a REQUEST FOR QUOTATION (RFQ) generally if the goods have to be designed or manufactured to the buyer's specification as outlined in the RFP. The seller prepares and sends the buyer a formal PROPOSAL including product specifications, quantities, prices and terms and conditions.

(4) The buyer and seller negotiate specifications, quantities, prices, terms and conditions.

(5) The buyer issues a LETTER OF ACCEPTANCE or signs an ORDER FORM.

(6) The buyer and seller prepare and sign a PURCHASE CONTRACT(see sample 4-1) or a CONTRACT FOR THE SALE OF GOODS(see sample 3-1).

(7) The seller prepares a COMMERCIAL INVOICE.

买方与卖方交易单证的制作流程通常如下。

(1) 进口商/买方向出口商/卖方发出询盘函,探询该公司是否有某种货物出售或是否愿意对某一项目进行投标。

(2) 卖方发出包括一份资质声明的回复信表明对递盘的兴趣。

(3) 一般来说，如果货物需要根据买方规格进行设计或生产的话，买方需报盘。卖方发给买方正式的报盘，包括产品规格、数量、价格、条款和条件。

(4) 买方和卖方就产品规格、数量、价格、条款和条件进行谈判。

(5) 买方发出接受函或签约订单。

(6) 买方和卖方签订购货合同（见样单 4-1）或销售合同（见样单 3-1）。

(7) 卖方备好商业发票。

4.3　Kinds of International Transaction Documents 交易单证种类

International transaction documents include letter of inquiry, request for quotation, proposal/bid/quotation/offer, pro-forma invoice, contract for the sale of goods (services), request for proposal and commercial invoice.

国际交易单证包括询盘函、报盘函、递价/递盘/报价/报盘、形式发票、商品或服务的销售合同、报价函和商业发票。

4.3.1　Letter of Inquiry 询盘函

This is a simple letter written by the buyer asking the seller if a product is available or if the seller will bid on the supply of a product. This letter is generally short and does not include detailed specifications.

询盘函是一封由买方拟订询问卖方是否有产品出售或卖方对某种商品投标情况说明的简单电函。函电一般比较简短，没有具体说明。

4.3.2　Request for Quotation 报盘函

Request for quotation (RFQ) is a letter written by the buyer asking the seller to submit a formal price quotation for a specified product and quantity. RFQ is generally used for a one time sale of an existing product from the seller's inventory or product line, or a fungible product (that is identical with other goods of the same nature).

报盘函由买方拟订，要求卖方对指定商品和数量做正式报价。报盘函一般针对卖方现有货物或者正在生产的产品，或可替代产品（也就是说与其他产品具有相同的本质）进行报价。

4.3.3 Proposal/Bid/Quotation/Offer
递价 / 递盘 / 报价 / 报盘

This is the seller's written offer to sell specified products under specified terms and conditions. This can be as simple as a one page letter listing stock number, quantities, price per unit and sales terms, or it can be a 100 page proposal complete with engineering drawings, and complicated terms and conditions. A limited term of validity of the proposal is given so that if business conditions change, the seller has the option of modifying the terms and conditions of the proposal.

在特定条款和条件下，此函由卖方拟订表明出售某类商品。该函电可用一页纸篇幅简单罗列出产品货号、数量、单价和销售条款；也可以用 100 页纸的篇幅说明配套的设计图纸、复杂条款和条件。发盘函的法律效力有限，但如果某些业务条件需要改变，卖方有权更改发盘函中的条款和条件。

4.3.4 Proforma Invoice
形式发票

This is a preliminary invoice made up by the exporter at the importer's request prior to a shipment of merchandise. It identifies the parties to the transaction and includes the kinds and quantities of goods to be sent, their value and specifications and shipping costs. The proforma invoice (see Sample 4-2) is used by the importer to see what the purchase will cost, obtain any necessary import licenses and international exchange approval, and to apply for a letter of credit. It is a statement of sales, issued before a transaction has been concluded rather than a record of sales already effected.

A proforma invoice is issued by the seller as a response to an inquiry from the potential buyer. It is a document similar to a commercial invoice and it contains the same information as those in the commercial invoice. It is a statement of sales, issued before a transaction has been concluded rather than a record of sales already effected.

A proforma invoice is needed in the following circumstances. If an irrevocable letter of credit is required by the exporter, the importer will use the proforma invoice to substantiate the need for a letter of credit to his bank. Sometimes it is needed by the importer to apply for the import license and international exchange. A proforma invoice, in some other circumstances, may be required by the importer to help him apply for the relevant letter of credit. Therefore, a proforma invoice has no legal status and serves only as a means to facilitate the buyer to accomplish the above-mentioned tasks.

形式发票（见样单 4-2）是在货物装运之前，出口商应进口商的要求开具的一份初步明确双方交易货物的种类、数量、价值、规格和运输成本的发票。形式发票用于进口商了解购买商品所需成本、获得必要的进口许可证、外汇证明和信用证申请。该单证在交易达成前签发,作为销售清单使用,而不是实际销售的记录。

形式发票由卖方开具以回应潜在买家的询盘。形式发票在格式和内容上都非常接近于商业发票。形式发票是在正式履行合同之前所开出的一种销售单据,而不是一份已经执行了的销售记录。

以下情况需提供形式发票。如果出口商要求将不可撤销信用证作为结算方式,进口商需使用形式发票向银行证实其开证需求。形式发票有时被进口商用来申请进口许可证和外汇。在其他情况下,进口商要求卖方出具形式发票来申请相关信用证。因此,形式发票不具有法律效力,只相当于一份备忘录,可促使买方完成以上所提及的工作。

形式发票在以下情况下使用。如果出口商要求开立不可撤销信用证,那么进口商将使用形式发票向银行证实其开证需求。有时候,形式发票在进口商申请进口许可证和购买外汇时使用。在其他情况下,进口商可能需要使用形式发票来申请相关的信用证。因此,形式发票不具备真正的法律地位,它只是促进进口商完成以上任务的一种工具。

4.3.5 Contract for the Sale of Goods (Services) 商品或服务的销售合同

This is the formal, legal agreement between the exporter and the importer stating products and prices, responsibilities and rights, and terms and conditions. It is issued by either the seller or the buyer, with the drafter having the advantage of claiming greater influence on contract terms, but the disadvantage of being subject to strict interpretation of the terms should there be a dispute.

Regardless of whether you draft the terms of the contract by yourself, or hire an attorney, you need to be aware of key contract provisions. It is up to you to insist on the protection of your own interests. The best course of action is to define all of the provisions of your agreement in writing at the tie you enter into it.

The following provisions are for a complete international contract for a one time sale of goods. Not every provision is applicable to every transaction.

(1) Contract date.

(2) Identification of parties.

(3) Goods——description, quantity, price.

(4) Payment——method of payment, medium of exchange, and exchange rate.

(5) Costs and charges——duties and taxes, insurance, handling and transport.

(6) Packaging arrangements.

(7) Delivery——date, place, transfer of title.

(8) Transportation——carrier, storage, notice provisions, shipping time, insurance.

(9) Import/export documentation.

(10) Invoice preparation and delivery.

(11) Re-exportation prohibition.

(12) Inspection rights.

(13) Indemnities.

(14) Intellectual property rights.

(15) Warranties.

(16) Enforcement and remedies.

(17) Arbitration provisions.

(18) Time is of the essence.

(19) Modification of contract.

(20) Cancellation.

(21) Liquidated damages.

(22) Attorneys' fees.

(23) Force majeure.

(24) Increment and assignment.

(25) Conditions precedent.

(26) Governing law.

(27) Choice of forum.

(28) Severability of provisions.

(29) Integration of provisions.

(30) Notices.

(31) Authority to bind.

(32) Independent counsel.

(33) Acceptance and execution.

Key Elements of Sales Contract:

(1) Names of commodity (ies) and specification(s).

(2) Quality of goods.

(3) Quantity.

(4) Packing of goods.

(5) Unit Price.

(6) Amount.

(7) Port of loading.

(8) Port of destination.

(9) Shipping marks.

(10) Time of shipment.

(11) Terms of payment.

(12) Insurance.

(13) L/C clause.

(14) Documents.

(15) Quality/Quantity Discrepancy.

(16) Arbitration.

(17) Other conditions.

销售合同是出口商与进口商订立的确定产品与价格、责任与权利、条款及条件的正式合法契约。销售合同可由卖方或买方拟订,拟订人的优势是可根据自身利益来拟订合同的条款,但其劣势是如果存在争议应严格解释条款。

不管合约条款由谁拟订,自己或是聘请律师,都需要注意关键的合同条款。保护自身利益最好的方式是明确合约中与自己相关联的所有书面规定。

以下是国际货物销售合同完整的规定内容。不是所有的规定都适合于每一次交易。

(1) 合同日期。

(2) 合同当事人。

(3) 货物的描述、数量和价格。

(4) 付款——付款方式、币种、外汇汇率。

(5) 成本和费用——税率、保险费、运输费。

(6) 包装安排。

(7) 交货——时间、地点和所有权转移。

(8) 运输——承运人、储存、通知条款、装运时间、保险。

(9) 进/出口单证。

(10) 准备发票和交付。

(11) 再出口禁止条款。

(12) 验收。

(13) 赔偿。

(14) 知识产权。

(15) 保证。

(16) 执行和救济办法。

(17) 仲裁条款。

(18) 时间是至关重要的。

(19) 合约的修改。

(20) 取消。

(21) 违约赔偿金。

(22) 律师费。

(23) 不可抗力因素。

(24) 增额与任务额。

(25) 先决条件。

(26) 适用的法律条款。

(27) 法院的选择。

(28) 条款的分离性。

(29) 完整的协议条款。

(30) 注意事项。

(31) 约束力。

(32) 独立检察官。

(33) 接受和执行。

销售合同的要点如下。

(1) 货物名称和规格。

(2) 货物质量。

(3) 数量。

(4) 包装。

(5) 单价。

(6) 金额。

(7) 装运港。

(8) 目的港。

(9) 唛头。

(10) 转运时间。

(11) 付款条件。

(12) 保险。

(13) 信用证条款。

(14) 单证。

(15) 质量/数量异议。

(16) 仲裁。

(17) 其他条款。

4.3.6 Request for Proposal (RFP) 报价函

RFP is a requested for a formal proposal for the sale, supply or manufacture of products. It include the following elements: name and address of importer/buyer (as on a letterhead), name and address of proposed exporter/seller, date, statement of request for a formal proposal and product specification.

The key element is the product specification list. This can be simple statement of a known item (such as a commodity known by international standards) or as complex as book-length listing of engineering drawings, raw material specifications, delivery schedules, packaging and shipping instructions, compliance documents inspection requirements and more.

报价函是一份针对产品销售、供给或生产拟订的正式要约的邀请。它包括以下要素：进口商/买方的名字和地址(与信头上的相同)、出口商/卖方的名字和地址、日期、正式报价声明、产品详细说明。

报价函中最重要的是产品详细说明表。它可以对商品进行简单说明(例如受国际标准认可的货物)，或是长达一本书厚度的复杂列表，包括工程图纸、原材料详细说明、交货时间表、包装和运输说明及符合检验要求的单证等。

4.3.7 Commercial Invoice
商业发票

When manufacture is complete and the product is ready for shipment, ordinarily the seller will prepare a commercial invoice(see Sample 4-3), which is the formal statement for payment to be sent directly to the buyer or submitted through banking channels for payment by the buyer. Such invoices may also contain the detailed terms or conditions of sale on the front or back of the form.

When the export goods are shipped, the exporter must prepare a commercial invoice, which is a statement to the buyer for payment. Usually English is sufficient but some countries require the seller's invoice to be in their language. Multiple copies are usually required, some of which are sent with the bill of lading and other transportation documents. The original is forwarded through banking channels for payment (except on open account sales, where it is sent directly to the buyer). On letter of credit transactions, the invoice must be issued by the beneficiary of the letter of credit and addressed to the applicant for the letter of credit. Putting the commercial invoice number on the other shipping documents helps to tie the documents together. The customs laws of most countries require that a commercial invoice be presented by the buyer (or the seller, if the seller is responsible for clearing customs), and the price listed on it is used as the value for the assessment of customs duties where the customs duties are based upon a percentage of the value (ad valorem rates). (Brazil, Egypt, Colombia, Guatemala, Senegal, Bahrain, Sri Lanka, Dominican Republic, Myanmar, and some other countries may assess duties on fair market value rather than invoice price.)

Perhaps the most important thing to note here is that many countries, like the United States, have special requirements for the information that, depending upon the product involved, must be contained in a commercial invoice. It is extremely important that, before shipping the product and preparing the commercial invoice, the exporter check either through an attorney, the buyer, or the freight forwarder to determine exactly what information must be included in the commercial invoice in order to clear International customs. In addition, certain items, such as inland shipping expenses, packing, installation, service charges, financing charges, international transportation charges, insurance, royalties, license fees, may have to be shown separately because some of these items may be deducted from or added to the price in calculating the customs value and the payment of duties. Many countries in the Middle East and Latin America require that commercial invoices covering shipments to their countries be "legalized". This means the export country's embassy or consulate must stamp the invoice. When an export control license is needed for the shipment (and on some other types of shipments), a destination control statement must be put on the commercial invoice.

1. Content of Commercial Invoice

Commercial invoice is the exporting firm's invoice, addressed to the International importer, describing key transaction details particularly the total value and claiming for payment. It is one of the most important documents used in international trade. It is used as the foundation for keeping accounts and making declarations to the customs. It is often one of the documents required for payment settlement. The commercial invoice serves as a record of the essential details of a transaction. Usually, it includes the basic information.

(1) Buyer's reference (order number/ indent number).

(2) Invoice number and date.

(3) Export or import license number.

(4) Method of dispatch.

(5) Shipment terms.

(6) Names and addresses of the seller and buyer.

(7) Country from which the shipment is made.

(8) Description of the goods——quantity, weight or measurements of the goods, unit price, total amount payable (including price of goods, freight, insurance and so on).

(9) Rebate or similar incentives.

(10) Signature of the exporter.

2. Major Invoices Adopted in Import-Export Trade

(1) Commercial invoice.

(2) Customs invoice.

(3) Proforma invoice.

(4) Consular invoice.

(5) Manufacturer's invoice.

3. Key Elements

This is the prime transaction document. It lists the date, buyer and seller, products, quantities, prices, delivery terms and other important information. It includes the following elements.

(1) Name and address of seller or buyer. Unless otherwise stipulated in the letter of credit, the commercial invoice must be made out in the name of the applicant (buyer). But in a transferable documentary credit the invoice may be made out to a third party.

(2) Date of issuance.

(3) Invoice number.

(4) Order or contract number.

(5) Quantity and description of the goods. It is virtually important that the description of the goods and the terms listed in the commercial invoice correspond precisely with the description of the goods in the contract of sale and with a documentary letter of credit.

(6) Any other information as required by the seller. The buyer, seller, and banks should all carefully check for discrepancies in the invoice. The details specified herein should not be inconsistent with those of any other documents and should exactly conform to the specifications of the credit.

(7) Shipping details including weight of the goods, number of packages, and shipping marks and numbers.

(8) Terms of delivery and payment.

(9) Unit price, total price, other agreed upon charges, and total invoice amount. The invoice amount should match exactly or at least should not exceed the amount specified in the letter of credit. Banks and buyers have the right to refuse invoices issued for amounts in excess of the amount stated in the credit. The exception is when a documentary credit specifies "about" in relation to the currency amount and quantity of merchandise, in which case the invoice may specify an amount equal to plus or minus 10 percent of the stipulated amount of the credit. The invoice should be made out in the same currency as the letter of credit.

4. Checklist for Commercial Invoice

(1) Is the commercial invoice in the name of the beneficiary?

(2) Is the commercial invoice addressed to the applicant named in the letter of credit?

(3) Did you sign the commercial invoice if required?

(4) Was the commercial invoice countersigned by any other party if required in the letter of credit?

(5) Does the commercial invoice conform to the letter of credit's terms relative to the following items:

a. Total amount, Unit prices and computations.

b. Description of merchandise and terms (FOB, CFR, CIF, and so on).

c. Description of packing(if required).

d. Declarations clauses properly worded.

e. The shipping marks on the commercial invoice agree with those appearing on the bill of lading.

f. If partial shipments are prohibited, is all merchandise shipped? Or, if partial shipments are permitted, is the value of the merchandise shipped? Or, if partial shipments are permitted, is the value of the merchandise invoiced in proportion to the quantity of the shipment when the letter of credit does not specify unit prices?

g. International language used for the merchandise description, if used in the letter of credit?

(6) Description of goods:

a. A credit only specifies the generic terms of the goods, invoice should show according to the sample, still can add column of the name of the goods in detail, but not contradictions with the generic terms.

b. If the commodity listed is more, they can be displayed in the invoice according to the L/C when there are generic terms of the goods in the L/C.

c. If the generic terms of the goods is not referred in the L/C, but the name is listed in detail, the invoice should be listed according to the regulation of the L/C, do not need to add the generic terms of the goods.

d. If a credit states that the name of the goods is not English expression, the invoice should show according to the original, also add column names in English.

e. When partial shipment is allowed and the actual shipment of the goods is only part of all the goods of the L/C, the invoice can only list actual shipment of the goods and can also be specified description of all the goods of the L/C, and then indicate the actual shipment of the goods.

f. Besides goods specified in the L/C, invoice can not show other goods, including samples, advertising material, even if they are free.

5. Functions of Commercial Invoice

(1) It is importer's and exporter's evidence of keeping accounts and verifying.

(2) It is the basis on which applying for the Customs entry and paying duties in places of exporting and importing.

(3) It is one of documents offered to handle insurance with the insurance company and to handle exchange settlement with the bank.

(4) It facilitates the importer to check and accept goods and make the payment.

6. Samples of Commercial Invoice Clauses

(1) Invoice to certify that the goods shipped and other details are as per supplier's S/C No.888 dated March 3rd 2015.

(2) Beneficiary's original signed commercial invoices at least 8 copies issued in the name of the buyer indicating of the merchandise, country of origin and any other relevant

information.

(3) All invoice must show FOB, Freight and Insurance Costs separately.

(4) Combined invoice is not acceptable.

(5) 5% commission invoice is not acceptable.

(6) Invoice to certify that the goods shipped are exactly equal to the samples presented to the buyer.

(7) 4% discount should be deducted from total amount of the commercial invoice.

(8) All invoice must show break down value: ① FOB value; ② freight prepaid; ③ insurance premium prepaid.

(9) Your declaration that no wood container has been used in packing of the goods listed on the invoice is required.

(10) Commercial invoice must indicate the following: ① That each item is labeled "made in China"; ② That one set of non-negotiable shipping documents has been airmailed in advance to buyer.

当货物准备装运时，卖方通常会准备好商业发票（见样单 4-3）。商业发票是由卖方直接向买方开具并递交给银行，由买方付款的一种正式单据。商业发票的正面或背面可能会包含具体的条款或条件。

当出口货物需要装运时，出口商应出具商业发票，作为买方的支付凭证。通常情况下，英文单证是通用的，但有些国家要求卖方以买方国家的语言来开具发票。通常要求开具多份发票，其中一些会连同提单或其他运输单证一起寄送。商业发票的原件通过银行渠道转寄作为付款单据（除了赊账销售之外，商业发票的原件将直接寄给买家）。信用证交易下的商业发票必须由信用证中规定的受益人出具，开证的申请人为抬头人。其他单证上需标示商业发票号码，这有助于把全套单证联系起来。多数国外海关法要求在清关时由买方出具商业发票（如果由卖方负责清关的话，应由卖方出票），发票上的价格清单用于海关计算关税之用，计税的方法是基于商品价值的一定百分比（从价税）来计算。（巴西、埃及、哥伦比亚、危地马拉、塞内加尔、巴林、斯里兰卡、多米尼加共和国、缅甸和一些其他国家通过市场价值而不是发票的价格来评估关税）。

需要注意的是，在大部分国家（比如美国），对产品本身的特别要求必须在商业发票里标示。在装运货物之前尤为重要的是备好商业发票，出口商可通过律师、买家或货运代理行检查所有的信息是否准确无误地标示在商业发票中，目的是货物在国外港口得以顺利清关。除此之外，通常某些条款，例如内陆的装运费、包装费、安装费、服务费、财务费、国际运输费、保险费、版税、许可证费也必须分别罗列出来。因为某些条款可能要在计算关税价值及支付税费时从价格中扣除或加到价格上。中东和拉美的许多国家要求在商业发票中必须标示装运到这些国家的货物是"合法"的。这就意味着这些国家在出口国的大使馆或领事馆必须在发票上盖章。当装运需用出口配额许可证时（或其他类型装运时），目的地国的配额证书也必须在商业发票中标示。

1. 商业发票的内容

商业发票是出口商公司写给国外进口商的发票，发票上说明交易的主要信息（尤其是商品的总值）并提示买方应支付的金额。这是国际贸易中最重要的单证之一，不仅是做账和向海关申报的基础，也是结算时必需的单证之一。另外，商业发票还可以作为一笔交易基本资料的记录。一般来说，一份商业发票应标示以下基本内容。

(1) 买方参考（订单号码/契约号码）。

(2) 发票号码和日期。

(3) 出口或进口许可证号码。

(4) 发货方式。

(5) 装运条款。

(6) 买卖双方的名称和地址。

(7) 货物起运国。

(8) 货物描述——数量、重量或体积、单价、应付总金额（包括商品的价格、运费、保险费等）。

(9) 折扣或类似奖励。

(10) 出口商的签名。

2. 进出口贸易中使用的主要发票

(1) 商业发票。

(2) 海关发票。

(3) 形式发票。

(4) 领事发票。

(5) 厂商发票。

3. 核心要点

这是主要的交易单证。其要列出日期、买方和卖方、产品、数量、价格、交货条件和其他重要的信息，具体包括以下要点。

(1) 卖方或买方名称和地址。除非信用证另有约定，商业发票必须以申请人（买方）为抬头开具，但可转让跟单信用证发票的买方可以填写为第三方。

(2) 出票日期。

(3) 发票号码。

(4) 订单或合同号码。

(5) 货物的数量和描述。事实上，尤为重要的是商业发票中的货物描述和条款要和销售合同中的货物描述相一致，同时也要和信用证相一致。

(6) 卖方要求的其他信息。买方、卖方和银行都应该认真核实发票的分歧点。所有细节都应该与其他单证相符，应该完全与信用证的规定相符。

(7) 装运细节，包括货物重量、包装号码、唛头和号码。

(8) 交货和付款条件。

(9) 单价、总价、合约达成一致的其他费用和总发票金额。发票的总额应该准确无误或至少不超出信用证中规定的总额。银行和买方有权拒绝超出信用证规定总额的发票。例外情况是：当跟单信用证在涉及金额、数量时注明"约"字样，发票总额可以等于信用证规定总额加减 10%。发票也应该填写与信用证相同的货币。

4. 商业发票的审核内容

(1) 商业发票的抬头是否为受益人的名字。

(2) 商业发票的抬头是否与信用证申请人的名称相一致。

(3) 如果需要的话，是否已在商业发票上签名。

(4) 如果信用证有要求，商业发票是否已由第三方会签。

(5) 商业发票是否遵循信用证的如下条款：

a. 总金额、单价和估算。

b. 货物和条款的描述 (FOB、CFR、CIF 等)。

c. 包装的描述 (如果需要)。

d. 报关条款准确表述。

c. 商业发票中的唛头与提单相一致。

f. 如果货物允许分批装运，并且信用证没有明确注明货物单价的话，发票中所注明的装运数量是否值得分批装运。

g. 如果已在信用证中使用，货物描述是否必须使用国际语言。

(6) 货物描述：

a. 信用证规定了货物的统称，发票除照样显示外，还可加列详细货名，但不得与统称矛盾。

b. 如果所列商品较多，信用证上标有统称时，发票可在具体名称上方按信用证显示统称。

c. 如果信用证未规定货物统称，但列举的货名很详细，则发票应照样按信用证规定列明，不需加统称。

d. 如果信用证规定的货名非英文表述，发票应照原文显示，也可同时加列英文名称。

e. 当货物允许分批装运，实际装运的货物只是信用证全部货物的一部分时，发票可只列实际装运的货物，也可列明信用证规定的全部货物描述，然后注明实际装运的货物。

f. 除了信用证规定的货物外，发票不能显示其他货物，包括样品、广告材料，即使它们是免费的。

5. 商业发票的作用

(1) 商业发票是进出口商记账和通关检验的凭证。

(2) 商业发票是申请通关和在进出口地付税的基础。

(3) 商业发票是与保险公司处理保险问题及与银行进行结汇的单证之一。

(4) 商业发票便于进口商验收货物和付款。

6. 商业发票条款样例

(1) 发票应证明装运货物和其他有关细节与 2015 年 3 月 3 日第 888 号销售合同书相符。

(2) 受益人签署的商业发票正本一式八份，以买方为抬头，标示商品、原产国和其他相关资料。

(3) 所有发票均应列出 FOB 价、运费和保险费。

(4) 不接受联合发票。

(5) 不接受从发票金额中扣除 5% 的佣金。

(6) 发票应证明装运货物与已交付买方的样品相符。

(7) 应从商业发票总金额中扣除 4% 的折扣。

(8) 所有发票应标明分类价格：①FOB 价；②预付运费；③预付保费。

(9) 发票上需声明所列货物未使用木制容器包装。

(10) 商业发票必须标示以下内容：①每件商品标明"中国制造"；②一套非议付装运单据已预先航空邮寄给买方。

Assignment 4.1   a Sample of Error Correction of Commercial Invoice
练习 4.1   商业发票改错示范

　　DOC. CREDIT NUMBER：044/307587
　　APPLICANT：EEN CO., VANCOUVER, CANADA
　　BENEFICIARY：GUANGDONG HUALIAN TRADING CORPORATION 60 HUHAI ROAD GUANGZHOU CHIN A
　　AMOUNT CURRENCY：USD5 256.00
　　AVAILABLE WITH/BY：FREELY NEGOTIABLE AT ANY BANK BY NEGOTIATION
　　LADING IN CHARGE：CHINA
　　FOR TRANSPORT TO：VANCOUVER VIA HONG KONG
　　LATEST DATE OF SHIPMENT：150131
　　DESCRIPTION OF GOODS：
　　2.920DS OF 100PCT COTTON DENIM-80Z-ROPE DYED INDIGO(CT-121)
　　DOUBLE P/SHRUNK RESIDUAL AHRINKAGE NOT MORE THAN 3-4PCT 82×50/14S×14S-WIDTH：58/59'
　　AT USD1.80/YD AS PER PURCHASE ORDER NO. FAB10-20030087/01-12, CIF VANCOUVER
　　DOCUMENTS REQUIRED：+SIGNED COMMERCIAL INVOICE IN TRIPLICATE

COMMERCIAL INVOICE				
TO MESSRS.：EEN CO., VANCOUVER, CANADA			INVOICE NO.：SHE01/7203	
L/C NO.：044/387587			DATE：Jan. 28th, 2021	
SHIPPED FROM GUANGZHOU TO VANCOUVER			P.O. No.：FAB10-20030087/01-12	
MARKS & NOS.	DESCRIPTION	QUANTITY	UNIT PRICE	AMOUNT
P.O. NO.： FAB10-20030087/01-12 COLOR：INDIGO	GOLDTRON GARMENTS SDN. BHD. 100PCT COTTON DENIM-80Z- ROPE DYED INDIGO (CT-121) DOUBLE P/SHRUNK RESIDUAL AHRINKAGE NOT MORE THAN	2 928 YARDS	USD1.80/YARD	USD5,256.00

```
R/NO.: 1-4, 6-36    3-4PCT 82×50/14S×14S-WIDTH: 58/59'
                    AS  PER  PURCHASE  ORDER  NO.  FAB10-
                    20030087/01-12

                    TOTAL: US DOLLARS FIVE THOUSAND TWO HUNDRED FIFTY SIX ONLY

                          GUANGDONG HUALIAN TRADING CORPORATION
                                            张三
```

7. A Sample of Making out a Commercial Invoice according to the Following Information 缮制商业发票样例

FIRST BANGKOK CITY BANK LTD. HEAD OFFICE
20 YUKHON 2 ROAD, BANGKOK 10100, THAILAND BANGKOK Nov. 13th, 2021
This credit is sent to the advising bank by airmail.
Irrevocable documentary credit No. 001-10397-2014

      Advising Bank   Applicant
Bank of China, Qingdao Branch,   Nan Heng International Trading Co. Ltd.
Qingdao, China   104/4 Lardp Rd. Wangt BANGKAPI. BKK
Beneficiary
Shandong Imp./Exp. Corp.
62 Jiangxi Rd, Qingdao, China
Amount: USD6 622.00 (SAY US DOLLARS SIX THOUSAND SIX HUNDRED AND TWENTY-TWO ONLY) CFR BANGKOK
Expiry date: Jan 15, 2021
Dear Sirs,
We hereby issue an irrevocable documentary credit in your favour which is available by negotiation of your draft (s) at SIGHT DRAWN ON US, for 100% invoice value marked as drawn under this credit accompanied by the following documents:

■ Signed Commercial Invoice in 9 copies, mentioning separately F. O. B. value, freight charge.

■ Full set clean on board ocean Bills of Lading in triplicate with two non- negotiable copies made out to the order of First Bangkok City Bank Ltd., Bangkok, notify applicant and marked Freight Prepaid.

■ Packing List in six copies.
Evidencing shipment of TRI-CIRCLE BRAND BRASS PADLOCKS 900 DOZ.
DETAILS AS PER ORDER DATED NOVEMBER 9, 2014 (S/C NO. 16A15AAL5029)
Shipment from China port to Bangkok Latest Dec. 31, 2021
Partial Shipment: Permitted   Transshipment: Permitted
Special conditions:
All documents mentioning this credit number.
All charges incurred outside Thailand are for buyer's account.
Negotiations under this credit are restricted to the advising bank.
Instructions to Negotiating Bank:
(1) The amount of each drawing must be endorsed on the reverse hereof.
(2) All documents and drafts are to be dispatched in two sets by consecutive airmails to us.

(3) Please claim reimbursements by method marked X

by debiting our account with you

by drawing on

First Bangkok City Bank Ltd.

We hereby agree with the drawer, endorsers and bona fide holders that drafts drawn and negotiated in conformity with the terms of this credit will be duly honoured on presentation and that drafts accepted within the terms of this credit will be duly honoured at maturity.

YOURS FAITHFULLY
For FIRST BANGKOK CITY BANK LTD.

Some Data:

1. S/C No.: 16A15AAL5029
2. Commodity: Tri-Circle Brand Brass Padlock
3. Unit Price: USD 7.357 per dozen CFR Bangkok
   (FOB Value: USD6 290.90, Freight Charges: USD330.40)
4. Total value: USD6 621.30
5. Packing: In wooden cases of 100 doz. Each
6. Vessel: East Wind V. 19
7. Shipping Mark: <u>NHIT</u>
   BANGKOK
   NO. 1-9
8. Gross weight: 1 800KGS
9. Measurements: 6.628M^3

Key

答案

COMMERCIAL INVOICE					
TO: NAN HENG INTERNATIONAL TRADING CO. LTD. 104/ LARDP RD. WANGT BANGKAPI BKKNO.TS0895			**DATE**: Jan. 10th, 2021 **S/C NO**: 15A15AC5029 **L/C NO.**: 001-10397-2021 **TERMS OF PAYMENT**: L/C AT SIGHT		
TRANSPORT DETAILS: FROM QINGDAO. CHINA TO BANGKOK, THAIL AND VIA H.K.SHIP BY EAST WIND V.19						
Marks and Numbers	Number and kind of package Description of goods	Quantity	Unit Price	Amount
<u>NHIT</u> BANGKOK NO.1-9	TRI-CIRCLE BRAND BRASS PADLOCKS PACKING: IN WOODEN CASES OF 100 DOZ. EACH GROSS WEIGHT: 1 800KGS MEASUREMENTS: 6.628CUM	900 DOZ/9 WOODEN CASES	CFR Bangkok USD7.357/DZ	USD6 621.30
(FOB VALUE USD6 290.90 FREIGHT CHARGES: USD330.40) SAY TOTAL: US DOLLARS SIX THOUSAND SIX HUNDRED AND TWENTY-ONE THIRTY CENTS ONLY				

SHANDONG IMP/EXP CORP
王丽丽

Case Analysis 4.1 the Description of the Goods in the Commercial Invoice Disagrees with That of Credit
案例分析 4.1 商业发票中货物描述与信用证规定不符纠纷案

April 5, 2021, H Bank in Karachi opened L/C No. 602348 with the amount of £4 757.58 to import rosin from China, payable at sight, date of shipment May 31, date of expiry June 15, upgraded rosin, packed in metal barrels, CFR Karachi.

On June 2, the export company presented the documents for negotiation. All items on the documents were found to be in accordance with the L/C except the name of the goods. The documents showed the name as "Gum Rosin" which corresponded with the one specified in the contract. The negotiating bank advised that the documents should be made out with the name "Rosin" as specified in the L/C, that the word "Gum" should not be added, or there would be a disagreement between the documents and the L/C. However, the export company insisted that the L/C was incomplete and the contract should be strictly followed. No dispute would arise because the import company was clear about this matter. Therefore, the negotiating bank gave up and sent the documents for settlement. On June 15 (the expiry date), the issuing bank sent a telegram notifying its refusal of payment. The reason was "description of goods showing Gum Rosin instead of Rosin, the documents not accepted." Though the exporter argued with the importer more than once, the problem remained unsolved. The issuing bank claimed in telegrams "the importer definitely refuses to make the payment, and the demurrage has been incurred as the goods reach the ports." Up until now, the exporter was put in a passive position. The case ended up with the exporter cutting the price by 28% and paying US $1 080 of warehouse rent charges.

Analysis:

As provided in UCP 600, Article 18.c, "The description of the goods in the commercial invoice must correspond with description in the Credit. In all other documents, the goods may be described in general terms not inconsistent with the description of the goods in the Credit".

In this way, now that the L/C used "Rosin" as the name of the goods, the documents presented for negotiation must conform to the description of the credit rather than the stipulation of the contract; otherwise, the documents would disagree with the credit terms. Alternatively, the exporter could have asked the importer to inform the issuing bank to amend the L/C.

The exporter thought that since the original commercial contract specified the goods' name as "Gum Rosin", it was unnecessary to amend the L/C. As a result, the bank refused to make payment for the reason of "inconformity" between the documents and the credit terms. UCP 600 clearly defines the relationship between the Credit and the contract: once the Credit is established, it is not subject to the original contract. The importer's refusal of payment was based on the relationship under the Credit rather than the original contractual relationship.

Although the importer's refusal of payment was well grounded, the ulterior motive was apparent. That is, the importer wanted to take advantage of pressure of the high warehouse rent to force the exporter to reduce the price. The importer was apparently unfriendly and had done harm to his credibility. One should be on guard against this type of business partner and try to avoid doing business with them or pay careful attention to every detail of the contract.

In spite of the importer's unfriendly intention, which led to the loss, the key point of the case lies in that the exporter has misunderstood the provisions of UCP 600 and consequently dealt with the issue so hastily. This is an important lesson to be remembered.

2021 年 4 月 5 日卡拉奇 H 银行开立了金额为£4 757.58 的即期信用证 602348 号，从中国进口上等松香，装船日期为5月31日，有效期为6月15日，金属桶装，付款条件为CFR卡拉奇。

6月2日出口公司交单议付。除了商品的名称外，单据上的所有项目都是按照信用证来缮制的。单据显示商品名称为"Gum Rosin"，这与合同相符。议付行建议单据上的商品名称应该是信用证中标明的"Rosin"，而不应增加"Gum"这个词，否则单据和信用证不相符。然而，出口公司坚持信用证是不完整的，应严格遵守合同。同时认为不会产生争议，理由是进口公司清楚这一点。因此，议付银行放弃了劝说出口公司，并把单据寄出进行议付。6月15日(有效期)，开证行发来一封电报通知拒付。原因是货物描述是"Gum Rosin"而不是"Rosin"，单据不接受。虽然出口商与进口商争议不止一次，但这个问题仍然没有解决。在电报中开证行声称"进口商绝对拒绝付款，由于货物到达港口，滞期费已经发生"。至此，出口商处于被动局面。此案最终以出口国削减28%价格和支付1 080美元仓租费结束。

分析：

UCP 600第18条c款规定："商业发票中的货物描述必须与信用证中的描述一致。在所有其他单据中，货物的描述可以与信用证的描述不相符。"

这样的话，既然信用证使用"Rosin"作为商品名称，提交议付的单据必须符合信用证的描述而不是合同规定；否则，将与信用证的条款不相符。或者，出口商要求进口商通知开证行修改信用证。

出口商认为，由于原商业合同规定了商品名称是"Gum Rosin"，没有必要修改信用证。因此银行拒付，理由是单据与信用证条款不相符。UCP 600明确规定了信用证与合同之间的关系：一旦建立了信用证，它不受原合同限制。进口商拒付是基于信用证关系，而不是原来的合同关系。

尽管进口商拒付是有理由的，但其不可告人的动机是明显的，即进口商想利用高仓租金的压力迫使出口商降价。进口商显然是不友好的，这有害于他的信誉度。应该警惕这种类型的商业伙伴，并且尽量避免与他们做生意或注意合同的每一个细节。

尽管进口商不友好的意图会导致损失，案件的关键点在于，出口国误解UCP 600条款的规定，因此处理这个问题才如此草率。这是一个重要的教训，值得牢记。

Cases Analysis 4.2 No Excessive Amount of the Draft/Commercial Invoice Permitted by the Credit
案例分析4.2 商业发票金额不得超过信用证允许的金额

Under a Credit, 90 per cent of the total amount of the Credit should be paid against documents and 10 per cent against inspection certificate issued by the applicant. Under such circumstances, the draft amount shall be 90 percent of the Credit for the first presentation and such draft may be refused if it is made to the full value of the Credit.

Analysis：

As to Commercial Invoice, UCP 600, Article 18.b has the following provision, "A nominated bank acting on its nomination, a confirming bank, if any, or the issuing bank may accept a commercial invoice issued for an amount in excess of the amount permitted by the credit, and its decision will be binding upon all parties, provided the bank in question has not honoured or negotiated for an amount in excess of that permitted by the credit."

So we are informed with the above stipulation that the value of the invoice should not exceed the available balance of the Credit, unless otherwise stipulated in the Credit or there is a more or less clause.

信用证下，信用证总额90%的货款凭单支付并且信用证总额10%的货款凭申请人出具的检验证书支付。在此情况下，首次呈交的汇票金额应该是信用证金额的90%，并且如果汇票是按信用证全额缮制的话，这些汇票可能遭拒收。

分析：

关于商业发票，UCP 600第18条b款规定：按指定行事的指定银行、保兑行(如有的话)或开证行可以接受金额大于信用证允许金额的商业发票，其决定对有关各方均有约束力，只要该银行对超过信用证允许金额的部分未作承付或者议付。

所以，根据上述规定我们得知：除非信用证有增减条款，否则发票金额不应超过信用总额。

Assignment 4.2 Make out a Commercial Invoice According to the Following L/C

练习4.2 根据以下信用证缮制商业发票

DOC. Credit Number * 20: KRT2899302

Date of Issue 31 C: 210912

Expiry*31 D: DATE 211205 PLACE CHINA

Applicant *50: CURRENT FUNDS LIMITED
　　　　　　ROOM 1110 CHINACHEM GOLDEN PLAZA
　　　　　　NO. 77 MODY ROAD, TSIM SHA TSUI EAST, KOWLOON, HONG KONG

Beneficiary*59: GUANGDONG TEXTILES IMPORT AND EXPORT KNITWEARS COMPANY LIMITED
　　　　　　15/F., GUANGDONG TEXTILES MANSION, 168 XIAOBEI ROAD, GUANGZHOU, CHINA

Amount * 32 B: CURRENCY USD AMOUNT 30 384.00

Available with / by * 41 D: CREDIT ISSUING OFFICE BY PAYMENT

Partial Shipments 43 P: FORBIDDEN

Transshipment 43 T: PROHIBITED

Loading in Charge 44 A: GUANGDONG, CHINA

For Transport to... 44 B: SANTOS, BRAZIL

Latest Date of Ship. 44 C: 141115

Descript. Of Goods 45 A: CHILDREN's 65 PERCENT COTTON 35 PERCENT POLYESTER KNITI'ED JOGGING SUIT

　　　QUANTITY: 720 DOZEN SETS

　　　　UNIT PRICE: USD42.2 PER DOZEN SET FOB GUANGDONG, CHINA

ALL OTHER DETAILS AS PER CONFIRMATION NO. DY-039 SHIPMENTS TO BE EFFECTED BY 1×20 CONTAINERS (FCL)

Documents Required: PACKING LIST IN TRIPLICATE SHOWING DETAILS OF PACKING, BREAK DOWN OF QUANTITY, GROSS WEIGHT, NET WEIGHT AND MEASUREMENT OF EACH CARTON.

Data:

① Invoice number: 1503SP023

② Invoice date: Nov.2nd, 2014

③ B/L No.: SA75214

④ Packing: 30DOZ/BALE

⑤ Shipped by: FANDU V.336

⑥ Loading Port: Guangzhou

⑦ NW: 180.00KGS/BALE
⑧ GW: 195.00KGS/BALE
⑨ Measurement: (100×100×120)CM/BALE

4.3.8 Special Provisions of the Commercial Invoice in Some Countries
某些国家对于商业发票的特殊规定

(1) The South Asian countries including India, Nepal and Sri Lanka: manually signed invoice is requested and the commodity Tariff number should be indicated.

(2) Latin American countries including Mexico, Peru, panama, Chile and Venezuela: name of commodity should be in Spanish. If based on CIF term, the freight, insurance premium and FOB should be showed separately on the manually signed invoice which should be certificated by the importer's consular. If there is no diplomatic and consular mission here, the invoice can be certified by CCPIT agent, but in a clear express, e.g. "There is no ××× country's consulate here".

(3) The Arab countries such as Kuwait, Bahrain and Iran: manufacturers' name and address should be shown on the invoice or certificate of origin, indicating goods tariff number, and the manually signed invoice should be certificated by the importer's consular. If there is no diplomatic and consular mission here, the invoice can be certified by CCPIT agent, but in a clear express, e.g. "There is no ××× country's consulate here".

(4) Lebanon: Real confirmed words and sentences should be filled on the invoice. "We hereby certify that this Invoice is authentic? Belong to the only one issued by us for the goods heron, That the value and price of the goods are correct without any deduction of payment in advance and its origin is exclusively to China".

(1) 印度、尼泊尔和斯里兰卡等南亚国家：发票要求手签，要注明商品的税则号。

(2) 墨西哥、秘鲁、巴拿马、智利和委内瑞拉等拉丁美洲国家：商品名称用西班牙文表示，如果是 CIF 术语的，则要在发票上分别显示运费、保险费和 FOB 价，发票手签并要求进口国使、领馆认证；如果出口地没有使、领馆，可以由贸促会代理认证，但要在发票上明示 "There is no ××× country's consulate here(本地无某国领事馆)"。

(3) 科威特、巴林、伊朗等阿拉伯国家：发票或产地证上显示制造厂商的名称与地址，注明商品税则号，发票手签并要求进口国使、领馆认证，如果出口地没有使、领馆，可以由贸促会代理认证，但要在发票上明示 "There is no ××× country's consulate here(本地无某国领事馆)"。

(4) 黎巴嫩：发票上加注真实性证实词句。"We hereby certify that this invoice is authentic? Belong to the only one issued by us for the goods heron, that the value and price of the goods are correct without any deduction of payment in advance and its origin is exclusively to China".

4.3.9 Special Customs Invoices
特别海关发票

In addition to the commercial invoice, some countries require a special customs invoice designed to facilitate clearance of the goods and the assessment of customs duties in that country. Such invoices list specific information required under the customs regulations of that country. It is similar in some ways to the consular invoice, except that it is prepared by the exporter and does not need to be signed or certified by the consulate.

除了商业发票之外，一些国家要求提供特别海关发票，以便为货物清关与评估海关关税提供便利。这样的发票包含了那个国家海关法规之下的专门信息。除了是由出口商开具的并且不需要领事在发票上签名或证明之外，其他内容与领事发票相似。

Chapter 5
Transport Documents
运输单证

International shipments of goods can be made by coasters airplanes, rail, trucks, and barges on inland waterways, carrier or any combination of modes (multimodal). An individual shipment may also be placed or packed in an ocean container, or airfreight container, in less than container load (LCL) shipments, in dry or wet bulk (such as grain, iron ore or crude oil) or in drums, sacks, or crates.

There are various transport documents used in international shipments. They are bills of lading (in various form), packing list, shipping instructions, forwarder's instructions, stowage instructions, hazardous materials instructions/declaration, dock receipt, mate's receipt and captain's (or master's) protest. Among all the documents issued by different transport modes and packing means, the bill of lading (B/L) is the most important.

The following are the various transport documents used in international shipments. It's rarely seen that all of these documents are used in a single shipment, but we should understand that each exists conceptually as requirements.

国际货物运输可以通过海洋运输、航空运输、铁路运输、公路运输、内河运输、邮政运输或者多种运输方式的组合(多式联运)等方式实现。货物可装在海运集装箱、空运集装箱中运输，或通过拼箱及大宗货物运输的方式(如谷物、铁矿石或原油)进行。另外，其他的运输包装如桶、麻袋和板条箱等也是常用的方式。

国际运输有各种各样的运输单据。有提单(各种形式)、包装单、装船指示、货运代理的通知、装载通知、有害物质声明、码头收据、大副收据和船长声明。在各种运输方式和包装方式下所签发的单据中，海运提单(B/L)是最重要的一种单据。

下面将介绍国际货物运输中使用的各种单据。在一次单独运输中使用所有种类的单据并不常见，但是我们应该知道，每种规定的单据都有其独特性。

5.1 Bill of Lading
提单

5.1.1 Definition
定义

Bill of lading (see Sample 5-1) is a key transport document that identifies the consignor, the consignee, the carrier, the mode of transport and other facts about the shipment.

A bill of lading is a document issued by a carrier to a shipper (exporter/seller/consignor), signed by the captain, agent, or owner of a vessel, furnishing written evidence regarding receipt of the goods (cargo), the conditions of transportation (based on contract of carriage), and the engagement to deliver goods at the prescribed port of destination to the lawful holder of the bill of lading.

A bill of lading is, therefore, both a receipt for merchandise and a contract to deliver it as freight. There are a number of different types of bills of lading and a number of issuers that relate to them as a group of documents.

Negotiable document——a written document that can be transferred merely by endorsement (signing). Checks, bills of exchange, bills of lading, and warehouse receipts (if marked negotiable), and promissory notes are examples of negotiable instruments which can be bought, sold or traded. Endorsement of such a document transfers the right to use money or goods described in the negotiable instrument to the holder of the document.

提单 (见样单 5-1) 是证明发货人、收货人、承运人、运输方式和其他运输事项的重要单据。

提单是由承运人签发给托运人 (出口商 / 卖方 / 发货人)、由船长或其代理人或运输工具的所有人签发的单据，是签发人收讫货物和履行运输条件 (根据运输合同要求) 的书面证明。另外，提单还是提单签发人将货物送达约定目的港并交给提单合法持有人的书面承诺。

因此，提单既是一项收货凭证，又是一份运货合同。提单的种类很多，签发人也因实际情况有所不同。

可转让单据是指仅可以通过背书 (签字) 的方式转让的书面文件。支票、汇票、提单、仓库收据 (在标明可转让的情况下) 和本票都是可以转让的支付工具，这些可转让的单据不仅可以被购买、销售，还可用来交易。被背书后，这些单据上的金额或货物的使用权就被转让给单据的持有人。

5.1.2 Types of Bills of Lading
提单的种类

In a documentary letter of credit transactions, if multiple modes of transport are permitted, or partial shipments allowed and part of the goods will be shipped by one mode of transport and part by another, it is necessary to put "or" or "and/or" between the names of the required transport documents. For example, if the goods are to be shipped by both sea and air, the letter of credit might specify "ocean bill of lading (see Sample5-2) and / or air waybill (see Sample5-3)."

1. Straight Bill of Lading (Non-Negotiable)

1) Definition

A straight bill of lading indicates the name of consignee in the Consignee Item. In this case, the goods will be delivered to the consignee only. To claim the goods, the consignee only needs to present identification. A straight bill of lading is often used when payment for the goods has already been made in advance or when the goods are shipped on open account. A straight bill of lading, therefore, cannot be negotiated or transferred by endorsement.

2) Key Elements

(1) Name of carrier with a signature identified as that of the carrier, ship master, or agent for the carrier or ship master.

(2) An indication or notation that the goods have been loaded "on board" or shipped on a named vessel. Also, the date of issuance or date of loading.

(3) An indication of the port of loading and the port of discharge.

(4) A sole original, or if issued in multiple originals, the full set of originals.

(5) The terms and conditions of carriage or a reference to the terms and conditions of carriage in another source or document.

(6) No indication that "the document is subject to a charter party" and no indication that "the named vessel is propelled by sail only".

(7) Meets any other stipulations of the letter of credit(when applicable).

3) Notes

Because the non-negotiable bill of lading are not title documents, it eliminates many of the inconveniences of a bill of lading and offer advantages in situations where the rigid security of a bill of lading is not required. It reduces the opportunity for fraud and they remove the problems of goods arriving ahead of documents.

2. Shipper's Order Bill of Lading

A shipper's order bill of lading is a title document to the goods, issued "to the order of" a party, usually the shipper, whose endorsement is required to effect in negotiation. Because it is negotiable, a shipper's order bill of lading can be bought, sold, or traded while goods are in transit. These are highly favored for documentary letter of credit transactions. The buyer usually needs the original or a signed copy as proof of ownership to take possession of the goods.

3. Blank Endorsed Negotiable Bill of Lading

1) Definition

A blank endorsed negotiable bill of lading is one that has been endorsed without naming an endorsee. In simple terms, any person in possession of a blank endorsed negotiable bill of lading may claim possession of the goods. Possession of this document equals rights to possession of the shipment.

2) Key Elements

(1) Name of carrier with a signature identified as that of the carrier, ship master, or agent for the carrier or ship's master.

(2) An indication or notation that the goods have been loaded "on board" or shipped on a named vessel. Also, the date of issuance or date of loading.

(3) An indication of the port of loading and the port of discharge.

(4) A sole original, or if issued in multiple originals, the full set of originals.

(5) The terms and conditions of carriage or a reference to the terms and conditions of carriage in another source or document.

(6) No indication that "the document is subject to a charter party" and no indication that "the named vessel is propelled by sail only".

(7) Meets any other stipulations of the letter of credit(when applicable).

3) Notes

(1) Vessel name.

If the bill of lading includes the notation "intended vessel", it must also contain an "on board" notation of a named vessel along with the date of loading, even if the named vessel is the same as the intended vessel.

(2) Port of loading.

If the L/C only specify general loading port or the port of destination port, such as Chinese ports, or European ports, should fill in the specific port name according to the actual situation.

If the document indicates a place where the goods were received by the carrier different from the port of loading, the document must also contain an "on-board" notation indicating the port of loading as named in the letter of credit and the named vessel, along with the date.

(3) Transport documents.

If a documentary letter of credit calls for a port-to-port shipment but does not call specifically for a marine bill of lading, the banks will accept a transport document, however named, that contains the above information. Banks will normally accept the following documents under this title: ocean bill of lading, combined transport bill of lading, provided it carries the notation "on board".

(4) Endorsement.

About endorser: If the documents are drawn up "the order of" the exporter or "to order", they must be endorsed by shipper. If the documents are drawn up "to ×××'s order" or "to order of ×××", they must be endorsed by ×××.

About means of Endorsement: ① blank endorsement: only fill in the endorser's name and address. ② special endorsement: fill in both endorser's name and address, and the endorsee's (transfer objects of ocean Marine bill of lading) name and address. ③ registered indicating endorsement: fill in both the endorser's name and address and the name and address of "TO ORDER OF + the endorsee's (ocean Marine bill of lading transfer objects)".

(5) Transshipment.

If the letter of credit prohibits transshipment, this document will be rejected if it specifically states that the goods will be transshipped.

(6) Transfer in transit.

Since this is a negotiable instrument, it may be endorsed and transferred to a third party while the goods are in transit.

(7) Signature.

① Signed by the carrier. if the carrier is COSCO, signature of a bill of lading should be COSCO (the signature of carrier on behalf of) AS Carrier. ② signed by the carrier agent. If the carrier is COSCO, agent is ABC SHIPPING Co., signature of a bill of lading should be (the signature of agent on behalf of ABC SHIPPING Co.) AS agent for the Carrier COSCO. ③ signed by the captain.If the carrier is COSCO, signature of a bill of lading should be COSCO (captain's signature) AS Master. ④ signed by the master agent (the name of the captain is XYZ). If the captain's name is XYZ and the agent is ABC SHIPPING Co., signature of a bill of lading should be ABC SHIPPING Co. (the signature of agent on behalf of) AS agent for the Master XYZ.

4. Air Waybill

1) Definition

An air waybill is a form of bill of lading used for the air transport of goods and is not negotiable.

2) Notes

(1) In a letter of credit payment situation the waybill should not be required to be issued "to order" and/or "to be endorsed" (since it is not a negotiable instrument). Also, since it is not negotiable, and it does not evidence title to the goods, in order to maintain some control of goods not paid for by cash in advance, sellers often consign air shipments to their sales agents or freight forwarders' agents in the buyer's country.

(2) About the shipper: When direct shipping, the shipper is the owner. When collective

shipping, the shipper is the freight agent. Under the payment by L/C, the shipper is the beneficiary. When consign dangerous goods, the shipper must be actual shipper, airlines don't accept freight agent checked.

(3) About the consignee: The air waybill must name a consignee (who can be the buyer). When direct shipping, the consignee is the actual consignee. When collective shipping, the consignee is the freight agent or overseas agent. The carrier is generally will not accept two or more than two consignees in one lot. In fact, if there are more than two consignees, the consignee is the first consignee and the notify party is the consignee.

(4) When loading airport or destination airport is not clear, the name of the city can be filled in.

5. Courier Receipt

A courier receipt is a document issued by a courier or delivery service evidencing receipt of goods for delivery to a named consignee and is not negotiable.

6. Post Receipt

A post receipt is a document issued by the postal service of a country evidencing receipt of goods for delivery to a named consignee.

7. Multi-Modal Bill of Lading

1) Definition

A multi-modal bill of lading (see Sample 5-4) is a single bill of lading covering a single shipment by more than one mode of transport (for example by truck, then by rail and then by ship to its final destination). It is issued by a freight-forwarder, logistics firm, or carrier. In some instances the document may be filled out by the exporter consignor, then signed by an agent of the carrier.

2) Notes

Even if a letter of credit prohibits transshipment, banks will accept a multi-modal transport document that indicates that transshipment will or may take place, provided that the entire carriage is covered by one transport document.

A multi-modal bill of lading issued by a freight forwarder is acceptable to banks in a letter of credit unless the credit stipulates specifically calls for a "marine bill of lading". The issuing freight forwarder accepts carrier responsibility for performance of the entire contract of carriage and liability for loss or damage wherever and however it occurs. As a rule, multi-modal transport documents are not negotiable.

8. Clean Bill of Lading

A clean bill of lading is one where the carrier has noted that the merchandise has been received in apparent good condition (no apparent damage loss, and etc.) and that does not bear such notations as "shipper's load and count", and etc. Most forms of documentary payments require a "clean" bill of lading in order for the seller to obtain payment.

9. Claused Bill of Lading

Opposite of clean bill of lading, a claused bill of lading is one that contains notations that specify a shortfall in quantity or deficient condition of the goods and/or packaging. There are some circumstances in which transport documents with clauses are acceptable. For example, in the steel trade, such notations are the rule rather than the exception. If this is the case, the letter of credit should explicitly state which clauses will be deemed acceptable.

10. Charter Party Bill of Lading

A charter party bill of lading is a transport document covering port to port shipments of goods issued by a party chartering a vessel. It is issued by the party chartering a vessel specifically not a carrier.

Notes: The charter party bill of lading may have preprinted wording indicating that the shipment has been loaded "on board" the "named vessel", but the document must still be signed by the ship's master or owner, or an agent for the ship's master or owner.

If preprinted wording is used, the date of issuance is deemed to be the date of loading on board. In all other cases the document must contain an "on board" the "named vessel" notation along with the date the shipment was loaded on board.

11. Courier Receipt

A courier receipt is a document issued by a courier or expedited delivery service evidencing receipt of goods for delivery to a named consignee.

Courier receipts should include the following elements: the name of issuer, stamp, sign or authentication by the service, name and address of the shipper/consignor(seller), name and address of the consignee, the date of pick-up or receipt of the goods by the service.

12. Post Receipt

A post receipt is a document issued by the postal service of a country evidencing receipt of goods for delivery to a named consignee. It is typically filled out by the exporter/seller/consignor, but then signed by an agent of the postal authority.

在跟单信用证项下，如果允许多式联运和分批装运，而且货物的不同批次由不同的运输工具装运，那么在信用证的"单据要求"中应使用"或"或者"和/或"字样。例如，如果货物通过海运和空运两种方式装运，那么信用证应注明"海运提单（见样单5-2）和/或航空运单（见样单5-3）"。

1. 记名提单（不可流通转让）

1）定义

记名提单的"收货人"一栏明确标示收货人的姓名。在这种情况下，货物只能交付给该收货人。收货人只要出示身份证件即可提货。在预付货款和赊销方式下可使用记名提单。记名提单不可流通，也不可通过背书的方式转让。

2）主要内容

(1) 承运人名称和签名，其中承运人、船长或两者的代理人均有签字权。

(2) 货物已装船或已装指定船只的说明、签发日期和装船日期。

(3) 装运港和卸货港名称。

(4) 一套单独正本提单或一整套一式几份正本提单。

(5) 运输条款或对另外运输单据的参考条款。

(6) 无"本单据受制于某一个租船合同"等内容；也无"该指名船只是帆船"等内容。

(7) 符合信用证其他条款的规定(在适用本提单的情况下)。

3) 注释

不可流通提单并非契约文件，因此该类提单删除了许多普通提单的烦琐之处。当一份提单不需要严格的安全保障时，这是很便利的。这种方式减少了利用提单进行欺诈的机会，也解决了货物早于提单到达的问题。

2. 托运人指示提单

托运人指示提单是一份契约文件。在这类提单中，收货人一栏应注明"由……指示"，通常为托运人。这时，托运人往往需要对提单进行背书，以使之流通转让。因其流通转让的特性，这类提单可以在货物运输过程中被购买、销售或交易。在跟单信用证交易中，这类提单被普遍使用。买方通常需要提单的正本或有签名的副本作为提货和拥有货物所有权的凭证。

3. 空白背书可转让提单

1) 定义

空白背书提单即在背书时不注明被背书人的提单。简而言之，任何持有空白背书提单的人都可以提货。得到提单就意味着得到货物。

2) 主要内容

(1) 承运人名称和签字。其中，承运人、船长或两者的代理人均有签字权。

(2) 货物已装船或已装指名船只的说明及签发日期和装船日期。

(3) 装运港和卸货港名称。

(4) 一套单独正本提单或一整套一式几份正本提单。

(5) 运输条款或对其他单证的运输条款的补充。

(6) 无"本单据受制于某一个租船合同"等内容，也无"该指名船只是帆船"等内容。

(7) 符合信用证其他条款的规定(在适用本提单的情况下)。

3) 注释

(1) 船名。

如果提单中含有"预期船只"字样，即使该指定船只与预期船只是同一条船，那么该提单必须同时标示某指名船只"已装船"字样及装运日期。

(2) 装运港。

如果信用证中只笼统规定装运港或目的港名称，如中国港口或欧洲港口，应根据实际情况填写具体港口名称。

如果提单中有承运人接货的地点，且该地点与装运港不同，那么提单在标明船名、装船日期及信用证中规定的装运港时必须同时注明"已装船"字样。

(3) 运输单据。

如果跟单信用证中仅要求港至港运输,而并未要求必须提交海运提单时,只要提交能体现以上信息的运输单据,银行即可接受。银行将接受以下类型的运输单据:海运提单、联合运输提单,只要这些单据注明"已装船"字样。

(4) 背书。

关于背书人:如果单据中注明"凭出口人指示"或"凭指示",那么该单据应由托运人背书。当收货人是"凭×××指示",由记名一方背书。

关于背书方式:①空白背书(不记名背书),只书写背书人名称及地址;②记名背书,既书写背书人名称及地址,也书写被背书人(海运提单转让对象)名称及地址;③记名指示背书,既书写背书人名称及地址,又书写"TO ORDER OF + 被背书人(海运提单转让对象)名称及地址"。

(5) 转运。

如果信用证禁止转运,而单据标示货物将被转运的话,单据将被拒收。

(6) 运输途中转让。

因为这是可转让支付工具,因此货物在运输途中时该单据即可背书和转让给第三方。

(7) 签署。

①承运人签署提单。如果承运人为 COSCO,则提单签署为 COSCO 承运人代表签名 AS Carrier。②承运人代理签署提单。如果承运人为 COSCO,代理人为 ABC SHIPPING CO.,则提单签署为 ABC SHIPPING Co.,代理人代表签名 AS agent for the Carrier COSCO。③船长签署提单。如果承运人为 COSCO,则提单签署为船长签名 AS Master。④船长代理签署提单(船长姓名 XYZ)。如果船长姓名 XYZ,代理人为 ABC SHIPPING Co.,则提单签署为 ABC SHIPPING Co.,代理人代表签名 AS agent for the Master XYZ。

4. 航空运单

1) 定义

航空运单是专用于航空运输货物的提单,该单据不可转让。

2) 注释

(1) 因其不可转让性,航空运单不具备物权凭证的性质。在信用证支付方式下,该单据不需要注明"凭指示"和/或"背书"。在非预付货款的情况下,卖方通常将空运货物的收货人填写为自己的销售代理或位于买方国家的货运代理,以便能在一定程度上对货物进行有效的控制。

(2) 关于托运人:直接托运时,托运人是货主;集中托运时,托运人是货运代理人。在信用证支付方式下,托运人是信用证受益人。托运危险货物时,托运人必须是实际托运人,航空公司不接受货运代理人托运。

(3) 关于收货人:航空运单必须填写收货人名称(买方)。直接托运时,收货人是实际收货人;集中托运时,收货人是货运代理人或者海外代理人。承运人一般不接受一票货物有两个或两个以上收货人。如果实际上有两个以上收货人,收货人是第一收货人,通知方是第二收货人。

(4) 在始发站机场或目的站机场不明确时，可填写城市名称。

5. 快件收据
快件收据是由快件公司或送货机构签发的证明签发人收到货物并送至指定收货人的不可流通单据。

6. 邮政收据
邮政收据是由邮政公司签发的证明其收到货物并送至指定收货人的单据。

7. 多式联运提单
1) 定义

多式联运提单 (见样单 5-4) 是指一批货物经由一种以上的运输方式运输而签发的单据 (例如，货物先由卡车运输，然后通过铁路运输，再由海运运至最终目的地)。多式联运提单可以由货运代理、物流公司或承运人签发。在某些情况下，可以先由出口托运人填好提单，然后由承运人代理签字。

2) 注释

即使信用证禁止转运，只要是同一份包括全程运输的运输单据，银行也会接受注明货物将被转运或可被转运的多式联运提单。

在信用证下，银行接受由货运代理签发的多式联运提单，除非信用证规定必须使用"海运提单"。签发提单的货运代理承担运输合同中的全部承运人责任，并对在任何地点和任何情况下货物发生的损失或损害承担赔偿责任。按照惯例，多式联运单据是不可流通转让的。

8. 清洁提单
清洁提单是指货物在装船时外表状况良好 (无明显损伤等)，承运人未加任何货损、包装不良等批注的提单，提单上无"由托运人装货和清点数量"等字样。在多数跟单支付情况下，卖方需提交"清洁"提单作为收付的条件。

9. 非清洁提单
与清洁提单相反，非清洁提单是指未加货物和/或包装存在短量、缺陷等问题的批注的提单。在某些情况下，附带有这些批注的提单是可以接受的。例如，在钢材贸易中，以上批注可以使用。在这种情况下，信用证应明确说明以上哪个条款是可以接受的。

10. 租船提单
租船提单是由租船方开立的港到港运输的运输单证。需要特别注意的是，是租船方不是承运人。

注释：租船提单可能有如货物"已装上×××船 (指定船只)"的内容，但是该提单必须由船长或船舶所有人或他们的代理人签名。

如果租船提单上有如上内容，那么提单的签发日即视为装船日期。在无如上内容的情况下，单据有货物"已装上×××船 (指定船只)"字样时，必须同时标明装船日期。

11. 快递收据
快递收据是由快递员或快递公司出具的收到货物并交付给指定收货人的单证。

快递收据应包括下列内容：开单人、邮戳、印章或服务标志的认证，托运人/发货人（卖方）的名字和地址，收货人的名称和地址，邮寄或收货日期。

12. 邮递收据

邮递收据是由国家的邮政公司开立的，证明送往指定收货人并收到货物的单证。一般由出口商/卖方/发货人填写，之后邮政公司代理人签署。

5.1.3 Checklist for B/L
提单核对内容

(1) Are bills of lading in negotiable form if required in the letter of credit?

(2) Are all originals being presented to the bank or accounted for?

(3) Are all originals properly endorsed when consigned "to the order" of the shipper?

(4) Are bills of lading clean (no notation showing defective goods or packaging)?

(5) Do bills of lading indicate that merchandise was loaded on board and loaded within the time specified in the letter of credit? If this provision is not part of the text but in the form of a notation, is the notation dated and signed by the carrier or its agent?

(6) Are the bills of lading made out as prescribed in the letter of credit (in other words, with names and addresses of beneficiary, applicant, notify parties, and flag, if any)?

(7) If freight was prepaid, is this payment clearly indicated by either "FREIGHT PREPAID" or "FREIGHT PAID"?

(8) If charter party, sailing vessel, on deck, forwarders, or consolidator's bills of lading is presented, does the credit specifically allow for them?

(9) Do marks and numbers, quantities, and the general description of goods agree with the commercial invoice and letter of credit, with no excess merchandise shipped?

(10) Does the bill of lading show transshipment if prohibited in the letter of credit?

(11) Is the document signed by the carrier or its agent? Is it correct?

(1) 如果信用证要求提交可转让提单，提单是否已经满足信用证要求？

(2) 是不是所有的正本提单都提交给银行或向银行说明了？

(3) 当收货人栏填写"凭发货人指示"时，是不是所有的正本提单已被正确地背书？

(4) 提单是否清洁（无货物或包装有缺陷的批注）？

(5) 提单是否标明货物已装运并且在信用证规定的时间内装运？如果这个内容不是提单的条款而是以批注的形式标示，那么这个批注是否附带装船期并由承运人或其代理人签字？

(6) 提单内容是否符合信用证的要求（换言之，如果有的话，是否标明受益人、开证申请人、通知人的名称和地址及标志）？

(7) 如果运费已预付，那么提单上是否标示"运费预付"或"运费已付"？

(8) 如果提交的是租船提单、帆船提单、甲板提单、货代提单或拼箱运输提单，信用证是否允许？

(9) 提单上的运输标志和标识号、数量和商品描述是否与商业发票和信用证规定的一致？货物是否多装？

(10) 如果信用证禁止转运，提单上是否有转运的信息？

(11) 提单是否由承运人或其代理人签字？如果已签，签字是否正确？

1. Sample of Making B/L according to the Following L/C
根据以下信用证缮制提单样例

Issuing Bank: METITA BANK LTD. FIN-00020 METITA, FINLAND
Term of Doc. Credit: IRREVOCABLE
Credit Number: KHL11–22457
Date of Issue: 210505
Expiry: Date 210716 Place CHINA
Applicant: FFK CORP. AKEKSANTERINK AUTO
P.O. BOX 9, FINLAND
Beneficiary: GUANGDONG RONGHUA TRADE CO., LTD.
168 DEZHENG ROAD SOUTH, GUANGZHOU, CHINA
Amount: Currency USD Amount 38 400.00
Pos. / Neg. Toll. (%): 5/5
Available with/by: ANY BANK IN ADVISING COUNTRY BY NEGOTIATION
Partial Shipments: Not Allowed
Transshipment: Allowed
Loading in Charge: GUANGZHOU
For Transport to: HELSINKI
Shipment Period: AT THE LATEST JULY 16, 2021
Description of Goods: 9 600PCS OF WOMEN'S SWEATERS
Unit Price: USD4.00/PC, CFR HELSINKI
Packing: 12PCS/CTN
Documents Required: FULL SET OF CLEAN ON BOARD MARINE BILLS OF LADING, MADE OUT TO ORDER OF METITA BANK LTD., FINLAND, MARKED "FREIGHT PREPAID" AND NOTIFY APPLICANT

Data:
(1) B/L No.: KTT0245678
(2) GW: 6 500K GS
(3) Measurement: 25CBMS
(4) Date of B/L: July 10th, 2021
(5) Container No.: SIHU365487—2(20') SEAL No.123456 CY/CY
(6) Place of signature: GUANGZHOU
(7) Shipper: ABC SHIPPING CO.
(8) Signer: 张三
(9) Marks & No.: ABC
HELSINKI
No.1-800

Key

答案

Shipper GUANGDONG RONGHUA TRADE CO.，LTD. 168 DEZHENG ROAD SOUTH，GUANGZHOU，CHINA		B/L No. KTT0245678	
Consignee TO ORDER OF METITA BANK LTD.，FINLAND		**Combined Transport Bill Of Lading**	
Notify Address FFK CORP. AKEKSANTERINK AUTO P.O.BOX 9. FINLAND			
Pre-carriage by HK	Place of Receipt HK		
Ocean Vessel Voy.No. MAKIS V.002	Port of Loading GUANGZHOU，CHINA	For Delivery of Goods Please Apply to：	
Port of Discharge HELSINKI，FINLAND	Place of Delivery	Final Destination for the Merchant§Reference only	
Container.Seal No. & Marks&No. ABC HELSINKI NO.1—800 SIHU365487—(20') SEAL N0.123456 CY/CY FCL	No.of Package&Description of Goods SHIPPER'S LOAD&COUNT&SEAL S.T.C. 800CARTONS WOMEN'S SWEATERS TOTAL：EIGHT HUNDRED CARTONS ONLY "FREIGHT PREPAID"	Gross Weight 6 500KGS	Measurement 25CBMS
Freight & Charges	Revenue Tons	Rate Per	Prepaid	Collect
		Prepaid at	Payable at	Place and Date of Issue GUANGZHOU，CHINA JULY 1ST，2021
		Total Prepaid	No.of Original Bs/L THREE(3)	Stamp&Signature AS THE CARRIER 　　ABC SHIPPING CO. 　　　张三

2. Sample of Making Correction of B/L according to the above L/C

根据以上信用证，提单改错样例

　　Issuing Bank：METITA BANK LTD.FIN–00020 METITA，FINLAND
　　Term of Doc. Credit：IRREVOCABLE
　　Credit Number：LRT9802457
　　Date of Issue：210505
　　Expiry：Date 210716 Place CHINA
　　Applicant：ABC CORP. AKEKSANTERINK AUTO
　　　　P. O. BOX 9，FINLAND
　　Beneficiary：GUANGDONG RONGHUA TRADE CO.，LTD.

Chapter 5   Transport Documents 运输单证

168 DEZHENG ROAD SOUTH, GUANGZHOU, CHINA

Amount: Currency USD Amount 36 480.00 (SAY US DOLLARS THIRTY SIX THOUSAND FOUR HUNDRED AND EIGHTY ONLY.)

Pos. /Nag. Toll. (%): 5/5

Available with/by: ANY BANK IN ADVISING COUNTRY BY NEGOTIATION

Partial Shipments: Not Allowed

Transshipment: Allowed

Loading in Charge: GUANGZHOU

For Transport to: HELSINKI

Shipment Period: AT THE LATEST JULY 16, 2021

Descript. of Goods: 9 600PCS OF WOMEN'S SWEATERS
 UNIT PRICE: USD3.80/PC
 PACKING: 12PCS/CTN TOTAL 800CTNS

OTHER DETAILS AS PER S/C NO. 98SGQ468001 CFR HELSINKI

Documents Required: FULL SET OF CLEAN ON BOARD MARINE BILLS OF LADING, MADE OUT TO ORDER OF METITA BANK LTD., FINLAND, MARKED "FREIGHT PREPAID" AND NOTIFY APPLICANT (AS INDICATE ABOVE)

Additional Cond.:

(1) T. T. REIMBURSEMENT IS PROHIBITED.

(2) ALL DOCUMENTS MUST BE MARKED THE S/C NO..

(3) SHIPPING MARKS: ABC
 HELSINKI
 NO. 1-800

Shipper GUANGDONG RONGHUA TRADE CO., LTD. 168 DEZHENG ROAD SOUTH, GUANGZHOU, CHINA ①			BILL OF LADING B/L No.KFT 2582588	
Consignee ABC CORP. AKEKSANTKRINK AUTO P.O.BOX9, FINLAND ②			中国远洋运输公司 中国远洋运输公司 **CHINA OCEAN SHIPPING** original	
Notify Party METTA BANK LTD., FIN-00020 METTA, FINLAND ③				
Pre carriage by DONGFANGHONG ⑨	Place of Receipt ⑩			
Ocean Vessel Vow. No. SUISUN 103 11	Port of Loading GUANGZHOU ⑫			
Port of discharge HELSINKI VIA	Final destination	Freight payable at	Number original Bs/L	
Marks and Numbers N/M ④	Number and kind of packages; Description 9 600PCS WOMEN'S SWEATERS ⑤ TOTAL: EIGHT HUNDRED CARTONS ONLY ⑥ S/C NO.LRT9802457 ⑦		Gross weight 13 600.00KGS FREIGHT COLLECT ⑧	Measurement(m^3) 25CBMS

Applicable only when document used as a Through Bill of Loading				
Freight &Charges	**Revenue Tons.**	**Rate Per**	**Prepaid**	**Collect** ⑬
		Prepaid at	Payable at	Place and Date of Issue GUANGZHOU, CHINA May. 20th, 2021
		Total Prepaid	No.of Original Bs/L THREE(3)	Stamp&Signature ABC SHIPPING CO. 刘五 AS MASTER

Key

答案

Shipper GUANGDONG RONGHUA TRADE CO., LTD. 168 DEZHENG ROAD SOUTH, GUANGZHOU, CHINA			**BILL OF LADING B/L No.** **KFT2582588**	
Consignee *TO ORDER OF METITA BANK LTD., FINLAND*			中国远洋运输公司 中国远洋运输公司 **CHINA OCEAN SHIPPING** original	
Notify Party *ABC CORP. AKEKSANTERINK AUTO P.O.BOX 9, FINLAND*				
Pre carriage by DONGFANGHONG ⑨	**Place of Receipt** ⑩			
Ocean Vessel Vow. No. SUISUN 103 11	**Port of Loading** GUANGZHOU, CHINA ⑫			
Port of discharge HELSINKI VIA, FINLAND	**Final destination**	**Freight payable at**	**Number original Bs/L**	
Marks and Numbers ABC HELSINKI NO.1-800	**Number and kind of packages; Description** 800CTNS WOMEN'S SWEATERS TOTAL: EIGHT HUNDRED CARTONS ONLY ⑥ S/C NO.: *98SGQ468001*		**Gross weight** 13 600.00KGS *FREIGHT PREPAID*	**Measurement (m³)** 25CBMS
Applicable only when document used as a Through Bill of Loading				
Freight &Charges	**Revenue Tons.**	**Rate Per**	**Prepaid**	**Collect** ⑬
		Prepaid at	Payable at	Place and Date of Issue GUANGZHOU, CHINA May. 20th, 2021
		Total Prepaid	No.Of Original Bs/L THREE(3)	Stamp&Signature ABC SHIPPING CO. 刘五 AS MASTER

Chapter 5　Transport Documents 运输单证

Case Analysis 5.1　How does the Carrier's Agent Issue B/L
案例分析 5.1　承运人代理是如何签发提单的

A Bill of lading issued by COSCO was required by the credit. The B/L presented by the beneficiary was issued by Shantou COSCO Container Transportation Co., the agent of the carrier. The B/L indicated that COSCO was the carrier.

The issuing bank dishonored.

Analysis:

The issuing bank was justified in doing so because the B/L should be issued by COSCO instead of the agent according to the credit. In this case, however, there was no COSCO (or its branch) in Shantou and Shantou COSCO Container Transportation Co. was its only agent of COSCO in Shantou, thus the L/C clause amended as "B/L can be issued by COSCO or its agent". If the credit requires the B/L to be issued by the master, while the signature on B/L is "for the master", the issuing bank can refuse the B/L because a signature for the master is not a signature by the master.

信用证规定需提交由中国远洋运输公司签发的提单。由受益人提交的提单是由承运人的代理机构汕头中国远洋运输公司签发，同时，提单标示，中国远洋运输公司是承运人。

该单据遭到开证行拒付。

分析：

开证行的做法是正确的。根据信用证规定，提单应由中国远洋运输公司签发，而不是其代理人签发。然而，在此案中，中国远洋运输公司（或分公司）没有在汕头，汕头中国远洋集装箱运输公司是其在汕头唯一的代理。因此，正确的做法应是：将信用证的条款改成"提单可以由中国远洋运输公司或其代理人签发"。如果信用证要求提单应由船长签发，而提单上的签名是"代船长"，那么开证行会拒付该提单，因为代船长签名不能代替船长的签名。

Case Analysis 5.2　Ante-dated B/L Resulting in Large Sum of Compensation
案例分析 5.2　倒签提单造成巨额赔偿

In October 2014, a Hong Kong Import and Export Company signed with a West German company a contact valued at US＄150 000. The West German company opened the L/C stipulating that the date of shipment was Dec. 31, and the port of destination was Rotterdam. The Hong Kong export company booked the shipping space of vessel "A" at a shipping company. Shortly before the loading, they found that there were some defects in the package of the goods that had to be fixed at once. They consulted with the shipping company to change their booking of shipping space of vessel "A" to vessel "B". But vessel "B" arrived late for some reasons at the port of shipment, and the loading was further delayed because of the bad weather. Vessel "B" did not depart until the end of January.

In order to meet with the date of shipment required on L/C, the export company obtained the B/L dated Dec. 31 with a letter of guarantee. They presented the B/L to the correspondent bank for negotiation and got the payment on Feb. 15.

However, the West German company received the cable notice from the seller saying that the goods would be shipped by vessel "A" at first. Later they received another cable notice saying that the shipment has been changed to vessel "B". The West German company examined the time of the two cables and became doubtful about the actual date shipment. They sent a cable to the export company on Mar. 5, requiring them to provide the loading evidence of shipment on Dec. 31. The export company replied that it was unnecessary to provide such a kind of evidence since the shipment on Dec. 31 was definite and the B/L was correct.

Vessel "B" arrived at Rotterdam on Mar. 23. If the date of shipment on B/L was correct, the goods had been under way for 80 days. The West German company recognized that there must be some problems with the date of B/L, so he refused to pick up the goods and launched a claim. The export company refused to accept the claim. The West German company engaged a lawyer soon after that. The lawyer got on to vessel "B" and examined the log of this ship, verifying vessel "B" had arrived at the port of shipment on Jan. 10, and departed on Jan.31. The lawyer took a photo of the log as a strong proof, started a lawsuit against the carrier and required the local court to detain the ship lawfully. The local court accepted the lawsuit and detained vessel "B" in Rotterdam.

The shipping company ran the responsibility to the export company immediately after knowing the detainment of vessel "B". Since the export company had obtained the B/L with a letter of guarantee, it has to assume all the responsibilities. After the continuous consultations by cables, both parties reached an agreement that the export company should pay US＄35 000 as compensation. At that time, the German company withdrew the lawsuit.

Analysis:

The date of shipment on B/L, strictly speaking, should be the accurate date (including the day, month and year) when the cargo is safely loaded aboard the vessel. Generally, the date of loading is also the issuing date of B/L. It is not only the proof of shipment but also the commencing point of carrier's liabilities.

The date of B/L is of vital importance to the buyer, seller, the correspondent bank, the customs and insurer. To the seller, it defines the date of shipment as well as his fulfillment of the contract; to the bank, it sometimes serves as a basis to determine the date of settlement of a time draft; to the customs, it tells whether the date of shipment falls within the useful life of the export license. As for the effectiveness of the insurance contract, it even has a closer relationship with the date of B/L.

Why does the ante-dated B/L still exist? There are quite a few reasons. Firstly, the shipper, for some reasons (as in the case that if the shipper cannot present B/L promptly, L/C will expire and the contract will be terminated), required the carrier to sign a date on B/L earlier than actual date of shipment, i.e. the date within the time limit of L/C. Secondly, because of port congestion, the goods cannot be shipped as scheduled. Under such circumstance, although both the shipper and carrier are fault-free, the shipper is afraid that the contract will be terminated, so he has to surrender a letter of guarantee to the carrier against the latter's insurance of an ante-dated B/L. Thirdly, in the case of vessel delay, the carrier is willing to sign an ante-dated B/L or B/L without cargo in order to attract more loads.

No matter what might lead to an ante-dated B/L, it is commonly regarded as a kind of document forgery. When the importer gets enough proof, he has the right to refuse the payment and start a lawsuit. Then, the carrier has no excuse for this malpractice. If the carrier signs the B/L at the sight of shipper's guarantee letter, he may transfer such risks and responsibilities to the shipper. At this time, the shipper has to make indemnity not only to the court as per the judgment, but also to the carrier for the loss occurred, just as the loss the carrier in this case suffered when vessel "B" was detained in Rotterdam.

Although the malpractice of signing an ante-dated B/L may not necessarily develop into such a bad situation as described in this case, it will damage the shipper's commercial credit at least, and further badly influence the future business transactions of the company.

2014年10月，一家香港进出口公司与一家西德公司签了一份价值15万美元的合同。西德公司开立了信用证，并在信用证中规定装运期为12月31日，目的港是鹿特丹。香港出口商在一家船公司订了舱位，船名为"A"。在装运即将开始时，出口商发现货物的包装有缺陷，必须立刻处理。于是出口商与船公司商量，将船由"A"船改成"B"船。但是由于某些因素的影响，B船到达装运港时迟到了，后来由于天气恶劣，装运一直被拖延。直到1月底，B船仍未离开装运港。

为了使装运日期与信用证规定相符，出口商在出具保函的条件下获得了12月31日装运的提单。之后，出口商向通知行交单议付并于2月15日得到货款。

西德公司从出口商最先发来的电报中得知，该批货物将由"A"船装运，之后，又收到通知，说明运输船只已改成"B"船。西德公司仔细对比了两封电报的时间，并对实际装运日期产生了怀疑。他们于3月5日向出口商发电报，要求提供货物于12月31日装船的证据。出口商回复没有必要提供此类单据，理由是装船日期确实是12月31日，而且提单是正确的。

"B"船于3月23日到达鹿特丹。如果提单标示的日期是正确的话，那就意味着这艘船已经航行了80天。西德公司意识到装船日期是有问题的，他们拒绝提货并提出索赔。出口公司拒绝赔偿。至此，西德公司专门聘请了律师。该律师登上"B"船，检查了航海日志，发现该船于1月10日到达装运港，至1月31日才离开。律师将航海日志拍下来作为装运延迟的有力证据，向承运人提起诉讼并请求当地法院依法扣留船只。当地法院受理此案并在鹿特丹扣留了"B"船。

知道"B"船被扣留后，船公司立刻将责任推到出口商身上。因对提单出具了保函，出口商需承担全部责任。通过多次的电报协商，买卖双方最终达成一致，由出口商赔偿3.5万美元。与此同时，德国公司撤销了诉讼。

分析：

严格地说，提单上的装运日期应该是货物安全地装到船上的日期（该日期应包括具体的日、月、年）。通常来说，装运日期即提单的签发日期。装运日期不仅是装运的凭证，也是承运人责任的起讫点。

提单的签发日期对买方、卖方、通知行、海关和保险人都很重要。对卖方来说，提单的签发日期是装运日期，也是履行合同义务的日期；对银行来说，这往往是银行决定远期汇票的结算日期的依据；对海关来说，这是审查装运货物出口许可证是否过期的依据。而对于一份有效的保险合同而言，提单的签发日期显得更为重要。

为什么倒签提单依然存在？这是由一些因素导致的。首先，因为某些原因（本案中如托运人不能及时提供提单，信用证将到期，合同也会终止），托运人会要求承运人签发一份早于实际装运日期的提单，也就是说，签发的装运日期是符合信用证期限的。其次，因为港口拥挤，货物往往不能按计划装运。在这种情况下，即使托运人和承运人都无过错，托运人也会担心合同将被终止。于是托运人不得不出具一份保证函，以作为船方签发倒签提单的担保。第三，由于船舶延误，承运人也愿意签发倒签提单或预借提单以便揽到更多的货源。

不管导致倒签提单的因素是什么，这类行为通常被视为单据伪造。如果买方拥有足够的证据，他有权利拒绝付款和提起诉讼。届时，承运人将无法推托其失职行为。如果倒签提单的签发是建立在托运人保函的基础上，那么承运人可以将所有的风险和责任转移到托运人身上。这时，托运人除了赔偿法院判决的罚款之外，还要赔偿承运人的损失。在此案中，承运人的损失即"B"船被扣留导致的损失。

尽管签发倒签提单这样的失职行为不一定会导致如本案的严重后果，但至少会损害托运人的商业信用，从而进一步影响该企业未来的贸易发展。

Assignment 5.1 Make out a Bill of Lading according to the following L/C.
练习5.1 根据以下信用证缮制一份提单

DRESENER BANK，BREMEN BRANCH
DATE: Jul. 4th, 2021
CREDIT No. TS—36376

EXPIRY: Aug. 31th, 2015
APPLICANT: SCHLITER.CO.BREMEN.
3601AW. HERO ROAD, BREMEN, GERMAN
BENEFICIARY: HANJIN ARTS AND CRAFTS I/E CORP. TIANJIN, CHINA
AOVISING BANK: BANK OF CHINA, TIANJIN, CHINA
AMOUNT: DEM6 600.00 (SAY DEM SIX THOUSAND SIX HUNDRED ONLY)
DEAR SIRS,
   WE OPEN THIS IRREVOCABLE DOCUMENTS CREDIT AVAILABLE AGAINST THE FOLLOWING DOCUMENTS:
   FULL SET OF CLEAN ON BOARD BILL OF LADING MADE OUT TO ORDER AND BLANK ENDORSED MARKED "FREIGHT PREPAID", NOTIFY OPENER.
   SHIPMENT FROM TIANJIN TO BREMEN LATEST ON AUG.25, 2021 COVERING:
   600SETS(3PCS OF EACH) "WILLOW PRODUCT" ART NO. ISSR-16 @ EUR11 PER SET, CIF BREMEN.
   PARTIAL AND TRANSSHIPMENT ARE NOT ALLOWED.
   SHIPPING MARKS:
         BREMEN
         NO.1—UP

Data:
① 600sets,150 CTN in 15 pallets, 3PCS in one set
② 28Kgs/CTN, M=0.04M^3
③ loading port: XINGANG, TIANJIN
④ destination: BREMEN
⑤ B/L NO: 123
⑥ ocean vessel vow. No.: PAUL RICKERS
⑦ date of issue: 2021.8.1
⑧ Container. Seal No.: 1×20' HQ FCL/FCL CY/CY
   TGHU7036445/54660

5.2 Packing List
装箱单

A packing list (see Sample 5-5) is a document made out by the seller stating the detailed content of each individual shipment. It is a supplementary document to the commercial invoice used to make up the deficiency of an invoice by giving all the necessary particulars of the goods. A packing list is one of the documents required for mandatory inspection and negotiation of payment. It is also used to facilitate the general checking of goods before shipment by the seller. The buyer also needs the packing list to check the goods on their arrival at the destination.

   Packing lists are utilized to describe the way in which the goods are packed for shipment, such as how many packages the shipment is broken into, the types of packaging used, the weight of each package, the size of each package, and any markings that may be on the packages. Forms for packing lists are available through packing companies who prepare export shipments. Sometimes packing lists are required by the customs laws of International countries, but even if they are not, an important use of the packing list is for filing insurance claims if there are some damages or casualty to the shipment during transportation.

1. Contents of Packing List

A packing list usually contains the following details.

(1) Invoice number.

(2) Buyer and consignee.

(3) Country of origin.

(4) Vessel or flight date.

(5) Port of airport of loading and discharge.

(6) Place of delivery.

(7) Shipping marks.

(8) Container number.

(9) Weight and / or volume of the goods.

(10) Full details of the goods.

2. Types of Packing List

(1) Packing List.

(2) Specification List.

(3) Weight List/Weight Memo.

(4) Measurement List.

(5) Neutral Packing List.

(6) Packing Declaration.

(7) Packing Specification.

(8) Packing Summary.

(9) Weight Certificate.

(10) Assortment List.

3. Key Elements

(1) Name and address of seller (consignor): Names should correspond with stipulations of the L/C.

(2) Name and address of buyer (consignee): Names should correspond with stipulations of the L/C.

(3) Date of issuance: it should be corresponded with the invoice's.

(4) P/L number: it should be corresponded with the invoice's.

(5) Order or contract Number.

(6) Quantity and description of the goods.

(7) Weight of the goods: The gross weight, net weight, total gross and net weight should be listed and the numbers should correspond with other documents.

(8) Number of packages.

(9) Shipping marks and number.

(10) Quantity and description of contents of each package, carton, crate or container.

(11) Any other information as required in the Shipper's Instruction (e.g. country of origin): generally, the unit price and the total amount are not stated.

4. Checklist for Packing List

(1) Does the packing type shown agree with the commercial invoice?

(2) Does the quantity, or do the units, match the commercial invoice?

(3) Is the exact breakdown of merchandise per individual packages shown, if required?

5. Main Points of Making out Packing Lists

(1) Names should correspond with stipulations of the L/C.

(2) The gross weight, net weight, total gross and net weight should be listed and the numbers should correspond with other documents.

(3) Generally, the unit price and the total amount are not stated and the number and issuing date should correspond with the invoices.

装箱单(见样单5-5)是由出口商缮制，说明装运细节的单证，是商业发票的补充单证。在强制检验和议付货款时，装箱单是必备单证之一。对出口商来说，装箱单有助于货物装运前进行总体清点。进口商同样需要装箱单，以便在货物到达目的地时进行检查。

装箱单是描述货物装运方式的单据，如装运的包装数量，包装方式，每个包装的重量、尺寸及包装上可能出现的任何标志。装箱单的表格由负责准备出口装运的包装公司提供。有的国外海关法中会规定提供装箱单，但即使无此规定，装箱单也有一个很重要的用途：当货物在运输途中受到损害或灭失时，装箱单是填写保险索赔的依据。

1. 装箱单的内容

装箱单通常包括以下内容。

(1) 发票号码。

(2) 买方和收货人。

(3) 原产国。

(4) 船舶或航班日期。

(5) 装运和卸货的港口或机场。

(6) 交货地点。

(7) 运输标志(又称唛头)。

(8) 集装箱号码。

(9) 货物的重量和/或体积。

(10) 货物的详细信息。

2. 装箱单的种类

(1) 装箱单。

(2) 规格单。

(3) 重量单/磅码单。

(4) 尺码单。

(5) 中性包装单。

(6) 包装声明。

(7) 包装说明。

(8) 包装提要。

(9) 重量证书。

(10) 花色搭配单。

3. 主要内容

(1) 卖方(托运人)的名称地址：名称必须与信用证规定一致。

(2) 买方(收货人)的名称地址：名称必须与信用证规定一致。

(3) 签发日期：必须与商业发票日期一致。

(4) 装箱单号码：必须与商业发票号码一致。

(5) 订单或合同号码。

(6) 商品描述和数量。

(7) 货物重量：必须明确列出各类商品的毛重、净重及毛重和净重的总值，装箱单上的重量必须与其他单据中的重量一致。

(8) 包装数量。

(9) 运输标志和数量。

(10) 每个包装、纸箱、板条箱或集装箱所装商品的数量和描述。

(11) 托运人指示要求的其他信息(如原产地)：一般来说，商品的单价和总值不标示在装箱单上。

4. 装箱单核对内容

(1) 包装方式是否与商业发票标示的一致？

(2) 数量或单位是否与商业发票标示的一致？

(3) 如果有规定，是否每个包装内所装商品的详细目录都根据要求标示？

5. 缮制装箱单的要点

(1) 装箱单上标示的名称应与信用证规定的一致。

(2) 必须明确列出各类商品的毛重、净重及毛重和净重的总值，装箱单上的重量必须与其他单据中的重量一致。

(3) 总体来说，装箱单上不标示单价和总金额；装箱单号码和签发日期应与商业发票一致。

Assignment 5.2 Make a packing list according to the following L/C.
练习 5.2 根据以下信用证缮制一份包装单

DOC. CREDIT NUMBER * 20: KRT2899302
DATE OF ISSUE 31 C: 210912
APPLICANT * 50: CURRENT FUNDS LIMITED
　　　　ROOM 110 CHINACHEM GOLDEN PLAZAS NO. 77 MODY ROAD, TSIM SHA TSUI EAST, KOWLOON, HONG KONG
BENEFICIARY * 59: GUANGDONG TEXTILES IMPORT AND EXPORT KNITWEARS COMPANY LIMITED
　　　　15/F., GUANGDONG TEXTILES MANSION, 168 XIAOBEI ROAD, GUANGZHOU, CHINA
AMOUNT * 32 B: CURRENCY USD AMOUNT 30 384.00
AVAILABLE WITH / BY * 41 D: CREDIT ISSUING OFFICE BY PAYMENT
PARTIAL SHIPHENTS 43 P: FORBIDDEN
TRANSSHIPMENT 43 T: PROHIBITED
LOADING IN CHARGE 44 A: GUANGDONG, CHINA
FOR TRANSPORT TO... 44 B: SANTOS, BRAZIL
LATEST DATE OF SHIPMENT 44 C: 141115
DESCRIPT OF FOODS 45 A: DESCRIPTION: CHILDREN'S 65 PERCENT COTTON 35 PERCENT POLYESTER KNITIED JOGGING SUIT
　　QUANTITY: 720 DOZEN SETS
　　UNIT PRICE: USD42.2 PER DOZEN SET FOB GUANGDONG, CHINA
　　ALL OTHER DETAILS AS PER CONFIRMATION NO: DY-039
　　SHIPMENT TO BE EFFECTED BY 1 ×20 CONTAINERS (FCL)
DOCUMENTS REQUIRED 45 A:
　　PACKING LIST IN TRIPLICATE SHOWING DETAILS OF PACKING BREAKDOWN OF QUANTITY, GROSS WEIGHT, NET WEIGHT AND MEASUREMENT OF EACH CARTON

Data:
　① invoice number: 1103SP023
　② invoice date: Nov.2nd, 2021
　③ B/L No.: SA75214
　④ Packing: 30DOZ/BALE
　⑤ Shipped by: FANDU V.336
　⑥ loading port: GUANGZHOU
　⑦ NW: 180.00KGS/BALE
　⑧ GW: 195.00KGS/BALE
　⑨ Measurement: (100×100×120)CM/BALE

Assignment 5.3 Mae Corrections of the following Packing List.
练习5.3   包装单改错

```
                PACKING LIST              ORIGINAL
Exporter:                          DATE: Oct. 28th, 2021
GUANGZHOU ARTS & CRAFTS IMP.       INVOICE NO.: 11KF335
AND EXP.CORP.                      B/L NO.: Oct. 31th, 2021
628 GUANGZHOU DADAO ZHONG          S/C NO.: 11AJ-KF002A
ROAD, GUANGZHOU, CHINA.            L/C NO.: M20K2710NS4)0032
                                              DSA11—1102
TRANSPORT DETAILS:
FROM GUANGZHOU TO PUSAN
BY VESSEL
224CTNS      3 632.00KGS    4 832.00KGS    35.84CBMS
TOTAL QUANTITY: 224CTNS
TOTAL: TWO HUNDRED AND TWENTY-FOUR CARTONS ONLY
```

(signed) GUANGZHOU ARTS & CRAFTS IMP.AND EXP.CORP.
628 GUANGZHOU DADAO ZHONG ROAD, GUANGZHOU, CHINA
王丽丽

Case Analysis 5.3   The Mistake about Figures
案例分析5.3   数量上的失误

A company in Nanning, China chooses to make shipment in Guangzhou for its high-efficiency. They mailed the full set documents for declaration to the agent declaration company in Guangzhou on June 30, 2015 and sent the contracted 1 000 cartons of products by truck 2 days later. When the products arrived in Guangzhou and ready for loading, they found that only 998 cartons can be shipped due to a miscalculation of volume. Under the request of the customhouse, the company immediately made a new set of shipping list and commercial invoice and drive to Guangzhou day and night and finally handed it to the customhouse before the ship set off.

Question: What's the mistake of the Nanning company?

Analysis: The figures on the packing list and commercial invoice must be the same with B/L. However, the number of products that will be actually loaded may be different with the predicted sometimes due to many reasons. Generally, the shipper should give the agent declaration company several empty and signed packing list forms and invoice forms with the ready-made ones. Once the number changes, the agent declaration company can use the empty forms and make the invoice and packing list with actual figures.

因为广州的通关效率很高，一家南宁的进出口贸易公司选择在广州装运。他们在2015年6月30日把全套报关单据寄出至广州的报关公司，并于2天后把1 000箱合同项下的货物通过卡车运到广州。当货物到达广州并准备装运时，他们发现因为对体积的计算失误，租赁的舱位实际只能装运998箱。在海关的要求下，该公司立即制作一套新的装箱单和商业发票，并日夜兼程赶到广州，终于在货物装运前将单据交给海关。

问题：这家进出口贸易公司的失误在哪里？

分析：装箱单和商业发票上的数字必须与提单上的一致。然而，因为各种原因，有时候

> 实际装运的数量与预期的不一致。一般来说，发货人向报关公司提供制作好的报关单据时，应同时提供空白、已签名的商业发票和装箱单若干份。万一装运数量有变化，报关公司可以使用空白签名的表格制作出与实际装运数量一致的单据。

Assignment 5.4 Make corrections of the following Packing List.
练习 5.4 装箱单改错

Date of Issue: 211020 Form of Doc. Credit: IRREVOCABLE
Doc. Credit Number: M20K2710NS00032
Expiry: Date 211215 Place IN BENEFICIARY'S COUNTRY
Applicant: SE BANG TRADING CO., LTD.
　　　　148 NAMCHEON-2 DONG, SUYOUNG – KU PUSAN, KOREA
Beneficiary: GUANGZHOU ARTS & CRAFTS IMP. & EXP. CORP.
　　　　628 GUAGNZHOU DADAO ZHONG ROAD, GUANGZHOU, CHINA
Partial Shipments: ALLOWED
Transshipment: ALLOWED
Loading in Charge: GUANGZHOU, CHINA
For Transport to...: PUSAN, KOREA
Latest Date of Ship: 211105
Descript. of Goods: CHINA ORIGIN CIF PUSAN ARTIFICIAL FLOWERS
　　　　AB–06001   5 184DOZ @ USD2.50/DOZ
　　　　AB–07049   2 880DOZ @ USD2.50/DOZ
AS PER S/C NO.11A/KF002A DATE OCT. 15 2014, ISSUED BY GUANGZHOU ARTS & CRAFTS IMPS & EXP. CORP.
Documents Required: PACKING LIST IN TRIPLICATE
Additional Cond.: ALL DOCUMENTS MUST INDICATE THIS CREDIT NUMBERS THE DETAILS SUCH AS ART NO. COLOR, QUANTITY SHOULD BE MARKED ON THE EACH INNER BOX AND CARTON EXACTLY
INV. NO.: 11KF335
INV. DATE: Oct. 28th, 2021
B/L NO.: DSA11-1102
SHIPPING MARKS: SE BANG/PUSAN
PACKING: AB-06001 36DOZ/CTN   G.W.: 23KGS/CTN   N.W.: 18KGS/CTN
　　　　AB-07049 36DOZ/CTN   G.W.: 19KGS/CTN   N.W.: 13KGS/CTN
NAME OF STEAMER: SUI 301/NORASIA V. 49-3   W/T HONG KONG
CONTAINER NO.: MSCU 4097560 (20'), MSCU 4097615 (40')
MEASUREMENT: (40×50×80) CM/CTN

```
                    PACKING LIST        ORIGINAL
Exporter:                               Date: Oct. 28th, 2021
  GUANGZHOU ARTS & CRAFTS               Invoice No: 2011KF335
IMP. AND EXP. CORP.                     B/L No.: Oct. 31th, 2021
  628 GUANGZHOU DADAO ZHONG             S/C No.: 11AJ-KF002A
  ROAD, GUANGZHOU, CHINA.               L/C No.: M20K2710NS40032
Transport Details: FROM GUANGZHOU TO PUSAN
                    BY VESSEL
```

Marks & Numbers	Description of goods	Quantity	N.W.	G.W.	Measurement
	ARTIFICIAL. FLOWERS				
	ART NO.: AB-06 36DOZ/CTN	@18.00KGS	@23.00KGS		@ (40×50×80)
	84DOZ/l44CTNS	2 592.00KGS	3 312.00KGS		23.04CBMS
	ART NO.: AB-07049 36DOZ/CTN	@13.00KGS	@19.00KGS		@(40×50×80)
	2 880DOZ/80CTNS	1 040.00KGS	1 520.00KGS		12.80CBMS
	224CTNS	3 632.00KGS	4 832.00KGS		35.84CBMS
	TOTAL QUANTITY: 224CTNS				

5.3 Other Certificates
其他证明书

(1) Certificate of Shipping Company.

(2) Certificate of Ship's Nationality.

(3) Certificate of Vessel's Age.

(4) Certificate of Classification.

(5) Black List Certificate.

(6) Master/Captain's Receipt.

(7) Beneficiary's Certificate.

(8) Beneficiary's Certificate for Dispatch of Documents.

(1) 船公司证明。

(2) 船籍证明。

(3) 船龄证明。

(4) 船级证明。

(5) 黑名单证明。

(6) 船长收据。

(7) 出口公司(受益人)证明。

(8) 出口公司(受益人)寄单证明。

Chapter 6
Export Documentation
出口单证

The successful completion of a single transaction may involve many documents. They may include government granted documents such as export license and quota, commercial documents such as commercial invoice and packing list, transportation documents such as bill of lading and shipping advice, insurance documents such as insurance policy or insurance certificate and financial documents such as letter of credit. Some documents are used for some very specific reasons and then only required at certain stages. Others such as commercial invoice and packing list are of more general use, appearing at most of the stages throughout the performance of a transaction.

To fully illustrate the sophistication of export documentation, the next part will develop an extensive discussion about the various kinds of documents, following the fulfillment of a CIF contract which requires payment by L/C. The reason to choose such a contract is two folded. On one hand, transactions of this type are very common in practice. On the other hand, such contract requires the use of documents of the greatest number and variety when comparing with others. It can provide a full picture of the documentation practice with consideration satisfaction.

一笔交易的成功完成可能会涉及许多种单证，如出口许可证和配额等政府授予的单证、商业发票和装箱单等商业单证、提单和装船通知等运输单证、保险凭证和保险单等保险单证及信用证等资金单证。有些单证由于特殊原因只在特定环节中运用，而商业发票和装箱单等单证则被普遍使用，贯穿整个交易的全过程。

为了将复杂的出口单证全面翔实地介绍给大家，本章的以下内容将对不同类型的单证进行广泛的讨论，随后将介绍一份以信用证为支付方式的 CIF 合同的填写方法。介绍这类合同，出于以下两个方面的原因。一方面，这类交易在实践中应用得非常广泛；另一方面，相对于其他合同，这类合同要求的单证数量和种类都是最多的。通过介绍，可以最大限度了解到制单的全部过程。

6.1 Documents Required Before or at Contract Negotiation
合同谈判中或之前所需单证

Before the negotiation of the contract, the seller is expected to apply for Export License or at least make sure that he is able to obtain it if the commodity he is to sell falls under the export control. During the negotiation of the terms and conditions of a contract, sometimes offers are made on a Proforma Invoice (see details in Section 4.3.4), which in this case should only be seen as a form of quotation. After acceptance is made at the end of the negotiation, the seller and the buyer will draft a sales contract can be referred back to chapter 1.

如果预售的商品受到国家出口管制，那么在合同谈判开始前，卖方应已经申请到或至少保证能申请到出口许可证。在合同条件和条款的谈判中，有时候发盘会做成形式发票（详见4.3.4节）的形式，这时它的作用仅是报价单。在谈判临近结束，双方都接受对方的条件时，买卖双方将起草一份销售合同，相关内容可以参考第1章。

Export License
出口许可证

Export licenses (see Sample 6-1) are issued by the export authority or government agency with regulatory authority of a country of export. They are often required for the export of certain natural resources, cultural relics, drugs, technology, live animals, food products, strategic commodities, and arms and armaments.

An export license is the first document a seller has to prepare when he intends to export commodities that are under export control of his country. Export licenses are issued by the government or its authorized institutions and required at the time of customs clearance. The goods under export control normally include the main raw materials, machinery or equipment in short supply, military or other goods relating to national security, and works of art and antiques which are of national, cultural or historical importance. In some cases the licensing system is used to implement government policy such as economic sanctions against certain countries.

1. Definition

An export license is a document granting an individual or business entity the general right to export or the right to export a specific shipment of a commodity or good to a named country.

2. Certain elements are likely to be included in all export licenses

(1) Name and address of seller, name and address of buyer.

(2) Date of issuance, validity date.

(3) Description of goods.

(4) Name of country of origin.

(5) Name of country of ultimate destination.

(6) Statement that the goods will not be diverted to another country contrary to the laws of the exporting country.

3. Notes

The license is a means of control, taxation and statistical reporting. In some cases, the lack of an export license can be cited as a reason why goods cannot be shipped, even though payment has been made. Buyers should be especially careful about buying sensitive goods from countries with a demonstrated lack of rule by law.

The export license is typically the seller's responsibility. However, a buyer who is dealing in sensitive goods should research the need for an export license beforehand. Failure to secure such a license can delay or prevent shipment and can jeopardize the validity of a payment such as a documentary letter of credit.

出口许可证（见样单6-1）是由出口监管机构或政府代理机构开立的。出口某些自然资源、文物、药物、技术、活的动物、食品、战略物品、武器及军备通常要求提供出口许可证。

如果卖方计划销售本国出口管制的商品，那么出口许可证将是第一个需要准备的单证。出口许可证由政府或其授权部门签发，并需在办理清关手续时出示。受到出口管制的商品一般包括主要的原材料、短缺的机器设备、军用物资或其他涉及国家安全的商品及对国家、文化和历史都有重要意义的艺术品和文物。有时候许可制度是国家执行政策的一种方式，如一国对某些特定国家实行经济制裁时，许可制度就是一个有效的方式。

1. 定义

出口许可证是授予某个人或企业有权出口某特定商品到指定国家的单证。

2. 出口许可证包括的内容

(1) 卖方的名称和地址、买方的姓名和地址。

(2) 签发日期、保质期。

(3) 商品说明书。

(4) 原产地名称。

(5) 终极目的地的国家名称。

(6) 货物不会转移到另一国而违反出口国法律的声明。

3. 注意事项

许可证是一种管理、税收和统计手段。在某些情况下，即使付款了，但缺乏出口许可证，也可成为货物不能装运的原因。买家应特别小心从缺乏法律论证的国家购买敏感货物。

出具出口许可证通常是卖方的责任。然而，购买敏感货物的买家应该事先研究是否需要出口许可证。无许可证会延迟或妨碍装运并且拖延跟单信用证的付款有效期。

6.2 Documents Involved in Goods Preparation 备货时涉及的单证

After the seller has got the goods prepared and packed, he will then issue a commercial invoice (see details in Section 4.3.7) and a packing list (see details in Section 5.2). Both documents are very important and required in all main stages of an export procedure.

当出口商将货物准备和包装好之后，他将会签发一份商业发票（详见4.3.7节）和一份装箱单（详见5.2节）。这两份单证都很重要，而且它们的应用将贯穿整个出口的过程。

6.3 Documents Concerning Mandatory Inspection 与强制检验有关的单证

If the goods need to go through mandatory inspection required by the stipulations of the government or the contract, the seller has to apply for it by filling out an inspection application form. After inspection, if the goods are up to the required standard, the seller will receive the relevant inspection certificate from the inspection body.

如果根据国家规定或合同的要求，货物必须进行强制检验的话，那么卖方应填写检验申请表。经检验，如果货物符合检验标准，那么卖方将收到一份由检验机构签发的相关检验证书。

6.3.1 Export Commodity Inspection Application 出口商品检验申请书

Export commodity inspection application is one of the essential domestic documents for the export of many commodities in China. The State Administration for Commodity Inspection, in the light of the needs in the development of international trade, makes, adjusts and publishes a list of import and export commodities subject to inspection by the commodity inspection authorities. The export of commodities on this list is not allowed until they have been inspected. Therefore, if the goods of the seller are on this list, he is required to fill out an application form to apply for inspection.

Upon submission, he will also be asked to present other documents such as the sales contract, the letter of credit, the commercial invoice, and the packing list. In some cases, only the inspection report supplied by the manufacturer is required.

出口商品检验申请书是众多中国出口商品必备的国内单证之一。国家商检机构根据国际贸易发展的需要制定、调整和发布必须由商品检验机构检验的进出口商品目录。在此目录上的商品未经检验不允许出口。因此，如果出口商预售的商品是目录内的商品，那么出口商必须填写申请表，申请检验。

提交表格时，出口商同时还需出示销售合同、信用证、商业发票和装箱单等单证。但是，有时候只需提交供货商提供的检验报告即可。

6.3.2 Certificate of Inspection
检验证书

1. Definition

The inspection certificate is document indicating the results of the inspection of the goods in terms of quality, quantity or any other element that has been specified. An inspection certificate may be issued by a government institution, surveyors of chamber of commerce or an independent service company. Inspection certificates are required when the goods are cleared for export and import and when the seller negotiates payment at the bank.

Its primary function is to ensure that the goods in question are meeting the relevant requirements stipulated by certain authorities.

Inspection and quarantine institutions are classified as follows:

Types of Inspection and Quarantine Institution	Implication	For Example
The official inspection and quarantine institution	Set up directly by the sovereign state or local government investment and the administrative institutions, in accordance with the relevant state laws and regulations, legal implement for import and export commodity inspection and quarantine, supervision and administration.	The General Administration of Quality Supervision, Inspection and Quarantine of the People's Republic of China
Semi-official inspection and quarantine Institution	The notary inspection organizations approved by the state, the government authorized, carry out commodity inspection and appraisal work and part of the management	China Import and Export Commodity Inspection Corporation
Folk inspection agency	Non-governmental civil commodity inspection organizations, such as chamber of commerce and industry association of professional inspection appraisal technical ability surveyor or company	SGS IITS UL

2. Kinds of Entry-exit Inspection and Quarantine Documents

(1) Entry Application Form for Inspection (see Sample 6-2).

(2) Entry Customs Clearance Bill.

(3) Entry Notification of Inspection and Quarantine.

(4) Export Application Form for Inspection(see Sample 6-3).

(5) Export Customs Clearance Bill.

(6) Export Receipt of Exchange.

(7) Certificate of Inspection.

(8) Certificate of Sanitary.

(9) Inspection Certificate of Veterinary.

(10) Inspection Certificate of Animals and Plants.

(11) Inspection Certificate of Means of Transport.

3. Application Procedure and Regulations of Entry-Exit Inspection and Quarantine

(1) Qualification of applicant.

(2) The range and the procedure.

(3) The period and locations.

(4) Documents attached.

4. Regulations of Filling in Export Application for Inspection

The export inspection application should be made by the inspection declarant who should fill in export inspection application form in accordance with the contract and related documents within 7 days before the customs declaration or shipment.

An inspection application form is made out for one batch of exports (one classification or one B/L). The form should be filled out completely and the "/" is used for the blank content. Any alteration is forbidden.

1. 定义

检验证书是说明货物的质量检验、数量检验或其他专项检验结果的单证。检验证书由政府机构、商会检验员或单独服务公司签发。检验证书在货物进出口通关时及出口商向银行议付货款时使用。

检验证书的基本职能是保证受检验货物达到特定机构所制定的相关标准。

检验检疫机构分类如下。

检验检疫机构类型	含义	举例
官方检验检疫机构	由主权国家或地方政府投资并直接设立的行政机构，按照国家有关法律法规对进出口商品实施法定检验检疫和监督管理	中华人民共和国质量监督检验检疫局
半官方检验检疫机构	由国家批准设立的公证检验机构，获得政府授权，执行商品检验鉴定工作和部分管理工作	中国进出口商品检验总公司

(续表)

检验检疫机构类型	含义	举例
民间检验机构	非政府的民间商品检验机构，如商会、行业协会等具有专业检验鉴定技术能力的公证行或检验公司	瑞士通用公证行 (SGS) 英国英之杰检验集团 (IITS) 美国安全试验所 (UL)

2. 出入境检验检疫单证种类

(1) 入境货物报检单（见样单 6-2）。

(2) 入境货物通关单。

(3) 入境货物检验检疫情况通知单。

(4) 出境货物报检单（见样单 6-3）。

(5) 出境货物通关单。

(6) 出境货物换证凭单。

(7) 检验证书。

(8) 卫生证书。

(9) 兽医卫生证书。

(10) 动、植物检疫证明。

(11) 运输工具检疫证书。

3. 进出口检验检疫的申请程序和规定

(1) 申请人资格。

(2) 范围和程序。

(3) 时间和地点。

(4) 附带单证。

4. 填写出口检验申请表的规定

检验申请人应在出口报关或装运前的 7 天内申请出口检验，同时根据合同和相关单证填写检验申请表格。

检验申请表仅用于一批出口货物（一类或一份提单）。表格内容应全部填满，在空白处使用"/"符号。填写的内容禁止修改。

6.4 Documents Involved in Transportation 运输时涉及的单证

For booking shipping space or chartering vessel, the seller is required to fill out a booking note. In return, the seller will receive a shipping order from the carrier or the agent.

1. Booking Note (B/N)(see Sample 6-4 and Sample 6-5)

A booking note is a form which is to be filled out by the exporter providing the carrier or the shipping agent all the necessary particulars about the shipment when an exporter intends to book shipping space on a liner or charter a ship for the carriage of export goods. When shipping space is booked or a ship is chartered, the carrier or the agent will inform the exporter of the particulars by means of a shipping order (S/O).

2. Shipping Order (see Sample 6-6)

A shipping order is a notice to the shipper (exporter) from the carrier or the agent, indicating that goods are received for loading. Thus a shipping order contains detailed information concerning the sailing, goods, place of loading, and etc., When the carrier or the agents are in receipt of the goods, they will mark and sign the shipping order properly so that the goods can be ready for export clearance. After the customs clearance, the Customs will stamp the shipping order evidencing that goods are cleared for export. This shipping order will be presented to the carrier at the time of loading. Without a shipping order, goods are not allowed to be loaded.

为了订舱位或租船，卖方需填写一份订舱单。作为回报，卖方会收到一份承运人或其代理人签发的托运单。

1. 订舱单（见样单 6-4 和样单 6-5）

订舱单是出口商计划租赁班轮舱位或租船装运出口货物时，填写的向承运人或船代理提供装运货物所有必要信息的单证。如果订舱成功或租船成功，承运人或其代理人将通过托运单通知出口商相关的细节。

2. 托运单（见样单 6-6）

托运单是承运人或其代理人给托运人（出口商）发送的，说明货物已收到待装运的通知。托运单包含航行、货物和装运地等内容的详细信息。承运人或其代理人收到货物后，就在托运单上做正确的标记和签字，以备通关之用。通关后，海关将在托运单上盖放行章证明货物已办理海关手续。这份托运单在货物装运时需向承运人出示。没有托运单货物不可装运。

6.5 Documents needed for Export Customs Clearance 出口清关需要的单证

The export goods cannot be loaded for shipment until they are cleared for export. To clear goods for export, exporters should declare the export goods to the Customs by filling the relevant customs forms such as the Customs Declaration for Export Commodity (used in China). After customs clearance, the Customs or the authorized institution will either stamp the shipping order or issue a customs clearance for export commodity to the seller, evidencing that goods are cleared for export.

出口货物获得放行前不可装船。为了办理放行手续，出口商应填写出口货物报关单（在中国使用）等报关表格以便向海关办理出口报关手续。通关后，海关或其授权机构将在托运单上盖放行章或向卖方签发一份《出口货物结关证书》，证明货物已办结海关手续。

6.5.1 Customs Declaration for Export Commodity 出口货物报关单

To clear the export commodity for export customs, the seller should fill out a customs declaration (see Sample 6-7), which will be submitted to the Customs or relative authorized institutions. In addition, some supporting documents may need to be submitted as well such as a commercial invoice, packing documents (a packing list, certificate of weight, and etc.), transport documents (ocean bill of lading, bill of lading, air waybill, cargo manifest, railway bill, and etc.). Also some special documents need to submit an export license (if required), processing and trade of electronic manual and electronic account, specific tax reduction or exemption certificate, certificate of origin, customs form, a copy of the sales contract and an inspection certificate (in case of, mandatory inspection) and a shipping order.

1. Definition of Customs Declaration

An exporter has to apply to the customs for declaration of the commodity before the shipment. The Customs officer will sign on the customs declaration form and release the goods if the goods are up to the requirement.

According to Customs law, Customs declaration and duty paying procedures of import/export goods shall be handled by Customs declaration enterprises approved by and registered with the Customs office or by enterprises entitled to do import/export business.

2. Objects of Customs Declaration

(1) Exit & Entry Conveyance.

(2) Exit & Entry Cargos.

(3) Articles of International Consignment.

3. The Main Contents and Notes of Customs Declaration Form

(1) No. of Pre-record: It is given by the Customs while the exporter is applying to Customs. It is given by computers automatically.

(2) No. of Customs: It is given by the computer system automatically or given by the Customs officer.

(3) Port of Export: It refers to the name and code of the Customs at final port of export.

(4) Record number for checking: It refers to the number of "Register Manual" or the number of "Certificate of Paid or Free Tax".

(5) Date of Export: It refers to the date of shipment. It is the applied date of departure of

the vessel.

(6) Date of Application: It is the date that the exporter applies for declaration.

(7) Executive Company: Fill in the company's name who signs and executes the S/C in Chinese (generally refers to the exporter), and the customs code of the company.

(8) Mode of Transportation: It refers to the final departure mode of transportation, such as sea, road, railway and air, and etc.

(9) Name of Transportation Tool: It refers to the name of departure tool of transportation (for example, sea for vessel and number of voyage, railway for the number of train and air for the number of flight).

(10) Delivery Numbers: It refers to all kinds of transportation documents numbers. Such as sea for B/L No., air for flight bill No. and road for receipt No., and etc.

(11) Entrusting Company: It refers to the manufacturer or exporter.

(12) Mode of Trade: Fill in the mode of trade stipulated in "Customs Modes of Trade Numbers" in brief style.

TRANSAC

Code	Name	Code	Name
1	CIF	4	C&I
2	CFR	5	the market price
3	FOB	6	ex warehouse

Notes: ① C&I is Cost and Insurance
② Market price is that specific transaction price is not indicated in the contract, but is subject to market fluctuation.
③ Mat warehouse is ex warehouse.

Corresponding Table of Mode of Trade and the General Principles of the "2010" Term

Group	group E	group F			group C				group D		
Terms	EXW	FCA	FAS	FOB	CFR	CPT	CIF	CIP	DAT	DAP	DDP
Mode of Trade	FOB				CFR				CIF		

(13) Kind of Tax: Fill in the kind of tax in brief style stipulated in "the Customs Tax Kinds", such as general tax or free of tax.

(14) Payment Style: It refers to the payment styles of L/C, D/P, D/A, T/T, and etc.

(15) License No.: If the export license is required, fill in the license number.

(16) Name of Destination Country (Region): It is the final destination, generally the import country.

(17) Designated Destination Port: It is the destination of port.

(18) Original Place of Delivered Goods.

(19) Number of Approved Documents: Fill in the approved documents and numbers except the export license. (If there is no other approved documents, it does not need to fill)

(20) Trade Terms: Fill in according to the code of price terms stipulated in "Customs Trade Terms Codes", for example, FOB, CFR, and CIF.

(21) Freight: They are the charges paid to the shipping company for transportation. Indicate type of the International currency.

(22) Insurance Premium: The premium is paid for the goods' insurance on CIF or CIP terms. Indicate type of the International currency.

(23) Additional Expenses: It refers to the other charges except the freight and insurance premium. Fill in with RMB.

(24) Contract No..

(25) Number of Packages.

(26) Type of Package: Fill in carton, bale, drum, case, and etc.

(27) Gross Weight: It refers to the gross weight with packing weight, the unit is kg.

(28) Net Weight: It refers to the net weight without packing weight, the unit is kg.

(29) Container No..

(30) Attached Documents: They are the other documents except customs declaration form, such as copy S/C, invoice, packing list, and etc.

(31) Manufacturer: It is the final firm that produces the goods for export. It may be filled in the exporter if it is unknown.

(32) Marks, Nos and Remarks: Fill in the shipping marks printed on packing. "N/M" is made out if there are no marks.

(33) Item No. and Number of Commodity: Item No. is refers to the order of this type of commodity in this customs declaration form. The number of commodity is made out according to commodity classification for China Customs Statistics.

(34) Quantity and Unit: Fill in the quantity of package and measurement of unit, For example 200 dozen, 10 000 kilograms, and etc.

(35) Final Destination Country (Region): It refers to the country (region) that consumes, use and processes the delivered goods.

(36) Unit Price: Made out according to the terms of price, such as USD600.00/MT CIF Rotterdam.

(37) Tax Paid or Not: This column is made out by the customs officer.

(38) Applying Company (Seal): Sign with seal. The seal is special used only for customs.

4. Customs Declarer

A customs declarer is a person who controls the aircraft or sea-going ship, or the ship agent. Documents to be submitted by a customs declarer shall include:

(1) A customs declaration.

(2) Detailed lists of goods.

(3) A written request of the customs declarer.

(4) A copy of bill of lading.

5. Notes on Customs Declaration

(1) The customs declarer shall be responsible before the law for using the temporarily-imported components and spare parts in accordance with the declaration.

(2) An exporter has to apply to the customs for declaration of the commodity before the shipment. The customs officer will sign on the customs declaration form and release the goods if the goods are up to the requirement.

(3) The person who asks for declaration is required to be qualified. That is to say, he/she should have the certificate of customs declaration. The examination is held by the General Administration of Customs of China.

(4) The customs declaration form is in different colors. For example, the white one is made out for general trade and the pink one is used for processing trade. The contents of these documents are similar. We take the specification of an export customs declaration form for general trade as an example to show the method of making out the document.

要办理出口报关手续，卖方需填写出口报关单（见样单6-7）并交给海关或相关的授权机构。另外，需提交的基本单证还包括商业发票，包装单据（装箱单、重量证书等），运输单据（海运提单、提货单、装货单、空运单、载货清单、铁路运单等）。除此之外，还需提交的特殊单证包括出口许可证（如果需要）、加工贸易电子化手册和电子账册、特定减免税证明、原产地证明书、通关单、销售合同副本、检验证书（若是法定检验商品）和托运单等。

1. 报关单的定义

出口商必须在货物装运之前申请报关。如果货物符合要求，海关官员会在报关单上签名，货物将予以通关。

根据海关法，报关和进出口货物付税的程序应由海关当局认可的报关企业或登记在案的报关企业或被冠名为从事进出口业务的公司来办理。

2. 报关的标的物

(1) 出入境交通工具。

(2) 出入境货物。

(3) 国际托运协议。

3. 报关单的主要内容和注意事项

(1) 预先登记号码：当出口商申请报关时，由海关的计算机系统自动给出。

(2) 海关号码：由计算机系统自动给出或由海关官员提供。

(3) 出口港：最终出口港海关的名称和代码。

(4) 商检号码："人工登记"的号码或"付款凭证或免税"号码。

(5) 出口日期：装运日期，是船启程的生效日期。

(6) 申请日期：出口商报关日期。

(7) 执行公司：用中文填写签约公司和执行合同公司的名字（一般为出口商），以及公司的报关代码。

(8) 运输方式：最终离岸的交通方式，例如海运、陆运、铁路运输和空运等。

(9) 交通工具名称：离岸交通工具的名称（例如：海运船只及航号、铁路运输的列车车次、空运的航班号）。

(10) 交货号码：多种运输单证的号码，如海运提单号码、航空运单号码以及铁路运单号码等。

(11) 委托公司：生产厂商或出口商。

(12) 贸易方式：按照合约规定以简洁明了的方式来填写贸易方式。

成交方式代码表

成交方式代码	成交方式名称	成交方式代码	成交方式名称
1	CIF	4	C&I
2	CFR	5	市场价
3	FOB	6	垫仓

注：① C&I 即成本加保险。
② 市场价即贸易合同中未注明货物具体成交价格，而是随行就市。
③ 垫仓即仓库交货价。

成交方式与《2010 通则》术语对应表

组别	E 组	F 组			C 组				D 组		
术语	EXW	FCA	FAS	FOB	CFR	CPT	CIF	CIP	DAT	DAP	DDP
成交方式		FOB			CFR				CIF		

(13) 税收种类：以简洁明了的方式按照合约规定填写"海关税收种类"，例如一般税或免税。

(14) 付款方式：这是指信用证、即期汇票、承兑交单和电汇等的付款方式。

(15) 许可证号码：如果需要出口许可证，须填写许可证号码。

(16) 目的地国别（地区）：最终目的地，一般来说是进口国。

(17) 指定目的地港：目的地港口。

(18) 装运货物的原产地。

(19) 被认可单证的号码：除了出口许可证之外，填写被认可的号码（如果没有其他的被认定的单证，则不需要填写）。

(20) 贸易条款：根据"海关贸易条款代码"来填写价格条款的代码，如离岸价格、离岸加运费价格和到岸价格。

(21) 运费：付给运输公司的费用。注明外币的类型。

(22) 保险费：支付货物到岸价格的货物保险。注明外币的类型。

(23) 额外的费用：除了运费和保险费之外的其他费用。以人民币填写。

(24) 合同号码。

(25) 包装号码。

(26) 包装类型：以箱、捆、卷和盒等为单位填写。

(27) 毛重：包括包装在内的重量，单位为千克。

(28) 净重：除去包装后的重量，单位为千克。

(29) 集装箱号码。

(30) 附加单证：除了报关单之外的其他单证，例如合约副本、发票和装箱单等。

(31) 生产商：生产出口货物的最终企业。如果不知道生产商的话，填写出口商。

(32) 唛头、备注：如果没有唛头，需要在运输唛头栏目填写"无唛"字样。

(33) 条款号码和货物号码：条款号码指的是该类型货物在报关单上的号码。货物的号码是指中国海关统计货物分类号码。

(34) 数量和单位：填写包装数量和测量单位，例如：200 打、10 000 千克等。

(35) 最终目的地国别：客户使用和加工运输货物的所在国。

(36) 单价：根据价格条款定出单价，比如每公吨 600 美元鹿特丹 CIF 价。

(37) 税款的支付与否：这一栏由海关官员来填写。

(38) 申请公司（盖章）：签名、盖章。盖章仅特别用于报关。

4. 报关员

报关员是空运、海运的运输代理人。报关员需要递交的单证包括：

(1) 报关单。

(2) 详细的货物单。

(3) 一份书面的报关员的要求。

(4) 提单的副本。

5. 报关的注意事项

(1) 报关员应确保临时出口的零部件在执行相关法规之前与报关的内容相一致。

(2) 出口商必须在货物装运之前申请货物报关。如果货物符合要求，海关官员会在报关单上签名并予以货物通关。

(3) 报关员必须要有报关资格证书。报关员证的考试由海关总署主办。

(4) 报关单有不同的颜色，例如，白色报关单用于一般的贸易，粉红色报关单用于加工贸易。这些单证的内容相似。我们采用一般贸易出口报关单做详细说明来展示报关单缮制的方法。

Assignment 6.1 According to the following information, make out a customs declaration

练习 6.1 根据以下信息缮制一份出口货物报关单

THE SELLER: QINGDAO DADI GARMENT CO., LTD.
THE BUYER: BAI DO CO.LTD, 123-55, YANGCHUN-GU, SEOUL, KOREA
PORT OF LOADING: QINGDAO, CHINA

```
FINAL DESTINATION: SEOUL, KOREA,
CARRIER: TSDD/1265F
TERMS OF PAYMENT: T/T
NOS OF PACKAGES DESCRIPTION      QTY/UNIT       UNIT PRICE      AMOUNT
                                                FOB QINGDAO
    50CTNS LADY'S JACKET         1 000PCS       @10.00          USD10 000.00
    75 CTNS MAN'S JACKET         1 500PCS       @12.00          USD18 000.00
                                                TOTAL: USD28 000.00
B/L NO.: TSDD 894521         INVOICE NO.: AX01806
NW: 3 100KGS, GW: 3 512KGS    1×40 CONTAINER NO.: FUTT5499216
PROCESSING TRADE CONTRACT NO.8466127, MANUAL NO.B87495612385
International Exchange Management and Control Form NO.: 579864879
ENTRY NUMBERS: BIUY564258
MANUFACTURER: QINGDAO XINHONG TEXTILE GARMENT FACTORY
DECLARATION DATE: May. 20th, 2021
B/L DATE: MAY 28TH, 2021
FREIGHT: USD6 500.00
PREMIUM: USD3 200.00
INCIDENTALS: USD300.00
MAN'S JACKET H.S CODE: 6203.3570
LADY'S JACKET H.S CODE: 6204.3240
```

6.5.2 Customs Clearance for Export Commodity 出口货物结关证明

A customs clearance is issued by the Customs or the authorized institution evidencing the customs clearance for the export commodity. It usually shows customs clearance number, the information of the goods, the contract number, and the voyage. In some cases, a shipping order with the signature by the customs or their agent can serve the same purpose. A customs clearance is required when the goods are to be loaded.

出口货物结关证明是由海关或其授权机构签发的证明出口货物已清关的文件。该文件通常标示清关号码、货物信息、合同号码和航次。在某些情况下，由海关或其代理机构签字的托运单也拥有相同的效力。出口货物结关证明是货物装运必需的文件。

6.6 Documents Received after Shipment 装运后收到的单证

After they are cleared for export and the customs clearance is obtained, the goods can be arranged to be loaded on the vessel. For his goods to be loaded, the seller shall present the shipping order and/or the customs clearance to the carrier. To ensure sufficient notice about the shipment, a shipping time of loading shall be forwarded to the importer by the seller without delay. Upon completion of the shipment, the exporter will get a bill of lading (see details in Section 5.1) issued by the carrier.

办妥出口货物报关手续并清关后就可以安排装船了。装船前,卖方应向托运人出示托运单和/或出口货物结关证明。为了保证装运通知的有效性,出口商应毫不延迟地将装运时间通知进口商。装运完成后,出口商将收到承运人签发的提单(详见 5.1 节)。

6.6.1　Mate's Receipt　大副收据

A mate's receipt is a document issued and signed by the mate of the shipping vessel indicating that the goods have been received by the vessel for loading or that the goods have been loaded on board the vessel. The seller can exchange the mate's receipt for the on-board bill of lading at a later time.

大副收据是船舶大副签发的,说明货物已收到待装运或货物已装船的单证。之后,卖方可以将大副收据换成已装船提单。

6.6.2　Shipping Advice　装船通知

A shipping advice (see Sample 6-8) is a notice of the shipment details which is issued by the carrier when goods are loaded on board the vessel and given by the seller (shipper) to the buyer (consignee). The purpose of the shipping advice is to notify the buyer that goods are loaded and that he can proceed to prepare for making payment and for receiving the goods at the destination. If the contract is concluded under FOB, FCA, CFR or CPT, the seller also has to pass the shipping advice to the buyer so as to facilitate the buyer to arrange insurance.

A shipping advice should be delivered to the buyer with no delay, or within the period stipulated in the sales contract or letter of credit. Occasionally a copy of the shipping advice may be required for the purpose of payment. A shipping advice usually covers the information as follows:

(1) The number of packages shipped.

(2) The total gross and net weight.

(3) The packing.

(4) The date and number of the B/L.

(5) The container number and seal number (if container is used).

(6) ETD (estimated time of departure).

(7) ETA (estimated time of arrival).

(8) The name of the port of shipment and port of destination.

装船通知（见样单 6-8）是货物装船后，由卖方（托运人）缮制并发给买方（收货人），说明装船细节的通知。装船通知的目的是通知买方货物已装船，以便于其进行下一步工作，如准备付款和提货。如果合同采用 FOB、FCA、CFR 或 CPT 贸易术语成交，卖方也需向买方发送装船通知以便买方安排保险事宜。

装船通知必须毫不延迟地或在信用证或合同规定的期限内发送给买方。在少数情况下，在结汇时也需提供装运通知。一份装船通知通常包括以下内容：

(1) 已装船的包装数量。

(2) 总毛重和总净重。

(3) 包装。

(4) 提单日期和号码。

(5) 集装箱号码和封条号（使用集装箱的情况下）。

(6) 预计开航时间。

(7) 预计到达时间。

(8) 装运港和目的港名称。

6.7 Insurance Documents
保险单证

Under a CIF contract, it is the exporter's obligation to cover insurance for the export goods. Insurance is normally obtained after the completion of the loading at the port of shipment. To take out insurance, an insurance application form, also known as the proposal form, has to be filled out and submitted to an insurance company for the purchase of cargo insurance. When the application is accepted, an insurance policy or certificate will be issued by the insurer.

在 CIF 合同项下，出口商有义务对出口货物投保。保险通常是货物在装运港被装运后才生效。为货物购买保险，需要填写保险申请表，也称投保单，并向保险公司提出申请。申请表被接受之后，保险人将给申请人签发一份保险单或保险凭证。

6.7.1 Insurance Application Form
投保单

An insurance application form (see Sample 6-9), also known as insurance proposal form, is to be filled out by the insured, providing all information about the parties concerned and the shipment involved. The specific information may cover the name of the insured party, the description of the cargoes insured, the voyage insured, the insurance amount, the insurance coverage, and etc. Documents needed for submission are the commercial invoice, the packing list, and etc. After all necessary formalities concerning insurance is completed, insurance policy are to be issued by the insurance company or their agent.

投保单（见样单 6-9）也称保险申请表，是提供有关保险当事人和被保险货物详细信息的单证，应由被保险人填写。投保单上的信息应包括被保险人的名称、被保险货物的描述、航次、保险金额、保险范围等。投保时需要的单证包括商业发票和装箱单等。投保手续办妥后，保险公司或其代理人将签发一份保险单。

6.7.2 Insurance Policy
保险单

An insurance policy (see Sample 6-10) is the contract made between the insurer and the insured, which is issued by the insurer and confirmed by the insured. In an international trade transaction, an insurance policy or certificate forms part of the chief documents for transactions on a CIF or CIP basis. In addition, in case of loss or damage, the insurance policy or certificates is the essential basis for claim and claim settlement.

Marine (or ocean) and air insurance is important on export shipments. Under the Carriage of Goods by Sea Act, ocean carriers are responsible for the seaworthiness of the vessel, properly manning the vessel, and making the vessel safe for carriage of the cargo. The ocean carrier is not responsible for negligence of the master in navigating the vessel, fires, perils, dangers, accidents of the sea, acts of God, acts of war, acts of public enemies, detention or seizures, acts or omissions of shippers, strikes or lockouts, riots and civil commotions, saving or attempting to save a life or property at sea, inherent defect, quality or vice of the goods, insufficiency of packing, quarantine restrictions, insufficiency or inadequacy of marks, latent defects not discoverable by due diligence, and any other causes arising without the actual fault of the ocean carrier.

Without insurance, even when the carrier can be proven liable, responsibility is limited to $500 per "package" on ocean shipments and $20 per kilogram on air shipment unless a higher value is declared in advance and a higher transportation charge paid. Although abbreviated trade terms, such as FOB port of shipment, are supposedly designed to clarify which parties are responsible for arranging and paying for various aspects of an export shipment, often confusion and misunderstandings occur. It is extremely important to clearly determine who will pay for such insurance and who will arrange for it. It is necessary for a seller or buyer to have an "insurable interest" in the merchandise in order to obtain insurance coverage. Depending on the terms of sale, the seller may have an ownership interest up to a particular point or a financial interest in the safe arrival of the shipment up until the time it is paid.

A company can buy an open or blanket cargo marine or air insurance policy that has in continuous effect for its shipments, or a special onetime cargo policy that insures a single shipment. Alternatively, it can utilize its freight forwarder's blanket policy. There are many advantages for a company to have its own open cargo policy, but the quantity of exports must justify it, otherwise, it is probably more appropriate to utilize the freight forwarder's blanket policy. Some insurance brokers recommend that a company has its own policy when exports and/or imports reach $500 000 to $1 million. When a blanket policy is used, a separate certificate is issued by the insurance company or the holder of the policy to evidence coverage for each shipment.

Familiarizing oneself with such insurance policies is also important in the event that a casualty occurs and a claim needs to be filed. Generally, it is best to obtain "all risks" (rather than "named peril") and "warehouse-to-warehouse" (or "marine extension") coverage. Even "all risks" coverage does not include war risk or "strike, riot and civil commotion" coverage and the seller should specifically determine whether these risks and others, such as delay in arrival and change in customs duties, should be covered by rider. Under the Inco terms it is necessary to insure the shipment at 110 percent of the invoice value; in the case of some letter of credit sales, payment cannot be obtained unless insurance in that amount has been obtained.

In order to get paid under letters of credit or documentary collections through banking channels, it may be necessary for the seller to furnish a certificate to the bank evidencing that insurance coverage exists.

Marine insurance companies and insurance brokers can advise on the different types of coverage available and comparative premiums. The premium will depend on the type of merchandise, its value (risk of pilferage), its packing, the type of coverage (including riders), the method of transportation, the country of destination and routing, the loss history of the insured, the carriers used, whether transshipment will occur, and etc.

保险单（见样单6-10）是保险人和被保险人间订立的、由保险人签发、被保险人确认的合同。在国际贸易中，保险单或保险凭证是CIF或CIP合同交易的主要单证之一。另外，在发生灭失或损害时，保险单或保险凭证是索赔和结算的基础。

海运保险或空运保险对出口货物非常重要。根据《海上运输法》，在海运方式下，海运承运人应对船舶的适航性负责，应正确操作船只以保证运输船只的安全。但是，海运承运人不对以下情况负责：由于船长的过失、火灾、海上危险、海上意外事故、不可抗力、海上战争、海上公敌的扣押和掠夺行为、托运人的过失、罢工、暴动、骚乱，以及在海上抢救或试图抢救生命财产安全、商品内在缺陷、包装不良、检验检疫机构限制入境、运输标志不全或不正确、尽职调查后仍无法发现的潜在缺陷或其他非海运承运人的实际过失造成的损失。

如果不办理保险，即使是承运人的责任，他们的赔偿也是有限额的。比如承运人对每个单位包装的海运货物最高赔偿 500 美元，对空运货物每千克最高赔偿 20 美元，但托运人事先声明货物的价值更高并交纳了更高的运费的情况除外。即使如 FOB 装运港等贸易术语已经将各当事人在出口装运各方面的责任义务划分得很清楚，但还是经常发生混淆和误解的情况。明确说明由谁负责安排保险和支付保险费是非常重要的。对买卖双方来说，要得到保险的赔付，必须拥有货物的"保险利益"。根据销售条款，卖方对货物的所有权权益可能于某个点终止，或者卖方在货物平安到达目的地之后仍拥有财务利益，直到买方付款为止。

在海运或空运方式下，被保险人可以为货物购买预约货物保险单，这类保险单可以为货物提供间断性的保险服务，或专门为某一批货物购买一份保险。另外，也可以使用货运代理的统保单。使用本公司的预约货物保险单有很多好处，但是装船后需更改货物实际装船的数量，而使用货运代理的统保单时，单上的数字很可能就更准确。有些保险经纪人建议，如果一个公司的出口和/或进口数量达到 50 万到 100 万美元，就应该为本公司单独购买保险。若选择统保单方式，保险公司或保单的持有人将另外签发一份保险凭证，证明每次投保的承保范围。

熟悉保险单很重要，尤其是在货物发生了损失后需要办理索赔手续的情况下。通常来说，最好选择"一切险"(而不是"指定险别") 和"仓至仓"条款 (或"海运扩展条款")。但即使是"一切险"也不承保战争，或"罢工、暴动和民变"等，因此卖方还需另外决定这些风险以及其他如到达延迟、关税改变等风险是否需要以附加险的形式投保。根据《国际贸易术语解释通则》的规定，应投保发票金额的 110%；在信用证方式下，如果保险金额没有达到发票金额的 110%，将会遭到银行拒付。

在信用证或跟单托收方式下，要得到银行的付款，卖方需向银行提交保险的凭证，证明保险的实际承保责任和范围。

海运保险公司和保险经纪人可以为投保人建议不同类型的保险范围和相应的保险费用。保险费根据商品的类型、价值 (偷窃风险)、包装、险别 (包括附加险)、运输方式、目的国和运输路线、被保险人的损失记录、承运人、是否转运等内容的差异而有所区别。

6.7.3 Checklist for Insurance Policy 保险单审核内容

(1) Are you presenting an insurance policy or a certificate? (Acknowledgements or a broker's cover are acceptable only if expressly allowed in the letter of credit).

(2) Is the insured amount sufficient?

(3) Is the insurance coverage complete and in conformity with the letter of credit as it relates to:

a. Special risks when required?

b. Coverage of destination and time (in other words, carried through to proper point or covering the entire period of shipment).

　　c. Proper warehouse clauses.

　　d. Has the insurance document been countersigned when required?

　　(4) Was the insurance document endorsed in blank if payable to the shipper?

　　(5) Are shipping marks identical to those on the commercial invoice and bill of lading?

　　(6) The insurer may not agree to issue acknowledge of insurance declaration, so if there are this requirement in the arrival L/C, it should be required to ask to change.

　　(1) 出示的是保险单还是保险凭证？（只有信用证明确规定可以接受时，确认书或保险经纪人的暂保单方可使用）

　　(2) 保险金额是否充足？

　　(3) 承保范围是否完整，是否与信用证规定的一致，应注意以下几个方面的问题：

　　a. 如有要求，是否已投保特别风险？

　　b. 承保的最终地点和时间（换句话说，是到某个时间、地点还是包括运输的全程）。

　　c. 仓至仓条款。

　　d. 如需要，保险单证是否已被会签？

　　(4) 如果保险单证的抬头是托运人，它们是否已空白背书？

　　(5) 商业发票和提单上的运输唛头是否与实际的唛头完全一致？

　　(6) 保险人不一定同意出具投保回执，故如来证有此要求，应要求对方改证。

Case Analysis 6.1 The date of B/L Disagrees with That of Insurance Policy
案例分析 6.1 保险单与提单日期不符的纠纷案

　　Company W, an export company, received from its client an L/C with the following content: "... By order of T.P.C We open an irrevocable letter of credit No. 35691 in favor of W Trading Co... full set of shipping company's clean an board original bill of lading made out to order blank endorsed notify buyer marked Freight Prepaid. Insurance policy covering W. A. and war risks as per ocean marine cargo clause of P.I.C.C. dated 1/1/2007. Phytosanitary certificate in duplicate."

　　Company W shipped the goods as per the provisions of the Credit and presented the required documents to the negotiating bank for negotiation. After examining the documents, the negotiating bank found them in conformity to the Credit and then sent these documents to the issuing bank for reimbursement. Two weeks later, a telex was received from the issuing bank:

　　"Documents No. D3910 under Credit No. 35691 have been found not in conformity to the terms of the Credit, i.e. the original bill of lading and the phytosanitary certificate are absent; the issuing date of insurance policy is later than the shipment date on the bill of lading. The documents are now in our temporary custody."

　　Surprised to receive the notice, company W inquired the negotiating bank whether they had lost the original bill of lading and the phytosanitary certificate before mailing them. However, the negotiating bank's covering schedule showed that the original bill of lading in triplicate and the phytosanitary certificate in duplicate had been mailed. Immediately, company W and the negotiating bank answered the issuing bank jointly:

　　"The issuing date of the insurance policy is indeed later than the shipping date on the bill of lading. Nevertheless, there is an insurer's statement on the insurance policy: 'this cover is effective at the date of loading on board', which proves that insurance had been affected before shipment and the cover became effective on the date of loading on board. According to UCP 600 , 'The date of the insurance document must be no later than the date of shipment, unless it appears from the insurance document that the cover is effective form a date not later than the date of shipment.' Now that our insurance policy declares that the cover takes effect on the date of loading, you should accept the documents even though the issuing date of insurance policy is later than the shipping date on the bill of lading.

Regarding the absence of the original bill of lading and phytosanitary certificate, our negotiating bank had indeed mailed to you the original bill of lading in triplicate and the phytosanitary certificate in duplicate together with other documents. If you have received other documents, you should also find the original bill of lading and the phytosanitary certificate. You mentioned in your notice that 'the issuing date of insurance policy is later than the shipping date on the bill of lading', then if you have not received the bill of lading, how did you know this fact? Please check again."

In reply, the issuing bank said:

"Concerning the discrepant documents No.D3910, we acknowledge bill of lading in triplicate and phytosanitary certificate in duplicate. We meant in our previous correspondence that you failed to send us the original ones. The documents you presented were all copies."

Not knowing how the original documents presented changed into copies, company W made the following objection:

"Regarding the bill of lading and the phytosanitary certificate under documents No.D3910, we have checked and found that the bills of lading we presented bear the carrier's official signature on the face and formal provisions on the back. They are the documents of title issued by the carrier. The one who holds the documents can take delivery of the goods. How could they be considered as copies? We have also contacted the carrier who confirms that the bills of lading issued by them are originals.

As regards the phytosanitary certificate, what your credit requires is not the original, but only the certificate in duplicate. We have provided the certificate in duplicate according to your stipulation: one is made out with a typewriter; the other is a carbon copy.

As mentioned above, the alleged discrepancies do not exist. You should accept the documents and make the payment immediately."

Company W sent the above message with strong confidence to receive the payment. Unexpectedly, the issuing bank still refused to accept the bills of lading and the phytosanitary certificate:

"Concerning documents No.D3910, the applicant agrees to take the insurance policy. But we are unable to accept the bills of lading and the phytosanitary certificate.

UCP 600 provides: credits that require multiple document(s) such as 'duplicate', 'two fold', 'two copies' and the like, will be satisfied by the presentation of one original and the remaining number in copies except where the document itself indicates otherwise. And UCP 600 provides that: unless otherwise stipulated in the Credit, banks will also accept as an original document(s), a document(s) produced or appearing to have been produced: i. by reprographic, automated or computerized systems; ii. As carbon copies...The two articles above imply that at least one of the multiple documents required by the Credit should be original. As a requirement, the original document must bear the word 'Original'. Signature can be added when necessary. The bills of lading and the phytosanitary certificate you presented do not indicate the word 'original', therefore do not comply with the above provision of UCP 600. The documents are still in our custody. Please let us know your disposal."

Company W tried to find a solution through direct contact with the importer, but in vain. In the end, company W had to entrust the goods to its overseas office and suffered a great loss.

Analysis:

The issuing date of insurance policy must go before the shipping date as a means of showing that the insurance has been effected before shipment and the cover has come into effect. If the issuing date of insurance policy is later than the shipping date, the insurance company may be exempt from liability for compensation. In this case, company W presented an insurance policy issued late than the shipping date, which failed to meet the standard, so the issuing bank refused to accept the documents. But the issuing bank did not find the special statement on the insurance policy that "this cover is effective at the date of loading on board". UCP 600 has the following provisions, "unless otherwise stipulated in the Credit, or unless it appears from the insurance document that the cover is effective at the latest from the date of loading on board or dispatch or taking in charge of the goods, banks will not accept an insurance document which bears a date of insurance later than the date of loading on board or dispatch or taking in charge as indicated in such transport document."

Company W made good use of the UCP 600 provision that banks should accept insurance policy that bears such statement and made the issuing bank take the document. It is nothing new that some beneficiaries suffer from loss because they do not know how to use UCP 600 provisions to justify their documents.

About multiple documents, UCP 600 provides that, "unless otherwise stipulated in the Credit, banks will accept as a copy, a document either labeled copy or not marked as an original one, a copy need not be signed".

And UCP 600 Further states:

"Credits that require multiple document such as 'duplicate' 'two fold' 'two copies' and the like, will be satisfied by the presentation of one original and the remaining number in copies except where the document itself indicates otherwise."

Therefore, a document that is not marked "original" may be regarded as a copy to collect payment smoothly, export companies shall make sure that an original document must bear the wording as "original" therein.

出口公司 W 收到其客户开来的信用证，内容如下："根据 T.P.C 订单，我方开立 35691 号信用证，以 W 贸易公司为受益人……整套清洁已装船提单正本，指示抬头，空白背书，通知人为买方，提单上注明运费预付。根据中国人民财产保险股份有限公司海洋货运保险条款投保水渍险和战争险，投保日期是 2021 年 1 月 1 日。一式两份植物检疫证明书。"

W 公司根据信用证规定条款装运货物，然后向议付行交单议付。经过审查，议付行认为单证与信用证相符，然后将单证寄给开证行要求偿付。两个星期后，议付行收到开证行的电传：

"35691 号信用证项下的 D3910 号单证与信用证不相符，缺少正本海运提单和植物检疫证明书。保险单的签发时间晚于提单上的装运日期。这些单证暂时由我行保管。"

W 公司对这份通知感到很意外，同时咨询议付行是否是他们在邮寄前把正本海运提单和植物检疫证明书丢失了。然而，议付行的回复函表示，一式三份的海运提单和一式两份的植物检疫证明书已经邮寄给开证行。于是，W 公司和议付行立即联合向开证行回函：

"保险单的签发日期确实晚于提单上的装运日期。然而，保险单上有一份保险人声明：'这份保险单在货物装船日有效'，这就可以证明保险在装运前已经办理，而且保险单在装运日是有效的。根据 UCP 600 规定：'保险单日期不得晚于发运日期，除非保险单显示，保险责任不迟于生效。'我方所提交的保险单已表明保险单于装运日生效，所以即使保险单的签发日期晚于提单上的装运日期,你方也应接受此单证。

关于正本海运提单和植物检疫证明缺失的问题,我们认为一式三份的正本海运提单和一式两份的植物检疫证明已经和其他单证一起寄给你们。如果你们已经收到其他单证,也应该收到这两份单证。你们在通知中说:'保险单的签发日期晚于提单上的装运日期',那么,如果你们没有收到海运提单,你们是如何发现这个问题的?请再次核对。"

开证行回复如下:

"关于 D3910 号单证不符点的问题,我们承认收到一式三份的海运提单和一式两份的植物检疫证明。之前的函电我们是指你方未寄来这两份正本单证。你们提交的单证是副本。"

不知为何提交的正本单证变成副本,W 公司提出以下反对意见:

"关于 D3910 项下的提单和植物检疫证明书问题,我们已审核并发现,所提交的提单正面有承运人的签名,单证的背面有正式条款。这是承运人签发的提单。提单的持有人可以提货。你们怎么说这是副本?我们和承运人联系过了,他们也证实他们签发的提单是正本提单。

关于植物检疫证明问题,我们的意见是:信用证并没有规定提交正本,只规定提交一式两份。我们已经根据你们的要求提交一式两份:一份用打字机缮制,另外一份是复印件。

综上所述,并不存在所谓的不符点。你们应该接受我方的单证并立刻付款。"

W 公司很有信心地将以上信息发送给开证行索汇。意外的是,开证行仍然拒绝接受提单和植物检疫证明:

"关于 D3910 号信用证的单证问题,开证申请人已同意接受保险单。但是,我们还是不能接受提单和植物检疫证明书。

UCP 600 规定:信用证要求多份单证时,诸如'一式两份''两张''两份'等,可以交付一份正本,其余可交副本,但单证本身另做说明者除外。同时,UCP 600 规定:'除非信用证中另有规定,只要单证注明为正本,如有必要时,加签字,银行还将接受下述方法或用下述方法缮制的单证作为正本单证:i. 影印、自动处理或电脑处理;ii. 复写……'以上两个条款说明,信用证上所要求的多式单证应至少有一份是正本。根据要求,正本单证的表面必须有'正本'字样。必要时可加签名。你所提交的提单和植物检疫证明书表面没有'正本'字样,因此不符合 UCP 600 的要求。这些单证仍由我方保管。请告知如何处理。"

W 公司试图通过与进口商直接联系解决问题,但是徒劳无功。最后,W 公司只好将货物委托给海外办事处处理,遭受了巨大损失。

分析:

保险单的签发日期必须早于装运期,这是证明装运前货物保险已生效的一种方式。如果保险单的签发日期晚于装运日期,保险公司很可能免除赔偿责任。本案例中,W 公司提交的保险单签发日期晚于装运期,是不符合要求的,因此开证行拒绝接受单证。但是开证行并没发现保险单上的特别条款"本保险单于装运日生效"。UCP 600 有如下规定:"除非信用证另有规定,或除非保险单表明保险责任最迟于装船、发运或接受监管之日起生效,银行将拒收出单日期迟于运输单证注明的装船、发运或接受监管日期的保险单。"

W 公司很好地利用了 UCP 600 条款,即银行应接受有以上声明的保险单并且让开证行接受了这份单证。受益人因不知道如何使用 UCP 600 条款为自己的单证辩护而遭受损失的例子并不少见。

对于多式单证,UCP 600 规定:"除非信用证另有规定,银行将接受标明副本字样或没有标明正本字样的单证作为副本单证,副本单证无须签字。"

UCP 600 进一步说明:

"信用证要求多份单证时,诸如'一式两份''两张''两份'等,可以交付一份正本,其余可交副本,但单证本身另做说明者除外。"

因此,表面无"正本"字样的单证被视为副本。为了顺利结汇,出口公司应确认正本单证上有"正本"字样。

6.8 Documents for Bank Negotiation
银行议付单证

The last and the most important thing the seller has to do is to collect and check all documents specified in the L/C and present them within period required to the negotiating bank for payment settlement. While doing so, he should also fill out a bill of exchange (a draft). The documents needed for submission generally include the commercial invoice, the packing list, the bill of lading, the insurance policy, and etc. Apart from these documents, there are also other types of documents required by the buyer and submitted to the bank for negotiation. Among them, the certificate of origin, consular invoice and customs invoice are worth mentioning.

对于卖方来说，最后也是最重要的一件事就是收集和核对所有信用证上规定的单证并在有效期内交给议付行办理议付手续。同时，还需填写汇票。需要提交的单证通常包括商业发票、装箱单、提单、保险单等。除此之外，有时买方要求其他单证，议付时也需要提交，其中原产地证书、领事发票和海关发票最值得注意。

6.8.1 Bill of Exchange (B/E) or Draft
汇票

A bill of exchange (B/E) (see Sample 6-11) or draft is an unconditional order in writing signed by one party (drawer) requesting a second party (drawee/payer) to make payment in lawful money immediately or at a determined future time to a third party (payee).

Usually, a draft is drawn and presented by the seller to the buyer or their banks as the payment instrument. Strictly speaking, a draft drawn under L/C is a payment instrument rather than a kind of the documents, though in practice it is accepted as one of the documents required for payment.

It should be noted that a draft drawn under L/C is usually required to indicate the relevant L/C in the drawn clause and the B/E amount should in no case exceeds the L/C amount.

1. Drafts for Payment

If payment for the sale is going to be made under a letter of credit or by documentary collection, such as documents against payment ("D/P" or sight draft) or documents against acceptance ("D/A" or time draft), the exporter will draw a draft on the buyer's bank in a letter of credit transaction or the buyer in a documentary collection transaction payable to itself (sometimes it will be payable to the seller's bank on a confirmed letter of credit) in the amount of the sale.

This draft will be sent to the seller's bank along with the instructions for collection, or sometimes the seller will send it directly to the buyer's bank (direct collection). If the payment agreement between the seller and buyer is at sight, the buyer will pay the draft when it is received, or if receive issued under a letter of credit, the buyer's bank will pay the draft when it is received. If the agreement between the seller and the buyer is that the buyer will have some grace period before making payment, the amount of the delay, called the usance, will be written on the draft (time draft), and the buyer will usually be responsible for payment of interest to the seller during the usance period unless the parties agree otherwise. The time period may also be specified as some period after a fixed date, such as 90 days after the bill of lading or commercial invoice date, or payment simply may be due on a fixed date.

2. Clauses of Draft

(1) We hereby issue our irrevocable letter of credit No.194956 available with any bank in China, at 90 days after Bill of Lading date by draft.

(2) Credit available with any bank in China, by negotiation, against presentation of beneficiary's drafts at sight, drawn on applicant in duplicate.

(3) All drafts should be marked "Drawn under the Citibank, New York L/C No.1956717 dated 2021-03-10".

(4) This credit is available with The Hong Kong and Shanghai Banking Corporation Ltd., Shanghai by negotiation against beneficiary's drafts drawn under this L/C at sight basis.

(5) This letter of credit is to be negotiated against the documents detailed herein a beneficiary's drafts at 60 days after sight with Standard Chartered bank Shanghai.

(6) The drafts at 90 days sight drawn on Bank of Tokyo Ltd., Tokyo branch. Usance drafts drawn under this L/C are to be negotiated at sight basis. Discount charges and acceptance commission are for account of accountee.

3. Contents of Bills of Exchange

(1) Indicating the word "draft" or "exchange".

(2) An unconditioned order in writing.

(3) Certain amount.

(4) Payer's (drawee's) name, usually the buyer or its nominated bank.

(5) Payee's name, usually the seller or its nominated bank.

(6) Date and place of issue.

(7) Signature of the drawer, usually the seller.

汇票（见样单6-11）是由一个人（出票人）向另一个（受票人/付款人）签发的、要求其立刻或在将来某个时间向第三方（受款人）支付法定货币的书面无条件支付命令。

通常来说，汇票作为一种支付工具，由卖方向买方或买方指定的银行出具。严格来说，在信用证项下汇票是一种支付工具而不是一份单证，即使在实际中汇票通常是以单证的形式被接受。

需要注意的是，信用证项下的汇票通常需要在汇票条款中标示相关信用证号码。另外，汇票金额绝不能超过信用证金额。

1. 汇票付款

如果采用信用证或跟单托收等付款方式，如付款交单 (D/P 或即期汇票) 或承兑交单 (D/A 或远期汇票)，那么，在信用证方式下，出口商应向进口商指定的银行提交与销售金额相等的、以自己为受款人的汇票 (有时在承兑信用证项下也可以卖方指定的银行为受款人)；在跟单托收方式下，以上汇票应直接交给进口商。

汇票将根据托收指示交给托收行，或有时卖方直接将汇票寄给进口商指定的银行(直接托收)。如果买卖双方间签订的是即期协议，那么买方应收到汇票后立刻付款；如果使用信用证方式，那么买方指定的银行应在收到汇票后立刻付款。如果买卖双方的协议上允许买方在一定时间后付款，那么付款延迟的期限，也称票据期限，应在汇票 (远期汇票) 上标示。同时，除非双方另有协定，买方通常应在票据期限内向卖方支付远期付款的利息。付款期限一般被指定为某个日期后的一段时间，如提单日期或商业发票日期后 90 天，或直接简单规定为某个日期。

2. 汇票条款

(1) 我方在此开具 194956 号不可撤销信用证，此证可在中国的任何银行议付，同时应出具提单日期后 90 天的汇票。

(2) 若受益人提交以开证申请人为付款人的一式两份即期汇票，信用证可在中国的任何银行议付。

(3) 所有的汇票都应标记 "由纽约花旗银行开立，信用证号码 1956717，日期 2021 年 3 月 10 日"。

(4) 本信用证在上海汇丰银行议付，随附受益人即期汇票。

(5) 本信用证为可议付信用证，信用证项下的 60 天远期汇票为付款方式，付款人为上海渣打银行。

(6) 开立以东京银行东京分行为付款人的 90 天远期汇票。以本信用证为基础开立的远期汇票可即期议付。贴现费用和承兑手续费由开证申请人支付。

3. 汇票内容

(1) 标示 "draft" 或 "exchange" 字样。

(2) 无条件书面命令。

(3) 确定的金额。

(4) 付款人 (受票人) 名称，通常是买方或其指定银行。

(5) 受款人名称，通常是卖方或其指定银行。

(6) 开票日期和地点。

(7) 出票人 (通常是卖方) 签字。

Assignment 6.2　Make corrections according to the L/C
练习 6.2　根据信用证改错

TO: BANK OF CHINA, GUANGDONG
FROM: ARAB NATIONAL BANK

P.O.BOX 18745 JEDDAH SAUDI ARABIA
DEAR SIRS,
　　KINDLY ADVISE BENEFICIARY'S M/S GUANGDONG METALS AND MINERALS I/E CORP. 5 TIANHE ROAD, GUANGZHOU, CHINA OF OUR OPENING WITH YOU AN IRREVOCABLE DOCUMENTARY CREDIT DATED 10 MARCH, 2015 IN THEIR FAVOUR ON BEHALF OF M/S MIGHWLLI STEEL PRODUCTS CO. P.O. BOX 18741 JEDDAH SAUDI ARABIA FOR AMOUNT ABOUT USD75 683.00 VALID IN CHINA UNTILL 20 MAY 2015, AVAILABLE WITH YOU BY PAYMENT AGAINST PRESENTATION OF BENEFICIARYS' DRAFT(S) AT 30 DAYS AFTER B/L DATE DRAWN ON OURSELVES AND MARKED "DRAWN UNDER ARAB NATIONAL BANK CREDIT NO.254LK254" .5% COMMISSION MUST BE DEDUCTED FROM DRAWINGS UNDER THIS CREDIT.

BILL OF EXCHANGE

NO.　　　　　　　　　　　　　　　　DATE <u>JAN. 10TH, 2021</u>
DRAWN UNDER <u>ARAB NATIONAL BANK</u>
EXCHANGE FOR <u>USD14 200.00</u>
AT <u>×××</u> DAYS AFTER SIGHT OF THIS FIRST OF EXCHANGE (SECOND OF EXCHANGE BEING UNPAID)
PAY TO THE ORDER OF <u>BANK OF CHINA, GUANGZHOU BRANCH</u>
THE SUM OF <u>US DOLLARS FOURTEEN THOUSAND TWO HUNDRED ONLY</u>
TO　　HONGKONG ABC CO.
　　　3/F GUANGTEX BUILDING TAIKOKTSUI
　　　KOWLOON, HONGKONG
　　　　　　　　　　GUANGDONG HUADA FOOD CO., LTD.
　　　　　　　　　　　　　　　张三

Assignment 6.3　According to the following L/C, please make out a draft
练习6.3　根据以下信用证缮制一份汇票

FIRST BANGKOK CITY BANK LTD.HEAD OFFICE
20 YUKHON 2 ROAD, BANGKOK 10100. THAILAND
BANGKOK NOV.23TH, 2021
THIS CREDIT IS SENT TO THE ADVISING BANK BY AIRMAIL
IRREVOCABLE DOCUMENTARY CREDIT
NO.001-10397-2021
ADVISING BANK: BANK OF CHINA, QINGDAO BRANCH, QINGDAO, CHINA
APPLICANT: NAN HANG INTERNTAIONAL TRADING CO., LTD.
　　　　　　104/4 LANDP RD. WANG BANGKAPI BKK
BENEFICIARY: SHANDONG IMP/EXP CORP.
　　　　　　62 JIANGXI RD, QINGDAO, CHINA
AMOUNT: USD6 622.00 (SAY US DOLLARS SIX THOUSAND SIX HUNDRED AND TWENTY TWO ONLY) CFR BANGKOK
EXPIRY DATE JAN 15TH, 2021
DEAR SIRS,
　　WE HEREBY ISSUE AN IRREVOCABLE DOCUMENTARY CREDIT IN YOUR FAVOUR WHICH IS AVAILABLE BY NEGOTIATION OF YOUR DRAFT(S) AT SIGHT DRAWN ON US, FOR 100% INVOICE VALUE MARKED AS DRAWN UNDER THIS CREDIT ACCOMPANIED

BY THE FOLLOWING DOCUMENTS:
- SIGNED COMMERCIAL INVOICE IN 9 COPIES, MENTIONING SEPARATELY F.O.B.VALUE, FREIGHT CHARGE.
- FULL SET CLEAN ON BOARD OCEAN BILLS OF LADING IN TRIPLICATE WITH TWO NON-NEGOTIABLE COPIES MADE OUT TO THE ORDER OF FIRST BANGKOK CITY BANK LTD., BANGKOK, NOTIFY APPLICANT AND MARKED FREIGHT PREPAID.
- PACKING LIST IN SIX COPIES.

EVIDENCING SHIPMENT OF TRI-CIRCLE BRAND BRASS PADLOCKS 900 DOZ. DETAIL AS PER ORDER DATED NOVEMBER 9, 2021 (S/C NO.99A15AAI.5029)
PARTIAL SHIPMENT: PERMITTED TRANSSHIPMENT: PERMITTED
SPECIAL CONDITIONS:
ALL DOCUMENTS MENTIONING THIS CREDIT NUMBER.
All CHARGES INCURED OUTSIDE THAILAND ARE FOR BUYER'S ACCOUNT.
NEGOTIATIONS UNDER THIS CREDIT ARE RESTRICTED TO THE ADVISING BANK.
INSTRUCTIONS TO NEGOTIATING BANK:
(1) THE AMOUNT OF EACH DRAWING MUST BE ENDORSED ON THE REVERSE HEREOF.
(2) All DOCUMENTS AND DRAFTS ARE TO BE DISPATCHED IN TWO SETS BY CONSECUTIVE AIRMAILS TO US.
(3) PLEASE CLAIM REIBURSEMENT BY METHOD MARKED X.

Assignment 6.4 Make correction according to the following data
练习6.4 根据以下资料改错

BENEFICIARY: CHANGSHU ABC LEATHER GOODS CO. LTD.
　　　　　　HUANGHE ROAD, CHANGSHU, JIANGSU 215500 CHINA.
APPLICANT: GRAPHIC MAGE 305SPAGNOLI ROAD, MELVILLE, NEW YORK 11747 USA.
DRAFT CLAUSE: DRAFTS TO BE DRAWN AT 30 DAYS AFTER SIGHT ON ISSUING BANK FOR 90% OF INVOICE VALUE.
　　YOU ARE AUTHORIZED TO DRAW ON ROYAL BANK OF NEW YORK FOR DOCUMENTARY IRREVOCABLE CREDIT NO. 742863 DATED JUANUARY 15th 2021.
EXIPIRY DATE: 20140909 FOR NEGOTIATION BENEFICIARY.
INVOICE NO.: 34567.
LOADING PORT: SHANGHAI, CHINA.
INVOICE AMOUNT: USD108 000.00 FOB SHANGHAI.
DESTINATION: NEW YORK, USA.
SHIPPING DATE: AUG 16TH, 2021.
SIGNATURE: CHANGSHU ABC LEATHER GOODS CO., LTD. 张三.

```
凭
Drawn under _____.
信用证              第           号
L/C No. 742863(2) .
日期
Dated AUGUST 16th, 2021.
按息付款
```

Chapter 6　Export Documentation 出口单证

```
Payable with Interest@                              % per Annum
号码                金额         中国，江苏        年 月 日
No.: 34567 Exchange for USD108 000.00  CHANGSHU，CHINA.
见票                           日后（本汇票之副本未付）
At ****** Sight of This of Exchange (Second of Exchange being Unpaid)
Pay to the Order of _____       或 其 指 定 人
付金额
The Sum of US DOLLARS ONE HUNDRED AND EIGHT THOUSAND ONLY
To
```

Case Analysis 6.2　Real Draft or Not
案例分析6.2　真假汇票

On January 8, an oil company clerk whose name John, holding two bank drafts for amount of $1 million and $2 million respectively of a bank branch A (payment location has not stated) and a bank branch B of a $3.5 million for bill of exchange, he is planning to buy oil in the northeastern United States. On January 11, there is a man called Brown who came to contact the business with John. As a supplier, Brown asked John to show certification of payment. John offered three copies of bank draft which total $6.5 million to Brown without hesitancy. On January 15, Brown (fraud suspects) made use of forged bills exchange with the real draft of John under the "switching count" approach. With excuse of contacting another business, Brown went to the bank for crime.

On January 26, John returns to place of residence, because of unsuccessful purchase of petroleum. On January 27, when John went to refund, he found that the bills he was holding are faked, John reported to court and made a stop payment notice. On January 28, the whole bank branch A was to be informed by telex system, but it was too late. On January 24, Jenny (Brown's partners in crime) held John's fake ID and 3 million bank draft for settle payment in bank branch A, of which 2 million transferred to bank branch B, 1 million in the January 27 was to be deposited on personal card for one of staff member who worked in the credit card department of bank branch B, meanwhile, 1 million was extracted in cash for 5 times in 4 days, while Jenny transferred 2 millions which firstly deposited in bank branch B into another two commercial bank respectively. Till February 3, except for $0.8 million was frozen by police, another $1.2 millions was extracted in cash for 5 times respectively.

Case analysis：

Firstly, the company's businessman John is lack of basic knowledge of prevention and how to settle business. There was no conscious that company personnel directly gave three draft copies of $6.5 million to the criminals when the intermediary (criminal) came to company and asked certain amounts of proof, such as payee name, seal, account number and name list etc, which means that the most basic elements were available to the criminals who forged bank drafts, ID cards.

Secondly, with increasingly fierce competition, people who work in the financial institutions ignore certain regulation of cash management in order to grab customers and stabilize deposits. They make easier for customers withdraw large amounts of cash especially credit card department which is seen to be the weak part in cash management. In this case, the criminals extracted total cash of $2.2 Million for 10 times in 11 days, of which criminals extracted total 5 times from credit card department, and the largest sum is $0.5 million, criminals also extracted total $0.9million in four times from other two urban credit branches, the largest sum is $0.4 million; and finally criminals extracted $0.3 million from another branch and run away. Large withdrawals without strict audition provides much more convinces for criminals.

The case is good lesson for China's financial system and International trade system to learn, in order to avoid such case occurs, attentions should be paid as follows.

(1) Strengthen corporation's employees training in terms of basic knowledge of how to settle business, how to prevent draft stolen, and also help them to understand the format of the normal draft, recorded project, different types of draft, counterfeit bills and how to identify, and what actions should be taken once counterfeit bills to be found. On the other hand, employees have to realize that do not present important documents and certification to counterparty who first time to contact.

(2) The staff of financial institutions has to strictly implement the regulation of People's Bank of China about "To Establish The Register Of Large Cash Payments" and regulation of "The Notice Of Banning Public Funds Transfer Into Personal Savings Account", which means that it is not allow for bank of deposit receive money in the way of from company account transfer into personal saving account. Strictly examine cash utilization of enterprises, once questions to be found, staff of financial institution should report to the local People's Bank. For bank draft which states the word of "cash", registration is necessary. For the credit card which have function of deposit, settle, and exchange, it is also subject to cash management requirements, any companies will not be allowed to pay in cash, and public funds transferred into personal credit card is strictly prohibited. Settlement need to be reformed and have to be speeded up. If large bills payment of cross-system can be through e-bank alliance, the bill for payment location is fast to know, agent bank is rapidly to be informed to stop payment, freezing, recover damages.

1月8日，石油公司职员约翰持有3张银行汇票，其中2张价值分别为100万美元和200万美元，由某银行的A分行(未标示支付地点)签发，还有1张价值350万美元的汇票，由某银行的B分行签发。他计划购买美国东北部的石油。1月11日布朗与约翰联系。作为供应商，布朗要求约翰出示付款证明。约翰毫不犹豫地把3份价值共650万美元的汇票交给他查看。1月15日，布朗(诈骗嫌疑人)以"换算"的借口用伪造的汇票把约翰的真汇票调包，然后以联系另外一笔生意为借口去了银行。

购买石油不成功，约翰1月26日返回居住地。1月27日约翰退款时发现，他所持有的汇票是假的。他向警方报案并做出停止付款的通知。1月28日，A分行收到电传通知，但是太迟了。1月24日珍妮(布朗的同伙)带着约翰的假身份证明在该行办理了300万美元的业务，其中200万美元转到B分行，100万在1月27日被存到B分行信用卡部门的一个工作人员的私人卡上，并在4天内分5次以提现的方式取出。同时，珍妮将存到B分行的200万美元分别转到2个商业银行。直至2月3日，除了被警方冻结的80万美元，其余的120万美元已经分5次被提现取出。

案例分析：

首先，该公司的业务员约翰缺乏防骗和结算货款的基本知识。他没有意识到，公司员工应对方要求直接将3份价值650万美元的汇票复印件给中间人(罪犯)，就等于让犯罪分子掌握了伪造汇票和身份证件所需的受款人姓名、印章、账号和名单等基本信息。

其次，在日益激烈的竞争下，金融机构的工作人员为了招揽顾客和稳定存款，往往会无视相关的现金管理规定。他们让顾客很容易提取巨额现金，尤其在信用卡部门，这已成为现金管理的薄弱环节。在本案中，罪犯在11天内分10次提取了220万美元现金，其中有5次在信用卡部门，金额最大的一笔有50万美元。另外，罪犯分4次在另外2个城市信用机构提取90万美元，其中最大的一笔有40万美元。最后，罪犯从另外一家分行提取了30万美元后逃逸。巨额提款缺乏严格监管给犯罪分子提供了更大的便利。

中国金融系统和国际贸易系统应很好地从本案中吸取教训。要避免类似案件的发生，应注意以下问题。

> (1) 应加强公司员工对结算货款、防止汇票被偷窃等基本知识的培训，让他们了解正规汇票的格式、使用记录和种类，有辨别伪造汇票的能力，知道在发现伪造汇票之后应立刻采取什么行动。另一方面，公司员工应该知道，不能把重要的单证和证书出示给初次打交道的客户。
>
> (2) 金融机构工作人员必须严格执行中国人民银行关于"建立大额现金支付注册制度"以及"禁止将公款转至个人储蓄账户的通知"的规定，也就是说，开户银行禁止为个人储蓄账户接收来自公司账户的转账。金融机构的工作人员应仔细审查企业的资金使用情况，一旦发现问题应立刻报告当地的人民银行。标示"现金"字样的银行汇票必须注册。有存款、结算和兑换功能的信用卡，必须服从现金管理业务的规定，任何一家公司都不允许将现金和公款转入个人信用卡。应改革结算方式和加快结算速度。如果大额票据的跨行支付能通过电子联盟银行进行，那么知道票据支付地点后，代理银行就能够迅速收到通知并立刻停止付款和冻结账户以弥补损失。

6.8.2 Certificate of Origin
原产地证书

A certificate of origin (see Sample 6-12) is a document certifying the origin of the goods or the place/ country of manufacturing. It should state the nature, quantity, value, and the place of manufacture. In many countries, the certificate of origin is usually prepared by the exporter, signed in the presence of a notary public institution and certified by a non-governmental commercial organization acceptable to the destination country. In China, the certificate of origin is generally issued by two governmental authorities: one is the Entry-Exit Inspection and Quarantine of the People's Republic of China, and the other is the China Chamber of International Commerce.

There are normally two types of certificates of origin: one is the certificate of origin, and the other is the generalized system of preferences certificate of origin (GSP C/O). The GSP Certificate of Origin is a special type of certificate of origin used to obtain the preferential customs duty treatment imposed by some developed countries on import commodities from some developing countries.

Different types of certificate of origin may be made at different stages of the export procedure. In normal cases, the seller can start to prepare the certificate of origin when the commercial invoice is ready. However, in some cases, for example GSP Form E, the issuance of a certificate of origin is made based on the submission of both the commercial invoice and the bill of lading. In this case, the preparation of the certificate of origin may be deferred to a time after the seller obtains the B/L. Whenever it is available, the certificate of origin is normally only used when the seller presents documents for negotiation of the payment.

The main purpose of the certificate of origin is to prove the origin of the goods based on which the import Customs can set import duties and implement the applicable import controls such as sanctions, quotas, anti-dumping duties or favorable treatments.

Certificates of origin must be distinguished from country of origin marking. Many countries require that the products themselves and the labels on the packages specify the country of origin. The country of origin certificate may be in addition to or in lieu of that requirement. An important certificate of origin is the one required under the North American Free Trade Agreement(NAFTA).

NAFTA contains product-specific country of origin criteria which must be met to qualify for reduced duty treatment on exports to or imports from Canada or Mexico. In general, in order to be eligible for the duty-free or reduced duty rates under NAFTA, all items imported from outside of North America must have undergone the "tariff shift" during the manufacturing process for that product. In addition, some products must contain a specified "regional value content" usually of 50 or 60 percent. Finished goods and sometimes raw materials purchased from others often must be traced backward to establish their country of origin.

1. Duty-Free and Reduced Duty Programs

Before importing, the importer should ascertain whether or not the product is eligible for one of the special duty-free or reduced duty programs which Congress has allowed. The largest program is known as the Generalized System of Preferences (GSP).This program was designed to encourage the economic development of less-developed countries by permitting the importation of those countries' products duty-free. The Harmonised Tarrif Schedule(HTS) contains a list of the approximately 101 countries eligible for this program. Under the NAFTA, Mexico was eliminated as a beneficiary country as of January 1, 1994. The fact that a product will be imported from one of the GSP beneficiary countries, however, does not guarantee duty-free treatment. Some specific products even from eligible countries have been excluded, and it is necessary for the importer to identify whether the particular product is on the exclusion list. In addition, at least 35 percent of the final appraised value must be added in that country. The importer must claim the duty-free status by putting an "A" in the entry summary and, if requested by customs, obtain a GSP declaration from the exporter.

For imports from the twenty-four countries located in the Caribbean Basin, a similar duty-free program is available, along with imports from Israel under the Israel Free Trade Agreement, imports from Bolivia, Colombia, Peru, and Ecuador under the Andean Trade Preference Act, and imports from thirty-five countries under the African Growth and Opportunity Act.

The final program is a duty-free and reduced duty program, the NAFTA, which was implemented on January 1, 1994. Under the NAFTA, products of Canadian and Mexican origin eventually can be imported duty-free to the United States if various requirements are met. Usually, this means that the product must be of Canadian or Mexican origin under one of six eligibility rules and the exporter must provide the importer with a certificate of origin.

Many items were granted duty-free status immediately, but other items will be eligible for duty-free status over a phase-out period of five to fifteen years. Nevertheless, if the importer can comply with the requirements, the duty will be less than on ordinary imports from Canada or Mexico.

2. Country of Origin

Determination of the proper country of origin can affect the duty rate payable on imported goods or whether they are subject to quotas. In addition, Section 304 of the Tariff Act of 1930 requires that imported merchandise be clearly and conspicuously marked in a permanent manner with the English name of the International country of origin. Some types of merchandise are exempt from the marking requirement but, in such cases, usually the outermost container that will go to the end user must be marked. This is an important preliminary planning consideration because the Customs regulations specify that certain types of products must be marked in certain ways, such as die-stamping, cast-in-the-mold lettering, or etching, during the manufacturing process.

The importer should check the country of origin regulations prior to purchasing products to ascertain whether or not it must advise the supplier or seller of any special marking methods prior to the manufacture of the products. Sometimes off-the-shelf inventory manufactured in an international country cannot be modified after manufacture to comply with the U.S. country of origin marking requirements. Merchandise which is not properly marked may be seized by the U.S. Customs Service. In some cases, the products can be marked after such seizure, but only upon payment of a marking penalty, which increases the cost of importing the products. More seriously, sometimes Customs will release the merchandise to the importer, and the importer may resell it. Then, the U.S. Customs Service may issue a notice of redelivery of the products. If the importer is unable to redeliver the products, a substantial Customs penalty may be payable. The marking must remain on the product (including after any repacking) until it reaches the ultimate purchaser, which is usually the retail customer.

3. Checklist for Certificate of Origin

(1) Are names and addresses as per the commercial invoice and letter of credit?

(2) Is the country of origin, if required, as per the commercial invoice and letter of credit?

(3) Have they been issued by the proper party and signed?

(4) Do they show a description relative to the commercial invoice and letter of credit?

(5) Are they in exact compliance with the letter of credit and dated with a reasonably current date?

(6) About the standard of origin:

a. Completely origin, fill in "P".

b. For imported ingredients, but conform to the standards of country of origin, to the following countries, fill in the following ①The European Union, Norway, Switzerland, Liechtenstein, Japan, Turkey: fill in the "W", then fill in the four-digit tariff number of export products (such as 96.18 "W"); Part of imported raw materials belongs to benefit country can be regarded as its raw material of its country, therefore, if the imported ingredients of the product which carry imported component completely, the standard of origin still should be filled out the "P". ②Canada: imported components accounted for below 40% of the ex-factory price of the products, "F" should be filled out. ③Russia, Belarus, Ukraine, Kazakhstan: import component shall not exceed 50% of the product is fob, fill in "Y", then fill in the value of the imported raw materials and components in the export product fob percentage accounted for 35% (such as "Y"). ④Australia and New Zealand: if its raw material and labor service is less than 50% of the products' cost, the origin of the product standard should be blank.

4. Kinds of Certificate of Origin

(1) Certificate of Origin.

(2) Generalized System of Preference Certificate of Origin (see Sample 6-13).

(3) Certificate of Manufacturer's Origin.

(4) The Asia-Pacific Trade Agreement certificate of origin is applicable to exports of India, Korea, Bangladesh, and Sri Lanka and conform to the provisions of the product.

(5) The China-Asean Free Trade Agreement certificate of origin (FORM E) is applicable to exports of Indonesia, Thailand, Malaysia, Vietnam, Philippines, Singapore, Brunei, Cambodia, Burma, Laos and other countries and comply with relevant regulations.

(6) China-Pakistan Free Trade Agreement certificate of origin: China's export preferential products with this certificate to Pakistan can be obtained preferential duty treatment under the framework by Pakistan.

(7) China-Chile Free Trade Agreement certificate of origin (FORM F): Since October 1, 2006, China's exports to Chile under the trade between China and Chile agreement products have enjoyed treatment of Chile tariff reductions.

(8) China-New Zealand Free Trade Agreement certificate of origin: Since October 1, 2008, our exports to New Zealand in China-New Zealand FTA rules of origin of products have enjoyed giving preferential duty treatment.

(9) China-Singapore Free Trade Agreement certificate of origin: Since January 1, 2009, China's export to Singapore in China-Singapore FTA rules of origin of products have enjoyed giving preferential duty treatment.

(10) Peru in China Free Trade Agreement certificate of origin: Since March 1, 2010, our country export to Peru in China-Peru FTA rules of origin of products have enjoyed preferential duty treatment given by Peru.

(11) China-Costa Rica Free Trade Agreement certificate of origin: Since August 1, 2011, our country in China-to costa rica costa rica FTA rules of origin of products have enjoyed treatment of tariff reductions in costa rica.

(12) The Government of the People's Republic of China and the Government of the Republic of Costa Rica Free Trade Agreement took effect on August 1, 2011. According to this agreement, China-Costa Rica of the two sides carried out more than 90% of their respective products phased zero tariff, including China's textile raw materials and products, light industry, machinery, electrical equipment, vegetables, fruits, automobile, chemical industry, raw fur and leather products and Costa Rica's coffee, beef, pork, pineapple juice, frozen orange juice, jam, fish meal, minerals, raw hides and etc. , benefited from lower taxes arrangement.

5. Clauses of Certificate of Origin

(1) Certificate of origin separated.

(2) Generalized system of preference certificate of origin FORM "A".

(3) Certificate of origin shipment of goods of origin prohibited.

(4) Photocopy of original certificate of Chinese original GSP Form A required and such certificate combined with or referring to other documents not acceptable.

(5) Certificate of origin incorporated in the invoice is acceptable.

(6) For imports from the People's Republic of China, a separated Certificate of origin is required along with the advising therein of name and address of the manufacturers. This certificate must be legalized by chamber of commerce.

原产地证书(见样单6-12)是证明商品原产地/国的文件。该证书应标示商品的性质、数量、价值和产地等内容。在很多国家，原产地证书由出口商在公证机构在场的情况下填制和签字，由目的国接受的非政府商业机构认证。原产地证书在中国一般由两个政府机关签发：中华人民共和国出入境检验检疫局和中国国际商会。

原产地证书一般有两种：一般原产地证书和普惠制原产地证书(GSP C/O)。普惠制原产地证书比较特殊，对某些发展中国家来说，向某些发达国家出口商品时使用这种证书可以获得优惠关税待遇。

不同类型的原产地证书在出口的不同阶段制作。在正常情况下，出口商做好商业发票后就开始着手一般原产地证书的办理工作。但是，在某些情况下，原产地证书只能在出口商提交了商业发票和提单之后才能出证，例如普惠制东盟国家自由贸易区原产地证书。这样的话，原产地证书的准备工作就有可能拖延到出口商获得提单之后的某个时间。不管是什么情况，出口商只在交单议付货款时才使用原产地证书。

使用原产地证书的主要目的，是在进口国征收进口关税时和实施制裁、配额、反倾销税或优惠待遇等进口管制措施时证明货物的原产地。

必须将原产地证书和原产国标志区别开来。很多国家规定在产品上和包装的标签上标明原产国。原产地证书有可能是这些标志的补充或者可以代替它们。在《北美自由贸易协定》中，原产地证书是很重要的一个文件。

《北美自由贸易协定》中有特定产品的原产地标准，出口至或进口自加拿大或墨西哥的产品要达到这些标准才能享受减免关税的待遇。一般来说，从北美地区外进口的所有商品要得到《北美自由贸易协定》中关税减免的资格，就必须在生产的过程中满足"关税税则变更"要求。另外，一些商品必须包含特定的"区域价值成分"，一般要达到50%～60%。对成品和有些从外部地区购买的原材料必须追溯来源，以确定原产国。

1. 关税减免项目

进口前，进口商应明确这类产品是否能获得国会允许的关税减免。其中最大的关税减免是普惠制(GSP)。这个项目的目标是通过免除自不发达国家进口商品的关税来促进这些国家经济发展。HTS(税则号，相当于我国的HS Code)中列出大概101个有资格参与这个项目的国家。根据《北美自由贸易协定》的规定，墨西哥于1994年1月1日被取消了受益国资格。但事实上，即使是来自以上101个受益国的进口商品，也不一定能获得免税的待遇。某些特定的商品被排除在外，所以进口商必须先确定要进口的商品是否在排除之列。另外，该商品必须有35%以上的价值来自本国成分。如要申请免税，进口商必须在进口汇总申报单上填"A"，另外，如果海关有要求，还需提交一份由出口商提供的普惠制原产地证书。

1994年1月1日开始执行的《北美自由贸易协定》中的最后一个项目是关税减免。在该协定下，原产于加拿大和墨西哥的商品出口至美国时，只要满足一定的条件即可享受免税待遇。这就意味着6条资格条款中的商品必须是加拿大原产或墨西哥原产，同时出口商必须向进口商提供原产地证书。许多商品的免税待遇是只要申请即得，但是有一些商品的审核需要5～15年的时间。尽管如此，但只要进口商按要求办理，从加拿大或墨西哥进口的关税始终是比一般关税低的。

2. 原产国

对原产国的选择会直接影响进口商品的关税率以及对配额的适用性。另外，《1930年关税法案》304部分规定，进口商品上必须有清晰和明显的原产国英文名称的永久性标记。一些种类的商品不需要在商品上做这个标记，但必须在商品最外层的包装上标明。这是很重要的初步规划设想，因为海关规定，某些特定商品必须以某种方式标记，如在商品的生产过程中以模压印花、模具刻字或铜板刻画等方式。

进口商购买进口商品前应了解原产国标准的规定以便确定是否需要在货物生产前建议供货商或卖方使用特定的标记方法。在美国，有些产于国外的货物在生产工序完成后是无法根据美国原产地标记的要求更改的。无正确标记的商品有可能会被美国海关总署没收。有时候商品被没收后还可以补上标记，但是需要缴纳一笔标记罚金，这会增加进口成本。更严重的是，有时海关会把商品交给进口商，而有些不知情进口商会把商品转售。然后，海关总署会签发一份货物再交付通知书。如果进口商无法再交付货物，就要支付一笔金额很大的海关罚款。标志必须保留在商品上（即使重新包装）直到商品到达最后的销售环节，即到达零售商手中。

3. 原产地证书审核内容

(1) 名称和地址与商业发票和信用证上的是否一致？

(2) 如果有规定，原产国与商业发票和信用证规定的是否一致？

(3) 证书是否由正确的当事人出具和签名？

(4) 商品描述与商业发票和信用证标示的内容是否相关？

(5) 证书与信用证是否严格相符，签发日期是否是近期的和合理的日期？

(6) 关于原产地标准：

a. 完全原产的，填写"P"。

b. 含有进口成分，但符合原产地标准，输往下列国家时，填写如下。①挪威：填写"W"，其后填明出口产品的四位数税则号（如：96.18"W"）；属于受惠国成分的进口原料部分可视作本国原料，因此，如果产品的进口成分完全采用受惠国成分，则该产品的原产地标准仍填写"P"。②澳大利亚和新西兰：本国原料和劳务不低于产品出厂成本的50%，则该产品的原产地标准留空。

4. 原产地证书的种类

(1) 一般原产地证书。

(2) 普惠制原产地证书（见样单6-13）。

(3) 厂商产地证书。

(4)《亚太贸易协定》原产地证书：目前适用于印度、韩国、孟加拉国和斯里兰卡出口并符合规定的产品。

(5)《中国—东盟自由贸易协定》原产地证书(FORM E)：目前适用于印度尼西亚、泰国、马来西亚、越南、菲律宾、新加坡、文莱、柬埔寨、缅甸、老挝等国出口并符合相关规定的产品。

(6)《中国—巴基斯坦自由贸易协定》原产地证书：我国出口到巴基斯坦的该优惠框架项下的产品凭此证书可获得巴基斯坦给予的关税优惠待遇。

(7)《中国—智利自由贸易协定》原产地证书(FORM F)：自2006年10月1日起，我国出口到智利的《中国—智利自由贸易协定》项下的产品享受智利给予的关税优惠待遇。

(8)《中国—新西兰自由贸易协定》原产地证书：自2008年10月1日起，我国出口到新西兰的符合《中国—新西兰自由贸易协定》原产地规则的产品享受新西兰给予的关税优惠待遇。

(9)《中国—新加坡自由贸易协定》原产地证书：自2009年1月1日起，我国出口到新加坡的符合《中国—新加坡自由贸易协定》原产地规则的产品享受新加坡给予的关税优惠待遇。

(10)《中国—秘鲁自由贸易协定》原产地证书：自2010年3月1日起，我国出口到秘鲁的符合《中国—秘鲁自由贸易协定》原产地规则的产品享受秘鲁给予的关税优惠待遇。

(11)《中国—哥斯达黎加自由贸易协定》原产地证书：自 2011 年 8 月 1 日起，我国出口到哥斯达黎加的符合《中国—哥斯达黎加自由贸易协定》原产地规则的产品享受哥斯达黎加给予的关税优惠待遇。

(12)《中华人民共和国政府和哥斯达黎加共和国政府自由贸易协定》于 2011 年 8 月 1 日起开始实施。按照这一协定，中哥双方将对各自 90% 以上的产品分阶段实施零关税，中国的纺织原料及制品、轻工、机械、电气设备、蔬菜、水果、汽车、化工、生毛皮及皮革等产品和哥方的咖啡、牛肉、猪肉、菠萝汁、冷冻橙汁、果酱、鱼粉、矿产品、生皮等产品，将从降税安排中获益。

5. 原产地证书条款

(1) 单独出具的原产地证书。

(2) 普惠制格式"A"原产地证书。

(3) 产地证书不允许装运的产品。

(4) 提供中国原产地证书或普惠制产地证书格式 A 正本的影印本，该产地证书是独立的，不依附于其他单证格式。

(5) 与发票联合的原产地证书可以接受。

(6) 从中国进口货物应单独缮制产地证，并注明厂家名称、地址，由商会签证。

Assignment 6.5 Make corrections of Certificate of Origin.
练习 6.5 原产地证书改错

SELLER: GUANGDONG DONGFENG IMPORT AND EXPORT CORP.122 DONGFENG ROAD EAST，GUANGZHOU

BUYER: ANYEI HONG KONG 14/F., KAISER ESTATE 1, MANYUE STREET，HUNG HOM，SYDNEY, AUSTRALIA

1. 2 400PCS (STAINLESS STEEL SPADE HEAD)
2. 12PCS/BUNDLE
3. SHIPPING DATE: DEC 1ST，2021

1. Goods consigned from (Exporter's business name, address, country) CUANCDONG DONGFENG IMPORT AND EXPORT CORP. 122 DONGFENG ROAD EAST, GUANGZHOU	Reference NO.　　　　GZ9/12078/6311 **GENERALIZED SYSTEM OF PREFERENCES CERTIFICATE OF ORIGIN** (Combined declaration and certificate) **FORM A** issued in **THE PEOPLE's REPUBLIC OF CHINA** (COUNTRY) See Notes overleaf
2. Goods consigned to Consignee's name, address, country) SANYEI HONG KONG 14/F,. KAISER ESTATE 1, MANYUE STREET, HUNG HOM, SYDNEY	
3. Means of transport an Route as far as known FROM GUANGZHOU TO SYDNEY BY VESSEL	4. For official use

5. Item number 1	6. Marks and numbers of packages KMART SYDNEY NO.1-200	7. Number and kind of packages; description of goods TWO THOUSAND FOUR HUNDRED (2 400) PCS OF STAINLESS STEELSPADE HEAD	8. Origin criterion (see Notes overleaf) "P"	9. Gross weight or other quantity 2 400PCS	10. Number and date of invoice SM199901 NOV 11.2021
11. Certification It is hereby certified, on the basis of control carried out, that the declaration by the exporter is correct. GUANGZHOU NOV.21ST, 2021 Place and date, signature and stamp of certifying authority			12. Declaration by the exporter The undersigned hereby declares that the above details and statements are correct; that all the goods were produced in GUANGZHOU (country) and that they comply with the origin requirements specified for those goods in the Generalized System of Preferences for goods exported to SYDNEY (importing country) GUANGZHOU NOV 20.2021 Place and date, signature of authorized signature			

Cases Analysis 6.3 Indian Company Cannot Get Tariff Deducted With C/O
案例分析 6.3 印度公司持有原产地证书但未得到关税减免

An Indian trading company exported tools from India to China, and the production process of the exported tools were finished in India. They applied for a C/O before tools were being shipped 3 days ago. When these tools arrived in China, they apply for tariff deducted with C/O, but they get refused.

Analysis:

The Bangkok Agreement is an initiative under the Economic and Social Commission for Asia and the Pacific (ESCAP) to exchange tariff concessions among countries in the ESCAP region. India, Korea, Bangladesh and Sri Lanka were signatories to the Agreement since 1975, but China joined the Agreement in April, 2001. As a result of China becoming a signatory to the Agreement, bilateral negotiations for exchange of tariff concessions between India and China were concluded in the year 2003.

Therefore, in this case, it is normal that the India trading company get refused for deducted tariff with C/O, they should apply for a FORM B instead of it.

一家印度贸易公司出口一批工具至中国，这批工具的最终生产环节在印度完成。工具装运前3天，该公司申请了原产地证书。当工具到达中国时，他们申请关税减免但遭到拒绝。

分析：

《曼谷协定》是亚洲及太平洋经济社会委员会(ESCAP)为了让亚洲及太平洋区域内的国家能相互享受关税减让而采用的初步措施。印度、韩国、孟加拉国和斯里兰卡于1975年成为该协议的签约国，中国2001年4月才加入该协定。2003年印度与中国完成关于双边关税减让的双边谈判。

因此，在此案中，印度贸易公司持原产地证书被拒绝关税减让是正常的。要获得这个待遇，他们应该使用 FORM B 表格。

6.8.3 Consular Invoice
领事发票

A consular invoice is a form, usually only obtainable from the importing country's consulate in the exporting country, on which the seller or its agent must enter a detailed description of the goods being shipped. Such a form is required by certain countries in order to compile statistics, control imports, collect import duties and check the origin of goods and the credit of the exporter.

A consular invoice shall carry such information as the name of the goods, the number of the items, their weight, the value and origin of the goods and a declaration that the information given is correct. Most of the consular invoices are in the language of the country to which the goods are shipped so it is usually considered as the most difficult document of all and must be filled in with special care.

领事发票是一份通常由出口国所在地的进口国领事出具的表格，卖方或其代理人须在此表上详细描述已经装船的货物。某些国家要求提供这种单证，为了进行统计、控制进口、收集进口关税和检查货物原产地和出口商的信用。

领事发票应该包括以下内容，货物名称、数量、重量、价值、商品原产地以及所提供的内容正确性的声明。大部分的领事发票使用装运货物所在地语言，所以它通常也被认为是最难的单证，必须特别认真填写。

6.8.4 Customs Invoice
海关发票

A customs invoice is one of the documents made out on a special form prescribed by the Customs authorities of the importing country. Generally, the invoice may include information required by the import Customs that is not stated on an ordinary commercial invoice.

This invoice is usually required by some importing countries such as U.S.A, Canada, New Zealand, Australia and some African countries and used to clear customs, to verify the country of origin for import duty and tax purposes, to compare export prices and domestic prices and to fix anti-dumping duties.

Types of Customs Invoice:

(1) Canada Customs Invoice (see Sample 6-14).

(2) Special Customs Invoice.

(3) Certificate of Origin for Exports to New Zealand Form 59A.

(4) Combined Certificate of Value and of Origin and Invoice of Goods for Exportation to West Africa Form C. It applies to Senegambia, Sierra Leone and Liberia.

(5) Invoice and Declaration of Value Required for Shipment to Jamaica Form C 23. It

applies to Jamaica Honduras and Dominica.

(6) Carioca/Caribbean Common Market Invoice.It applies to 12 members of Carioca/Caribbean Common Market: Jamaica Dominica and Guyana.

(7) Uncertain format customs invoice.

There is no name of customs invoice and a designated name in this format. It applies to Malta Mauritius and etc. The content and format of West Africa customs invoice format is basically the same content. Words of origin and value can be filled to certify if commodities exported to the countries and L/C does not require supplying customs invoice or can avoid for. Australian customs invoice has stopped using. A statement can be filled on the developing countries in the commercial invoice. For example: "I declare that the final process of manufacture of the goods for which special rates are claimed has been performed in China and that not less than one half of the factory cost of the goods is represented by the value of labor and material of China."

海关发票是根据进口国海关指定格式出具的特殊单证之一。通常海关发票应包含进口国海关规定的内容，而这些内容在一般的商业发票上是不标示的。

美国、加拿大、新西兰、澳大利亚和一些非洲国家一般要求提供海关发票，可用于清关，也用于缴纳进口税时核对原产国、比较出口价格和国内价格以及确定反倾销税等。

海关发票种类：

(1) 加拿大海关发票(见样单6-14)。

(2) 美国海关发票。

(3) 新西兰海关发票格式59A。

(4) 西非海关发票格式C，适用于塞内加尔、塞拉利昂和利比里亚。

(5) 牙买加海关发票格式C23，适用于牙买加、洪都拉斯和多米尼加。

(6) 加勒比共同市场海关发票。它适用于里约热内卢/加勒比共同市场的12个成员国：牙买加、多米尼加和圭亚那。

(7) 无确定格式的海关发票。

海关发票没有特定的名称。马耳他和毛里求斯等国适用海关发票。西非各国海关发票的内容和格式几乎都是相同的。如果货物要出口到这些国家，要在海关发票上填写产地国和货物的价值，以证明其可靠性。另外，如果信用证不要求提供海关发票，这些内容就不用填写。澳大利亚海关发票已经停止使用。相关的声明在发展中国家的商业发票上要注明。例如："兹证明享受特殊税率的货物的制造是在中国进行的，而且货物的工厂成本不少于一半是加工费和材料费。"

6.9 Exporter's Instruction Documents
出口商指示单证

Instruction documents issued by the exporter are generally not required for export, but are highly recommended to facilitate the export process and make certain that everyone is performing according to the exporter's specific instructions.

Exporter's Instruction Documents include forwarder's instructions, shipping instructions, stowage instructions, hazardous materials/ dangerous goods instructions and bank instructions.

1. Forwarder's Instructions

A forwarder's instructions issued by the consignor contains instruction for booking the shipment of cargo and completing the transport documents.

2. Shipping Instructions

Shipping instructions issued by the consignor gives specific instructions to the shipping company or freight forwarder regarding the shipment. It is virtually identical to the forwarder's instructions. The bill of lading is typically drawn up from this information.

3. Stowage Instructions

It is issued by the consignor contains specific instructions regarding how or where a cargo should be stowed during transport. For example, a shipper may require that the shipment is placed below deck and amidships for greater protection from the elements.

4. Hazardous Materials/Dangerous Goods Instructions

It is issued by the consignor and contains information regarding a shipment of hazardous materials or dangerous goods. A hazardous material is a substance or product that has been determined to be capable of posing an unreasonable risk to health, safety and property when transported in commerce. Hazardous material is classified as dangerous goods when transported by air. Hazards are classified as "Other Regulated Materials" and include irritating, corrosive, caustic, flammable, radioactive and other life or health threatening materials. Special handling instructions must be provided and containers must be properly emblazoned with warning labels and stickers.

5. Bank Instructions

Bank instructions issued by the consignor contains information about how the exporter/ seller wishes to have payment secured for a shipment when a documentary collection or documentary letter of credit is used.

出口一般不需要由出口商出具的指示单证，但是在进出口过程中，强力推荐根据出口商的明确指示去操作，以便出口过程顺利进行。

出口商指示单证包括货代的指示、装运指示、理舱指示、有害物质/危险货物指示和银行指示。

1. 货代的指示
货代的指示由发货人开立，包括订货指示和货运指示单证。

2. 装运指示
装运指示是托运人签发的对船公司或货代发出的特定的指示。它实际上与货代指示相同。提单典型是以装运指示为基础起草的单证。

3. 理舱指示
理舱指示由发货人开立，包含在运输过程中，货物应该如何装或者放哪里的具体说明。例如，托运人可以要求货物放甲板船中间以便更好保护货物。

4. 有害物质 / 危险货物指示
由发货人开立的有害物质 / 危险货物指示是关于有害物质或危险货物的资料。危险材料是一种在运输中对人的健康、安全及财产造成不合理风险的物质或产品。航空运输时，危险材料被列为危险物品。危险划分为"其他可调节材料"，包括刺激性、腐蚀、磨损、易燃、辐射和其他对生命或健康有威胁的材料。必须提供特殊处理指示，而集装箱必须恰当贴有警告标签和贴纸。

5. 银行指示
由发货人签发的银行指示包含关于当使用跟单托收或跟单信用证时，出口商 / 卖方希望如何安全付款的信息。

6.10　Electronic Filling of Documents
　　　　电子填单

Increasingly, certain export documents are required to be filed electronically. Many systems are now in place whereby the same electronic document format may be used for exporting/importing between dozens of different countries. This standardization is proved to be of great benefit to the international exporter/importer.

越来越多的出口单据须由电子系统提交。现在有许多单证系统，但许多出口 / 进口国用同一单证系统。对于国际进、出口商来说，单证系统标准化被证明是非常有益的。

6.11　A Summary of Export Documents
　　　　出口单证小结

From the perspective of sellers, documentation is not only one of his basic obligations under the contract, but also an important task concerning the collection of the export cargo proceeds.

Generally speaking, the basic requirements for documentation are correctness, completeness, conciseness, cleanness and promptness.

Documents for an export transaction are to be prepared and checked on all the bases such as contract, credit, and original information from the manufacturers.

Any negligence in documentation may hinder the fulfillment of the contract and might result in serious problems.

Major export documents include the bill of exchange (draft), invoice, packing list, insurance policy, bill of lading, inspection certificate and certificate of origin, and etc.

As is discussed above, different types of documents are required at different stages of the export procedure. But as there are too many different documents involved in too many different stages, to study them one by one may only provide you a squirrel's view of the picture. To help you take a bird's eye of the picture, the main documents are summarized in Table 6-1.

Table 6-1 A Summary of Export Documents

Items	Good Preparation	Inspection	Booking Space	Export Clearance	Loading	Insurance	Payment Negotiation
Export license				√			
Sales Contract	√	√		√		√	
Letter of Credit	√	√					√
Commercial Invoice				√		√	√
Packing list				√		√	√
Inspection Application		√					
Inspection Certificate				√			√
Booking Note			√				
Shipping Order					√		
Customs Declaration				√			
Customs Clearance					√		
Shipping Advice							√
Bill of Lading							√
Proposal Form						√	
Insurance Policy							√
Bill of Exchange							√

(Continuation Table)

Items	Good Preparation	Inspection	Booking Space	Export Clearance	Loading	Insurance	Payment Negotiation
Certificate of Origin							√
Consular Invoice							√
Customs Invoice							√

从卖方的角度来说，单证制作不仅是合同的基本义务，也是收取货款需完成的重要任务。

一般来说，单证的基本要求是正确、完整、简洁、清洁和迅速。

对出口交易而言，制作和核对单证的基础是合同、信用证和制造商提供的原始数据。任何单证的错误都有可能阻碍合同的履行，甚至可能导致严重的问题。

主要的出口单证包括汇票、发票、装箱单、保险单、提单、检验证书和原产地证书等。

如上所述，不同的单证在出口不同阶段使用。但是单证的种类和环节太多，如果一步步去学，大家可能会感到困惑。为了使大家能更好地全面了解出口单证，表 6-1 对主要出口单证做了汇总。

表 6-1　出口单证汇总表

项目	备货	检验	订舱	清关	装货	保险	议付
出口许可证				√			
销售合同	√	√		√		√	
信用证	√	√					√
商业发票				√		√	√
包装单				√		√	√
检验申请表		√					
检验证明书				√			√
订舱单			√				
装货单					√		
报关申请表				√			
清关单					√		
装船通知							√
提单							√
投保单						√	
保险单							√
汇票							√

(续表)

项目	备货	检验	订舱	清关	装货	保险	议付
原产地证							√
领事发票							√
海关发票							√

Chapter 7

Import Documents
进口单证

For many basic transactions, import documentation is simple. Importers of non-regulated goods from many countries can present a commercial invoice, a bill of lading and an import declaration.

很多基本交易的进口单证都非常简单。对很多国家的进口商来说,如果进口的是非管制类商品,那么只要提交商业发票、提单和进口报关单即可。

7.1 Definitions
定义

Import documents are issued or secured by the exporter, the importer (or a customs broker working for the importer) or third parties.

进口单证由出口商、进口商(或为进口商工作的海关经纪人)或第三方开具或者担保。

7.2 Basic Requirement for Making Import Documentation
进口制单的基本要求

7.2.1 Terms and Conditions
条款和条件

(1) A written or verbal agreement has been made between the parties specifying the product, quantity, price, delivery date, delivery method and all other conditions of sale including who will pay for shipping, insurance, duties and other costs.

(2) The countries of export and import have normal trade relations.

(3) The country of export is economically and politically stable and does not have excessive international exchange regulations.

(4) The country of import does not require consular certificates or invoices.

(5) The goods traded are unregulated and do not require import licenses or permits.

(6) The buyer is familiar with the goods traded and has no reason to believe that these goods shipped will be anything other than the goods ordered.

(7) The parties to the transaction know each other, have traded successfully in the past, or have no reason to expect duplicity or dishonesty from the other party.

(8) The terms are payment in advance, by cash, check, wire-transfer, or credit card, or on open account with future payment by check, wire-transfer, or credit card.

(1) 买卖双方已事先就产品类型、数量、价格、装运日期、装运方式以及其他贸易条件(如谁支付运费、保险费、关税和其他费用)等问题达成书面或口头协议。

(2) 出口国和进口国有正常的贸易关系。

(3) 出口国经济和政治稳定，无过多的外汇管制。

(4) 进口国通关不需领事证书或领事发票。

(5) 交易的货物不受管制，不需要办理进口许可证。

(6) 买方对货物很熟悉，而且相信所装运的货物即所购货物。

(7) 交易各方了解彼此，曾经成功合作，或不会怀疑对方口是心非或不诚实。

(8) 付款条件是通过现金、支票、银行电汇或信用卡的方式预付货款或通过支票、银行电汇或信用卡的方式进行远期付款(赊销)。

7.2.2 Basic Import Documents
进口单证的基本种类

Basic import documents include commercial invoice, bill of lading, import declaration, packing list, certificate of origin and insurance documents.

进口单证包括商业发票、提单、进口报关单、包装单、原产地证和保险单。

7.2.3 Additional Import Documentation(Complicating Factor)
其他进口单证

While many import transactions require minimal documentation, others require that the importer issue or secure additional documents.

(1) Import Licenses (see Sample 7-1), Permits and Declarations (see Sample 7-2).

(2) Additional Documents Required by the Import Authority.

(3) Special Transport Documents.

(4) Banking and International Exchange Documents.

尽管很多进口贸易都要求单证简单化，但是在某些贸易中，还是要求进口商签发或担保一些额外的单证。

(1) 进口许可证（见样单 7-1) 和进口报关单（见样单 7-2)。
(2) 进口国官方要求的其他单证。
(3) 特别的运输单证。
(4) 银行单证和外汇单证。

7.3　Import Licenses, Permits and Declarations 进口许可证和进口报关单

All countries seek to control their imports for political, economic or security purposes. Governments also seek to control who imports, what is imported and the country of origin of their imports.

In some cases, an outright import ban on a commodity or product might exist. In other cases, import of a product may be banned only from certain countries, while sometimes it may be permissible to import a product only under certain specified conditions. In all cases, governments use various forms of import licenses, permits and declarations to control and track their imports.

所有国家都会因为政治、经济或安全的目的而对进口进行管制。除此之外，政府也会控制由谁进口、进口的是什么以及进口商品的原产地。

在某些情况下，某种商品可能会遭遇完全的进口禁令。而有时只是被禁止来自于某些特定国家，或者必须满足某种特定条件才允许进口。但是，所有的国家都会使用不同种类的进口许可证和进口报关单来管制和追踪进口活动。

7.3.1　Import License/Permit (Issued by the Import Authority) 进口许可证（进口国当局签发）

Import licenses and permits are either general or specific. In some instances, a general license to import and a specific permit to import a restricted product must both be obtained.

进口许可证有一般进口许可证和特种商品进口许可证两种。有时候，某种限制进口的商品需要同时提交以上两种证书。

7.3.2　Dangerous Goods Declaration(Issued by the Importer) 危险货物申报单（进口国签发）

Countries put special procedures in place for handling and documenting shipments of hazardous materials/ dangerous goods including biohazards and toxic and radioactive wastes. This declaration is a formal statement about the contents of a specific shipment and is used by both import authorities and the carrier.

对于生物危害物质、有毒物质和放射性废弃物等危险品的装运和制单,每个国家都有特别规定。进口国当局和承运人都会要求提供这类关于装运具体内容正式声明的申报单。

7.3.3 Exchange Control Documents
外汇管制单证

Certain countries seek to control the flow of their national currency by controlling imports and exports (i.e. Russia, Nigeria, and India). Such countries require that the importer make a statement or declaration that the flow of goods and payments follow prescribed regulations. Importers may be required to apply for prior approval (see Sample 9-2 and Sample 9-4) to obtain hard currency to pay for an import shipment.

一些国家试图通过管制进出口来控制国内货币的流动(如俄罗斯、尼日利亚、印度)。这些国家要求进口商做出声明,即商品和支付流动是符合规定的。在这种情况下,进口商如果想得到硬货币来支付一批进口货物的话,可能需要预先审批(见样单9-2和样单9-4)。

7.4 Documents Required by the Import Authority
进口国当局需要的单证

1. Special Certificate of Origin(Issued by the Shipper/Exporter or Special Authorizing Agency of the Country of Export)

This document certifies that the country of a shipment is within the context of a regional trade agreement(e.g. the NAFTA Certificate of Origin).

2. Customs Bond(Issued by Insurance Company)

This offers evidence that a financial guarantee by an insurance company has been made to the import authority regarding a particular import shipment.

3. Packing Declaration(Issued by the Shipper/Exporter or Forwarder)

This document certifies that packing materials are free from pests.

4. Certified Consular Invoice(Issued or Certifies by a Consulate of the Country of Final Destination Located in the Country of Export)

This establishes country of origin and description and value of goods shipped.

5. Insurance Certificate

This document offers proof of insurance for a shipment.

6. Inspection Certificate(Generally Issued by a Third-party Independent Testing Company)

This document certifies product quality, quantity or adherence to certain specifications. These certificates are required by certain nations as a means of controlling techniques commonly used to circumvent exchange control regulations(i.e. overstated quantities or underdeclared valuations). The import license usually requires a "clean report of findings" by an authorized inspection organization before goods can clear customs or payment can be made.

7. Quality Certificate (Issued by Independent Testing Companies)

This document certifies that the products continued in the shipment meet the standards of the importing country. Most countries require that this certification be provided by the exporter and be approved and filed by the appropriate governmental control agency(i.e. the exporting country Department of Consumer Safety)prior to shipment.

8. Phytosanitary Certificate(Generally Issued by a Third-party Independent Testing Company)

This document certifies that shipment of imported plants or plant products (i.e. seeds, bulbs, flowers, fruits, vegetables, and etc.) is free from pests or disease. This certificate requires on-site inspection of the plants during the growing season and is usually provided by the agricultural ministry or department of the country of export.

9. Fumigation Certificate (Generally Issued by a Third-party Independent Testing Company)

This document certifies that wood-based packing materials, used clothing or packaging (i.e. coffee or cocoa bean bags) and certain other commodities have been fumigated or sterilized to kill any pests. These certificates are issued by private companies authorized to carry out these procedures and include details of the specific process, temperature range, chemicals and concentrations used.

10. Veterinary Certificate(Generally Issued by a Third-party Independent Testing Company)

This document certifies that a shipment of live animals, fish, chilled and frozen meats (and sometimes even canned meats) has been inspected for disease.

11. Public Health Certificate (Generally Issued by a Third-party Independent Testing Company)

This document certifies that a shipment has been inspected for disease.

12. ATA Carnet (Generally Issued by a Third-party Independent Testing Company or Government Authority)

An international customs document is used for the temporary duty-free admission of certain goods into a country in lieu of the usual customs documents.

13. Free Sale Certificate (Issued by a Local Chamber of Commerce in the Exporter's Country)

This certifies that certain commodities (i.e. medicines, vitamins, other health products) are freely sold in the country of origin.

1. 专用原产地证书（由托运人/出口商或出口国特别授权机构开立）

这类证书证明装运国属于某个区域性贸易协定的范围之内（如北美自由贸易区原产地证书）。

2. 海关担保（由保险公司签发）

这类证书证明保险公司已经就某个特定批次进口货物向进口国当局出具财务担保。

3. 包装声明书（由托运人/出口商或货运代理签发）

这类单证证明包装材料无虫害。

4. 已证实的领事发票（由驻出口国的最终目的国领事馆签发或证实）

这类单证证明原产国、货物描述和价值。

5. 保险单证

这类单证是货物已被投保的证明。

6. 检验证书（一般由第三方独立的检验机构签发）

这类单证证明产品的质量、数量或符合某些特定的规格。由于某些国家的进口商广泛使用一些技术来规避外汇管制（如多报数量或低报价值），因此这些国家当局要求提供检验证书，作为一种控制手段。进口许可证通常要求在货物清关或者付款前由官方检验机构出具清洁检验报告。

7. 品质证书（由独立的检验机构签发）

这类单证证明装运货物满足进口国标准。大多数国家要求，这类证书应在装运前由出口商提供，由相应的政府管理机构批准和存档（如出口国的消费者安全部门）。

8. 植物检疫证明（一般由第三方独立的检验机构签发）

这类单证证明所进口的植物或植物产品（如种子、鳞茎、花朵、水果、蔬菜等）无虫害或无疾病。要签发这类证书，必须在植物的生长季节做现场检验，通常由出口国的农业部门提供。

9. 熏蒸证书（一般由第三方独立的检验机构签发）

这类单证证明木质材料的包装；二手服装或包装（如咖啡或可可豆袋子）和某些特定的其他商品已经被熏蒸消毒，产品上携带的害虫已被杀死。这类证书由被授权实施熏蒸程序的私营企业签发，证书上包括具体程序、温度范围、使用的化学制剂和浓聚物等内容。

10. 兽医证书（一般由第三方独立的检验机构签发）

这类单证证明所装运的活动物、鱼、冻肉（有时包括罐装肉）已经通过检验，不携带病菌。

11. 公共卫生证书（一般由第三方独立的检验机构签发）

这类单证证明所装运货物已经通过检验，不携带病菌。

12. 临时进口证（一般由第三方独立的检验机构或政府机构签发）

临时进口证是某些特定商品申请临时免税入境时使用的、可替代其他海关单证的国际海关文件。

13. 自由销售证书（由出口国本地商会签发）

这类单证证明某些特定商品（如药品、维生素和其他保健品）在原产国是允许自由销售的。

7.5 Special Import Transport Documents 特殊的进口运输单证

Special transport documents may be issued in place of a standard ocean bill of lading, used to notify the carrier and import authorities of special or dangerous cargo, or be prepared to certain transactions between the carrier and the consignor or consignee.

1. Special Bill of Lading

For example, the importer, in a letter of credit, may require presentation of an "air waybill" as proof of shipment by air.

2. Shipping Instructions (Generally Issued by the Consignor/Shipper /Exporter, but often at the Request of the Importer/Buyer/Consignee)

This form gives specific instructions to the shipping company about how to handle a shipment. The bill of lading is typically drawn up from this information.

3. Stowage Instructions (Issued by the Consignor/Shipper/Exporter)

This form gives specific instructions to the shipping line about how and where to stow cargo during transport and is typically used when shipping hazardous, oversize, fragile, live or other unusual cargo.

特殊的运输单证可以代替标准海运提单，用以通知承运人和进口国当局所装运货物为特殊货物或危险品，或用以证明承运人与收货人之间或承运人与托运人之间的某些交易。

1. 特殊提单

例如，信用证中的进口商要提交"航空运单"作为空运证明。

2. 装运指示（一般由发货人/托运人/出口商签发，但通常以进口商/买方/收货人的要求为前提）

这类单证向装运公司提供了装运的详细指示。提单一般以此说明为基础缮制。

3. 装载指示（由发货人/托运人/出口商签发）

这类单证向船公司提供货物运输的详细装载指示，一般用于危险货物、超大货物、易碎货物、活动物或其他非常规商品。

7.6 Banking and International Exchange Documents
银行单证和外汇单证

The importer's contact with banks is determined principally by the terms of payment agreed to with the exporter/seller. If the terms are payment in advance by cash, check, wire-transfer, or credit card, or on open account with future payment by cash, check, wire-transfer, or credit card, the importer's only contact with the banks will be to write a bank check, to have the bank send a wire transfer of funds to the exporter, or to process a credit card payment.

However, if a documentary collection or documentary letter of credit is used as the payment mechanism, much greater involvement with the bank is required.

进口商与银行的联系方式主要由进出口双方同意的付款条件决定。如果采用现金、支票、银行电汇或信用卡等方式预付货款或远期支付，那么进口商与银行的业务联系只包括填写支票、让银行向出口商电汇货款或使用信用卡支付。

然而，如果使用跟单托收或跟单信用证的方式，那么进口商与银行有更多的业务往来。

7.6.1 Electronic Filing of Documents
电子填单

Increasingly, customs documents are required to be filed electronically. Many systems are now in place whereby the same electronic document format may be used for exporting/importing between dozens of different countries. This standardization is proving to be of great benefit to the international trader.

目前，使用电子系统填制海关单证的比例逐渐增加。有几十个国家之间的进出口贸易单证查验系统已被电子系统代替。电子系统已被证明能给国际贸易商人带来极大便利。

7.6.2 Import Document Assistance/ Customs Brokers
辅助的进口单证/报关行

Import documentation can be extremely simple or exceedingly complex. Many importers rely upon the services of a customs broker for assistance. Even importers whose goal is to handle all import documents internally often rely upon these professionals until they become well versed in import requirements for their range of commodities.

If you do use a customs broker, you will be required to sign a LIMITED POWER OF ATTORNEY. This gives your customs broker the right to act on your behalf with the customs authority and to sign customs documents in your name.

　　进口单证可以很简单，也可以很复杂。很多进口商在报关领域主要依赖报关行的服务。即使那些希望独立处理单证的进口商也经常依赖专业报关行的服务，除非他们已对相关商品进口手续的要求非常熟悉。

　　如果你选择使用报关行服务，那么你需要在"有限授权委托书"上签字。这份委托书将授权相应的报关行以你的名义在海关办理相关手续和签署报关单证。

Chapter 8
Banking Documents
银行单证

8.1 Method of Payment
支付方式

Because international trade always involves the transfer of money between different business entities in different national jurisdictions using different currencies, banks are almost always involved and so are the all-important banking documents. In fact, documents is so much a part of the process that banks refer to them as documentary transaction. Bankers rely upon these packets of paper because they spell out every nuance of who, what, where, when and how much money will be paid.

Depending upon the method of payment, bank documentation can be minimal or extremely complex.

由于国际贸易的资金转移通常在不同国度的商业实体之间进行，而且通常涉及不同币种，因此一般需要通过银行办理，所以银行单证就变得非常重要。事实上，单证处理在业务中的分量很重，以至于银行通常将国际贸易称为单证买卖。银行的付款取决于这些单证，因为它们能明确说明付款的对象、内容、地点、时间和金额。

因付款方式的差异，银行的单证业务有简单的也有复杂的。

8.1.1 Prepaid/Cash-in-Advance/Cash with Order
预付 / 预付现金 / 订货付现

Prepaid terms are common, especially where the transaction value is not great or where the importer/buyer trusts the exporter/seller sufficiently to prepay for the shipment. Obviously, this is the best arrangement for the exporter/seller.

This is the most straightforward international transaction where the buyer negotiates the purchase of goods and prepays with cash, bank wire transfer, credit card, travelers' checks or perhaps even a personal or business check. The importer/buyer either picks up the goods on the spot, or they are shipped after payment has been received. In this case, the banks are hardly involved other than cashing a check, handling a bank wire transfer, arranging for traveler's checks or processing a credit card payment.

预付货款的现象很普遍，尤其在交易金额不高或进口商/买方非常信任出口商/卖方的情况下。很明显，对出口商/卖方来说，这是最好的付款方式。

同时，这也是国际贸易中最直接的付款方式。买方与卖方谈好购买事项后即用现金、银行电汇、信用卡或旅行支票的方式预付货款，有时也使用个人或公司支票。进口商/买方要么当场提货，要么允许卖方收到货款后再发货。在这种情况下，银行的业务只包括支票付现、办理电汇、处理旅行支票或办理信用卡支付。

8.1.2 Open Account
赊销

Open account terms are also common, especially where the exporter/seller sufficiently trusts that the importer/buyer will pay for the shipment at a later date. Obviously, this is the best arrangement for the importer/buyer.

On open credit terms, the exporter/seller ships goods to the importer/buyer on the expectation that payment will be made at a set future date. This can be 30, 60, 90 or even 180 or 360 days after shipment. Payment on the due date may still be made by cash, bank wire transfer, credit card, traveler's checks or even a personal or business check.

赊销方式也很普遍，尤其在出口商/卖方充分信任进口商/买方的情况下，即允许进口商/买方在货物装运后的一段时间内再付款。很明显，这对进口商/买方来说，是最好的付款方式。

在赊销条件下，出口商/卖方将货物装运给进口商/买方，并且相信进口商/买方会在未来的某个日期付款。这个日期有可能是装运后的 30 天、60 天、90 天甚至 180 天或 360 天。到期付款时，支付的方式有现金、银行电汇、信用卡、旅行支票、个人或公司支票。

8.1.3 Documentary of Credit
信用证

In a documentary collection transaction, the seller uses banks as intermediaries to ensure that the documents conveying title to the shipment are not transferred to the buyer until payment (or a suitable promise of payment) has been made. It is a "documentary" collection because documents form the basis of the procedure.

Documentary collection transaction requires a great deal of documentation.

在跟单托收交易中，卖方委托银行保证在买方付款(或做出合适的付款承诺)前不能将代表货物装运的单证交给买方。由于单证是履行程序的基础，因此此类托收称为"跟单"托收。

跟单托收交易中需要的单证数量较多。

8.1.4 Documentary Letters of Credit
跟单信用证

In a letter of credit transaction, the buyer uses banks as intermediaries to ensure that payment to the seller is made only after certain terms and conditions have been met. All the terms and conditions involve presentation of documents. This is why the technical name for this procedure is "documentary letter of credit."

在信用证交易中，买方委托银行保证仅在信用证的所有条款和条件都得到满足时才付款。所有的条款和条件都与交单相关。这就是为什么其有一个专门的名称"跟单信用证"。

8.2 International Banking Documents
国际银行单证

8.2.1 Documentary Collection Payment Documents
跟单托收付款单证

1. Documentary Collection Order

The collection order is the key document prepared by the seller specifying the terms and conditions of the documentary collection. It must be prepared with care and precision because banks are permitted to act only upon the instructions given.

The following are the key provisions of the collection order:

(1) The payment type and period as agreed with the buyer.

(2) The name and address of the buyer.

(3) The buyer's bank.

(4) Instructions, if any, about what to do with the accepted bill of exchange.

(5) Notation concerning payment of charges for the documentary collection.

(6) Instructions for the lodging of a protest in the event of non acceptance or nonpayment.

(7) Instructions for notification of agent or representative in the buyer's country.

1. 跟单托收委托书

托收委托书是卖方缮制的单证中非常重要的一项，是说明跟单托收的条款和条件的单证。由于它是银行执行托收手续的指示，因此委托书的缮制必须谨慎和精确。

以下是托收委托书中包含的主要条款。

(1) 买方同意的付款方式和期限。

(2) 买方的名称和地址。

(3) 买方银行。

(4) 如有指示，应说明汇票被承兑后应如何处理。

(5) 标注跟单托收的手续费支付情况。

(6) 买方拒绝承兑或拒付后的处理办法。

(7) 向卖方驻买方国家的代理或代表发出通知的指示。

2. A Sample of Collection Order 托收委托书样本

Sender					Documentary Collection Place/Date_____			
Our Reference We send you herewith the following documents for collection.					**Registered** ×××× Bank Corporation Documentary collections P.O. Box _____			
Amount			**Notify**		**Drawee**			
					Drawee's bank			
Draft/ Receipt	Invoice		Insurance Certificate	Certificate of Origin	Weight/ Packing List	Bill of Lading	Waybill	Postal/ Forward Receipt	Other Documents
	Commercial	Custom/ Consular							
Goods: By: Please follow the instructions marked "X"									
Documents/goods to be delivered against ☐ payment ☐ acceptance			Draft ☐ to be sent back after acceptance			State the exact due-data ☐ to be collected on due-data		
☐ **Your charges for drawee's account if refused**					☐ waive charges	☐ do not deliver documents		
☐ **Your correspondent's charges are for drawee's account if refused**					☐ waive charges	☐ do not deliver documents		
☐ Protest in case of	☐ non-payment		non-acceptance		☐ do not protest in case of	☐ non-payment		☐ non-acceptance
☐ Advise	☐ non-payment		☐ non-acceptance		☐ by airmail	☐ by cable		☐ giving reasons

Please credit the proceeds as follows:
☐ to our _____ account for _____
☐ remit to

Remarks：

(1) In case of difficulties，the collecting bank is requested to inform our representatives：Messrs. Beach & Co. Inc.，Broad Street 485，New York 34，who will be of assistance but who is not allowed to alter the above instructions.

(2) Negotiable bill of lading

(3) Document package for the importer/buyer

(4) Draft/bill of exchange

Signature：_____

8.2.2 Documentary Letter of Credit Payment Documents 跟单信用证支付单证

(1) Letter of credit(L/C) application (see Sample 8-1).

(2) Letter of credit(L/C).

(3) Letter of credit(L/C) advice/notification.

(4) Request for amendment(to the letter of credit).

(5) Amendment (to the letter of credit).

(6) Amendment notification (to the letter of credit).

(7) Negotiable bill of lading.

(8) Document package for the importer/buyer (prepared by the exporter). This is the group of documents that the exporter prepares for the importer and that are needed to secure the shipment from the carrier and clear customs in the country of import. At the least，this includes a commercial invoice and a certificate of origin，but may also include inspection，insurance and other documents. Technically，the negotiable bill of lading is part of the document package.

(9) Draft/bill of exchange.

(1) 信用证申请书（见样单 8-1）。

(2) 信用证。

(3) 信用证通知书。

(4) (信用证) 修改要求。

(5) (信用证) 修改函。

(6) (信用证) 修改通知书。

(7) 可转让提单。

(8) (出口商) 为进口商 / 买方准备的文件包。这是出口商为进口商准备的单证组合，用以说明货物已在承运人处装运并已办理进口国清关手续。这些单证至少包括商业发票和原产地证书，另外还有可能包括检验证书、保险单证和其他单证。严格来说，可转让提单也是文件包的一部分。

(9) 汇票。

8.3 Drafts, Bills of Exchange and Acceptances
汇票和承兑汇票

1. Drafts

The most common versions of drafts are : ①sight drafts which are payable when presented ; ②time drafts (usance drafts) which are payable at a future fixed (specific) date or determinable (e.g.30 days, 60 days, 90 days) date.

2. Acceptances

An acceptance is a time draft that has been accepted and signed by the drawee (the buyer or the bank) for payment at maturity. If a time draft is accepted by a buyer of merchandise, it is called a trade acceptance. If a time draft is accepted by a bank, it is called a banker's acceptance.

In most cases, obviously, a draft accepted by a bank enjoys higher credit standing than a draft accepted by a company or individual, since a bank is presumed to meet its obligation at maturity, and a company or individual in an International country may not as readily comply with its obligation.

3. Holding or Discounting Acceptances

In documentary transactions, the seller has two options, once its time draft is accepted. The seller may either hold it until maturity and collect full face value, or discount the draft, most likely with the accepting bank, and take the net value in cash immediately. In these ways, trade and bankers' acceptances often represent the easiest, least expensive way for a seller to provide credit to a buyer, while enjoying the security provided by the documentary transaction.

4. Financing Transactions Using Acceptances

International buyers may indicate that they wish to provide a "time" documentary credit (rather than a "sight" documentary credit). In the case of a time documentary credit, the buyer may agree to allow the seller to increase the sales price slightly in order to offset the acceptance commission and discount costs.

In most cases, the buyer and the buyer's bank will absorb the charges involved, and the seller will receive the full contract sales amount. Since the charges are usually lower than conventional financing charges, the buyer is still better off than if financing had been obtained through a traditional bank loan.

5. "Clean" Acceptance

A "Clean" acceptance is one that does not have any notations attached that would compromise its value. In a trade acceptance, the customer promises to pay the bank the full amount of the draft no later than the date of maturity, or upon demand of the bank. The accepted draft, when discounted, becomes a negotiable instrument that can be sold in the acceptance market, which is an over-the-counter market of brokers, dealers, and banks.

Bankers' acceptances are generally short-term (up to 80 days). Bankers' acceptances become money market instruments once they are accepted by a major bank, which means that the bank has undertaken to honor the note at its maturity. Because of this characteristic, bankers' acceptances often result in lower financing costs. The difference can range from 1 to 3 percent depending on the transaction and the bank involved. Thus they are important sources of financing.

1. 汇票

最普遍的版本包括：①即期汇票，即提示后立刻付款；②远期汇票，即在未来某个具体的日期或未来某个时间段（如 30 天、60 天、90 天）后付款。

2. 承兑汇票

承兑汇票是已由受票人（买方或银行）承兑和签字，以保证到期付款的汇票。被工商企业者承兑的汇票是商业承兑汇票；被银行承兑的汇票是银行承兑汇票。

在大多数情况下，因为银行到期履行义务的可能性更大，银行承兑汇票信用程度明显更高，而国外的公司或个人履行义务的可能性较小。

3. 持有或贴现承兑汇票

在跟单交易中，卖方在汇票承兑后有两个选择。他可以持有汇票直到到期日收取全额款项，或者对汇票进行贴现（一般在承兑行办理），即刻以提现的方式收取汇票的净值。在这种情况下，商业承兑汇票和银行承兑汇票就属于卖方给买方提供的最简易、最便宜的信用，而同时又能享受跟单交易带来的保证。

4. 使用承兑的融资交易

国外买主一般会要求使用"远期"跟单信用的方式（而不是"即期"跟单信用）。在远期跟单信用的情况下，买方有可能同意让卖方稍微提高销售价格，以便抵消承兑和贴现费用。

大多数情况下，相应的费用由买方或买方银行承担，卖方得到的是销售合同的全部金额。但是，这些费用低于传统融资的费用，因此相对于传统的银行贷款，托收方式对买方而言还是比较实惠的。

5. "清洁"承兑汇票

"清洁"承兑汇票是指不附带任何能让票面价值有协商余地的标注的汇票。在商业承兑汇票中，顾客承诺不晚于到期日向银行支付汇票的全部金额，或根据银行的要求支付。当承兑汇票被贴现时，它就变成一个可以在承兑市场销售的可转让支付工具（承兑市场是经纪人、经销商和银行的场外市场）。

8.4 Documentary Letters of Credit
跟单信用证

A letter of credit is the written promise of a bank, undertaken on behalf of a buyer, to pay a seller the amount specified in the credit provided the seller complies with the terms and conditions set forth in the credit. The terms and conditions of a documentary credit revolve around two issues: ①the presentation of documents that evidence title to goods shipped by the seller; ②payment.

In simple terms, banks act as intermediaries to collect payment from the buyer in exchange for the transfer of documents that enable the holder to take possession of the goods.

Letter of credit (L/C) is the historic and popular term used. However, the formal term is "documentary" letter of credit because of the importance of documents in the transaction.

信用证是银行以进口商的名义向卖方开立的书面承诺，只要卖方满足信用证上规定的条款和条件，银行即向卖方支付信用证规定的金额。跟单信用证的条款和条件主要围绕两个主题：①提交证明货物由出口商装运的单证；②付款。

简单地说，银行以中间人的身份向买方收取货款，作为向其交付可作提货凭证的单证的条件。

信用证是具有时代意义的、很受欢迎的支付方式。然而，由于单证在业务中非常重要，因此它的正式名称是"跟单"信用证。

8.4.1 Revocable, Irrevocable Letters of Credit
可撤销信用证和不可撤销信用证

A revocable letter of credit gives the buyer and /or issuing bank the ability to amend or cancel the credit at any time right up to the moment of intended payment without approval by, or notice to the seller. Revocable letters of credit are, therefore, of great advantage to the buyer.

An irrevocable letters of credit constitutes credit as issued. A firm contractual obligation on the part of the issuing bank to honor the terms of payment of the credit as issued. The buyer and issuing bank cannot amend or cancel the credit without the express approval of the seller. Irrevocable credits are of advantage to the seller. Virtually, all documentary credits issued are irrevocable and so state on their face.

可撤销信用证是指买方和/或开证行在付款前，可在未取得卖方同意或未通知卖方的情况下在任何时间修改或取消的信用证。因此，可撤销信用证对买方比较有利。

不可撤销信用证是指信用证开立之后，其支付条款就以正式合同条款的形式对开证行付款行为产生约束力。未得到卖方同意，买方和开证行都没有修改或取消信用证的权利。不可撤销信用证对卖方有利。事实上所有的跟单信用证都是不可撤销的,当然,信用证的表面也有相应说明。

8.4.2 Confirmed, Unconfirmed Letters of Credit
保兑信用证和不保兑信用证

Payment under an irrevocable letter of credit is guaranteed by the issuing bank. However, from the seller's perspective, this guarantee may have limited value as the issuing bank may be: ①in an International country; ②beholden to the buyer; ③small and unknown to the seller; ④subject to unknown International exchange control restrictions. The seller, therefore, might wish that another bank, a local one, adds its guarantee (confirmation) of payment to that of the issuing bank.

Unconfirmed letters of credit: In this form of letters of credit, only the issuing bank assumes the undertaking to pay, thus payment is the sole responsibility of the issuing bank.

Confirmed letters of credit: In this form of letters of credit, both the issuing and confirming banks carry the commitment to pay the seller.

The most popular letter of credit for sellers is the irrevocable confirmed letter of credit because it cannot be cancelled by the buyer, and a second bank (usually the seller's bank) adds its guarantee of payment to that of the buyer's bank.

不可撤销信用证的付款行为由开证行担保。然而,从卖方的角度来说,如果开证行有以下情况:①在另一个国家;②与买方来往较紧密;③是一个名不见经传的小银行;④受到未知外汇管制的约束,那么保证的程度是有限的。卖方就希望能有另一家银行,一般来说是本地的,能对信用证的开证行付款责任进行担保(保兑)。

不保兑信用证:在这类信用证项下,只有开证行承担付款责任,也就是说,付款是开证行自己的责任。

保兑信用证:在这类信用证项下,开证行和保兑行一起承担付款责任。

不可撤销保兑信用证是最受卖方欢迎的信用证,因为信用证开出后买方就不能取消,同时又得到第二家银行(通常是卖方银行)对买方银行付款行为的担保。

8.4.3 Special Documentary Letters of Credit
特殊跟单信用证

(1) Revolving credit: This is a commitment on the part bank to restore the credit to the original amount after it has been used or drawn down.

(2) Red clause credit: This credit has a special (red) clause that authorizes the confirming bank to make advances to the seller prior to the presentation of the shipping documents, in essence, extending pre-shipment financing to the seller.

(3) Transferable credit: In this credit, the original beneficiary transfers all or part of the proceeds of an existing credit to another party (typically the ultimate supplier of the goods). It is normally used by brokers as a financing tool.

(4) Back-to-back credit: This is a new credit opened on the basis of an already existing, nontransferable credit. It is used by traders to make payment to the ultimate supplier. A trader receives a credit from the buyer and then opens another in favor of the supplier. The first credit is used as collateral for the second credit. The second credit makes price adjustments from which comes the trader's profit.

(1) 循环信用证：原始金额被使用之后又自动恢复的信用证。

(2) 红条款信用证：信用证上有一个特别的红条款，授权保兑行在卖方提交货运单证前预付货款，这种条款事实上是特别给予卖方的装运前融资。

(3) 可转让信用证：在这类信用证项下，第一受益人可以将信用证的全部或部分转让给另一方(通常是实际供货人)使用。它通常是中间商融资的手段。

(4) 背对背信用证：这是信用证的新种类，是在已开立的、不可转让的信用证基础上开立的。它是贸易商向实际供货商支付货款的工具。贸易商从买方那里收到信用证之后，再开立一份以实际供货商为受益人的信用证。第一份信用证是第二份信用证的担保。为了从中获益，贸易商将对第二份信用证的价格进行调整。

8.4.4　Role of Banks
　　　　银行的角色

(1) In a documentary credit, banks act upon specific instructions given by the applicant (buyer) in the documentary credit application. Buyer's instructions left out of the credit by mistake or omitted because "we've always done it that way" don't count. The buyer, therefore, should take great care preparing the application so that it gives complete and clear instructions.

(2) In a documentary collection, banks act upon specific instructions given by the principal (seller) in the collection order. Seller's instructions left out of the collection order by mistake or omitted because "we've always done it that way" don't count. The principal, therefore, should take great care in preparing the collection order so that it gives complete and clear instructions.

(3) Banks are required to act in go faith and exercise reasonable care to verify that the documents submitted appear to be as listed in the letter of credit or collection order. They are, however, under no obligation to confirm the authenticity of the documents submitted.

(4) Banks are not liable for the acts of third parties. Third parties include freight forwarders, agents, customs authorities, insurance companies and other banks. They also are not responsible for delays or consequences resulting from Acts of God (floods, earthquakes,

and etc.), riots, wars, civil commotions, strikes, lockouts, or other causes beyond their control.

(5) Banks also assume no liability or responsibility for loss arising out of delays or loss in transit of message, letters, documents, and etc.

(6) Banks assume no responsibility regarding the quantity or quality of goods shipped. They are only concerned that documents presented appear on their face to be consistent with the instructions in the credit or collection order. Any dispute must be settled between the buyer and the seller.

(7) Without explicit instructions, the banks take no steps to store or insure the goods. This can be a problem for both the seller and the buyer. A seller who has not received payment still has ownership and an insurable interest in the goods.

(8) If a documentary collection remains unpaid or a bill of exchange is not accepted and the collecting bank receives no new instructions with 90 days, it may return the documents to the bank from which it received the collection order.

(9) So long as the documents presented to the banks appear on their face to comply with the terms and conditions of a letter of credit, banks may accept them and initiate the payment process as stipulated in the credit.

(1) 在跟单信用证中，银行根据开证申请人（买方）所提供的开证申请书上的详细指示办理业务。信用证一旦开出即成立，对于申请书中写错或遗漏的内容，买方不可以"我们一贯都是这么做的"之类的理由要求更改。因此，为了保证申请书的指示是完整和清楚的，买方在填写申请书时应非常仔细。

(2) 在跟单托收中，银行根据委托人（卖方）所提供的托收委托书上的详细指示办理业务。委托书一旦被接受即不可更改，对于委托书中写错或遗漏的内容，卖方不可以"我们一贯都是这么做的"之类的理由要求更改。因此，为了保证委托书的指示是完整和清楚的，卖方在填写申请书时应非常仔细。

(3) 银行应该以诚实的态度、合理的方式来核查所收到的单证是否与信用证或托收委托书上所列明的一致。但是，银行不对所收到的单证的真实性负责。

(4) 银行不对第三方的行为所造成的损失负责。第三方包括货运代理、代理商、海关机构、保险公司和其他银行等。另外，对于延误、不可抗力（洪水、地震等）、暴动、战争、骚乱、罢工、封锁或其他不在控制范围内的原因所造成的损失，银行概不负责。

(5) 对于信息、邮件、单证在运送途中的延误或遗失所造成的损失，银行概不负责。

(6) 银行不对所装运货物的数量或质量负责。银行只负责核对所提交单证的表面是否与信用证或托收委托书中的要求一致。除此之外的任何争议都应由买卖双方自行解决。

(7) 若无明确指示，银行不负责存储货物或给货物投保。这对买卖双方来说是个难题。未收到货款的卖方仍然拥有货物的所有权以及保险利益。

(8) 在跟单托收项下，如果代收行在汇票被拒付或被拒绝承兑后的 90 天内得不到任何指示，那么代收行将退还单证给向其发出托收委托的银行。

(9) 只要所提交单证的表面符合信用证上的条款和条件，那么银行就必须接受这些单证并开始办理信用证上规定的付款手续。

8.4.5 Electronic Applications for Documentary Credits
跟单信用证的电子申请书

Electronic application are becoming more and more common. Buyers install software on their office PCs that enable them to fill out an application and send it to their bank's processing center. Security is provided using encryption and password systems. Electronic applications enable the repeat letter of credit applicant faster turnaround and cuts paperwork for everybody.

电子申请书的支付方式正日趋普及。买方先在办公室的计算机上安装相应的软件，然后在计算机上填写开证申请书，并通过网络将申请书传送到银行数据处理中心。该程序的安全通过密码来保证。电子申请使重复申请信用证的申请人工作效率更快，减少了纸质工作。

8.4.6 Contract Provision Sample
合同条款范例

PAYMENT: TO SECURE PAYMENT, THE <u>BUYER</u> SHALL HAVE <u>ISSUING BANK</u> OPEN AN IRREVOCABLE DOCUMENTARY CREDIT NAMING <u>SELLER</u> AS BENEFICIARY.

THE DOCUMENTARY CREDIT IS TO BE <u>CONFIRMED</u> BY <u>CONFIRMING BANK</u>. THE DOCUMENTARY CREDIT MUST REMAIN VALID FOR <u>NUMBER OF MONTHS</u> AFTER ISSUANCE AND BE AVAILABLE <u>AT SIGHT</u> AGAINST PRESENTATION OF THE FOLLOWING DOCUMENTS: 1...2...3...ETC. THE COST OF THE CREDIT IS TO BE PAID BY <u>BUYER NAME</u>. THE CREDIT SHALL BE SUBJECT TO THE UNIFORM CUSTOMS AND PRACTICE FOR DOCUMENTARY CREDITS (2007 REVISION), ICC, PUBLICATION NUMBER 600.

The terms in <u>UNDERLINED CAPITAL LETTERS</u> are the variables.

付款：为了安全支付，<u>买方</u>应当要求<u>开证银行</u>开立一份以<u>卖方</u>为受益人的<u>不可撤销</u>跟单信用证。

跟单信用证<u>由保兑银行确认</u>。跟单信用证开立后必须保证有效期<u>几个月</u>，以下单证一旦提交就立即生效：1……2……3……等。信用证的费用是由<u>买方</u>支付的。信用证须以国际商会 600 号出版物《跟单信用证统一惯例》(2007 年修订本) 为准。

有下画线的字可变化。

8.5 Document Movement for Issuance of a L/C
信用证开立的单证流程

When the two parties of an international trade transaction finalize their deal a sales contract is established. This document is the basis for the importer to apply for a letter of credit. The content should directly or indirectly reflect the details of the sales contract. Upon its coming into force, however, the credit will become a completely separate document from the sales contract. The contractual relationship between the exporter and the importer has no impact on the credit operation what so ever. As a result, the exporter should pay special attention to examining the content of the credit so as to avoid any conflicting items.

Typically a letter of credit contains the following contents: name & address of the opening bank, date of issuance of L/C, number of L/C, credit amount, description of goods, type of L/C, full name & address of the parties concerned, documents that shall be provided, details of shipment, validity period for L/C, settlement instructions, fee clauses and special clause, if any.

At the stage of issuance of a documentary credit, four parties are involved and their relationships are illustrated in Figure 8-1. The procedure any happen in the order as described.

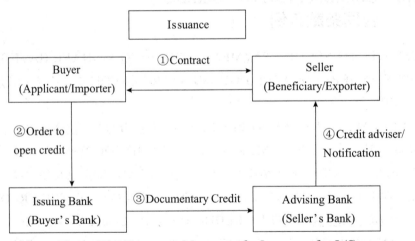

Figure 8-1 Document Movement for Issuance of a L/C

(1) After signing the sales contract with the seller, the buyer will present to his local bank the contract, an application letter and other documents required for the opening of L/C. The importer is the applicant of the credit.

(2) Depending on the buyer's credibility and relationship with the bank, the buyer may or may not be required to pledge a percentage of the value of the credit in cash funds or cash equivalents. The bank then issues the letter of credit to one of its branches or correspondent banks in the seller's country. The importer's local bank becomes the issuing bank of the credit and overseas branch or correspondent bank is the advising bank.

(3) The advising bank will notify the seller of the arrival of the credit. Once paying an advising fee, the seller receives the original of the documentary credit. He has to examine the credit closely before he accepts it.

贸易双方达成交易后会签订一份销售合同。它是开立信用证的基础。其内容应该直接或间接地反映出销售合同的细节。然而，一旦其生效，信用证将成为一个完全独立于销售合同的单证。出口商和进口商之间的合同关系不会影响信用证业务运作。因此，出口商应该特别注意检查信用证的内容，以避免条款冲突。

通常，信用证包含以下内容：开证行的名称和地址、开立信用证日期、信用证号码、信用证金额、物品的描述、信用证的类型、当事人的姓名和地址、应提供的单证、装运细节、信用证有效期、结算指示、费用条款和特殊条款。

在开立跟单信用证阶段，交易四方都要参与，它们的关系如图 8-1 所示。过程顺序如图 8-1 描述。

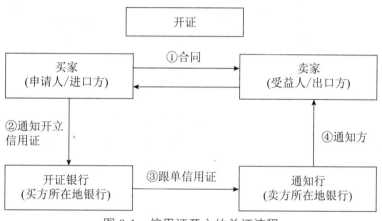

图 8-1　信用证开立的单证流程

(1) 与卖方签订销售合同后，买方将向他的当地银行提交合同、申请书和其他开立信用证的必要文件。进口商是信用证的开证申请人。

(2) 根据买方的信誉和与银行的关系，买方可能需要也可能不需要提供一定比例的信贷现金基金或现金等价物。然后，银行开立信用证给在卖方所在国的通知行。进口商的本地银行成为开立信用证的银行，其海外分行或代理行成为通知行。

(3) 通知行将通知卖方信用证的到达。一旦支付通知费，卖方就会收到正本跟单信用证。在接受之前，卖方必须仔细检查信用证。

8.6　Document Movement for Amendment to a L/C 信用证修改的单证流程

Due to its emphasis on the importance of documents, when the exporter receives a credit, it is crucial for him to inspect it thoroughly and carefully. If the beneficiary finds mistakes or terms and conditions which do not comply with the contract of sale, or he cannot fulfill in the future, he must contact the applicant and request for amendment of the credit without delay. If the applicant agrees to do so, a similar process as issuing a credit will be carried out again, until the beneficiary receives the amendment of credit from the same advising bank. Figure 8-2 shows the document movement for amendment to a L/C.

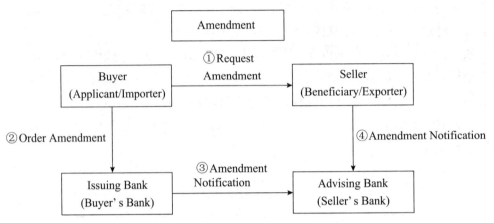

Figure 8-2　Document Movement for Amendment to a L/C

由于强调单证的重要性，当出口商接收信用证时，应仔细检查，这点非常重要。如果受益人发现信用证有误或条款和条件与销售合同不符，或他在未来不能履行合同义务，就必须联系申请人并要不延误地请求修正信用证。如果申请人同意这样做，类似开立信用证的过程将再次进行，直到受益人收到来自相同通知行的信用证修改书。信用证修改的单证转移流程如图 8-2 所示。

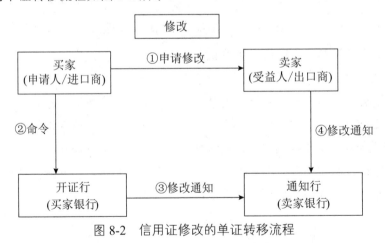

图 8-2　信用证修改的单证转移流程

8.7　Opening a Documentary Credit
　　　　开立跟单信用证

The documentary credit should not require documents that the seller cannot obtain;

nor should it call for details in a document that are beyond the knowledge of the issuer of the document. The documents specified should be limited to those required to smoothly and completely conclude an international sale of goods.

跟单信用证不应要求卖方提供其无法提供的单证，也不应要求单证提供超越单证签发人知识范围的内容。信用证规定的单证应该限于有助于国际贸易顺利完成的范围。

8.8 Document and Goods Movement for Utilization of a L/C
信用证下单证和货物的流转

Figure 8-3 shows the document and goods movement for utilization of a L/C.

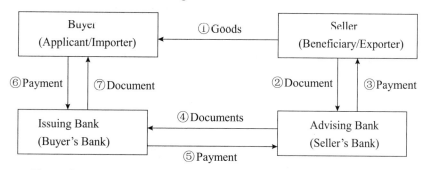

Figure 8-3　Document and Goods Movement for Utilization of a L/C

1. Irrevocable Straight Documentary Credit

Advantage/disadvantage：It is of greatest advantage to the buyer who does not incur a liability to pay the seller until his own bank reviews the documents.

Engagement clause：①We hereby engage with you that each draft drawn and presented to us under and in compliance with the terms of this documentary credit will be duly honored by us. ②This credit is subject to the Uniform Custom and Practice for Documentary Credits (2007 Revision)，International Chamber of Commerce，Publication Number 600，and engages us in accordance with the terms thereof.

2. Irrevocable Negotiation Documentary Credit

Advantage/disadvantage：this form of credit is of advantage to the seller who does not have to wait until the buyer's bank reviews the documents to get the credit paid.

Engagement clause：①Credit available with any bank，by negotiation for payment of beneficiary's draft at sight... ②This credit is subject to the Uniform Custom and Practice for Documentary Credits (2007 Revision)，International Chamber of Commerce，Publication Number 600，and engages us in accordance with the terms thereof.

3. Irrevocable Unconfirmed Documentary Credit

Advantage/disadvantage: There is a slight advantage to the buyer as the buyer is typically responsible for paying the documentary credit fees. Since confirmation incurs a fee, the buyer would have a small savings.

Engagement clause: ①This credit is subject to the Uniform Custom and Practice for Documentary Credits (2007 Revision), International Chamber of Commerce, Publication Number 600, and engages us in accordance with the terms thereof. ②the enclosed advice is sent to you without confirmation.

4. Irrevocable Confirmed Documentary Credit

Advantage/disadvantage: This is the most secure credit for the seller because it adds the guarantee of a second (and usually local) bank to that of the issuing bank. Confirmation by a second bank is the equivalent of added insurance, and insurance costs money, so this form of credit is more costly.

Engagement clause: ①This credit is subject to the Uniform Custom and Practice for Documentary Credits (2007 Revision), International Chamber of Commerce, Publication Number 600, and engages us in accordance with the terms thereof. ②Confirmation instructions: with confirm, or confirmed.

图 8-3 给出了信用证下单证和货物的流转图。

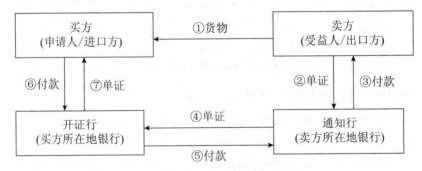

图 8-3　信用证下单证和货物的流转

1. 不可撤销直接付款信用证

优缺点：对买方非常有利，因为买方在其指定银行核查单证之前不需要承担付款责任。

表示文句：①我行保证及时对所有根据本信用证开具并与其条款相符的汇票兑付。②本信用证根据国际商会 2007 年修订本第 600 号出版物《跟单信用证统一惯例》开立，我行受信用证条款的约束。

2. 不可撤销议付跟单信用证

优缺点：这类信用证对卖方有利，因为卖方在买方银行审核单证之前即可得到货款。

表示文句：①信用证在任何银行都可以根据受益人的即期汇票议付……②本信用证根据国际商会 2007 年修订本第 600 号出版物《跟单信用证统一惯例》开立，我行受信用证条款的约束。

3. 不可撤销不保兑跟单信用证

优缺点：对买方稍有利，因为信用证相关费用通常由买方承担，在不保兑情况下，买方可省去一笔费用。

表示文句：①本信用证根据国际商会 2007 年修订本第 600 号出版物《跟单信用证统一惯例》开立，我行受信用证条款的约束。②附件中的通知已在未保兑的情况下发送给你方。

4. 不可撤销保兑跟单信用证

优缺点：它是对卖方最有保障的信用证，因为有另一家银行（一般是本地的）对信用证的开证行付款责任进行担保。第二家银行的保兑相当于额外的保险，这种保险不是免费的，因此它是昂贵的信用证。

表示文句：①本信用证根据国际商会 2007 年修订本第 600 号出版物《跟单信用证统一惯例》开立，我行受信用证条款的约束；②保兑指示：保兑或受保兑。

8.9 Discrepancies with Documents 单证不符点

If a bank involved in the transaction finds discrepancies in the documents, it has several options.

(1) The advising or confirming bank can refuse to accept the documents and return them to the seller (beneficiary) so that they can be corrected or replaced.

(2) The issuing bank, if it feels the discrepancy is not material to the transaction, can ask the buyer (applicant) for a waiver for the specific discrepancy, but must do so within seven banking days.

(3) The advising or confirming bank can remit the documents under approval to the issuing bank for settlement.

(4) The issuing or confirming bank can return the incorrect documents directly to the seller for correction or replacement and eventual return directly to the issuing or confirming bank.

(5) The confirming bank can proceed with payment to the seller but require a guarantee from the seller for reimbursement if the issuing bank does not honor the documents as presented.

If there is a discrepancy, the buyer and seller must communicate directly and then inform the banks of their decision. In the case of serious discrepancies, an amendment to the credit may be necessary.

The seller may request the opening bank to present the documents to the buyer on a collection basis. However, the buyer may refuse to accept the documents/merchandise.

如果银行发现单证的不符点，通常有以下选择。

(1) 通知行或保兑行拒绝接受单证并将其退还给出口商 (受益人)，以便于受益人修改或更换单证。

(2) 如果开证行认为不符点对交易影响不大，那么它可以请买方 (开证申请人) 放弃不符点，但是这个选择必须在 7 个银行工作日内做出。

(3) 通知行或保兑行可以在得到同意的情况下将单证寄给开证行结汇。

(4) 通知行或保兑行可以将不正确的单证直接退还给出口商，要求其更正或替换，最后出口商直接将单证寄给开证行或保兑行。

(5) 保兑行可以办理付款手续，但是卖方必须出具保函，担保如果开证行拒付货款，卖方将承担偿付责任。

出现不符点时，买卖双方必须直接沟通并将他们的决定通知银行。如果不符点非常严重，则需要修改信用证。

卖方可能会要求开证行以托收的形式将单证提示给买方。然而，买方一般会拒绝接受这些单证 / 货物。

8.10 Documentary Collections
跟单托收

Banks act as intermediaries to collect payment from the buyer in exchange for the transfer of documents that enable the holder to take possession of the goods. The procedure is easier than a documentary credit, and the bank charges are lower. The bank, however, does not act as surety of payment but rather only as collector of funds for documents.

银行以中间人的身份向买方收取货款，转让可用作提货凭证的单证。这种方式比跟单信用证简单，银行费用也更低。然而，虽然银行有凭付款交付单证的义务，但并不承担保证买方付款的责任。

8.11 Documentary Collections and Documentary Credits
跟单托收和跟单信用证

There are two major differences between a collection and a letter of credit: ①The draft involved is not drawn by the seller (the drawer) upon a bank for payment, but rather on the buyer (the drawee); ②The seller's bank has no obligation to pay upon presentation, but more simply, acts as a collecting or remitting bank on behalf of the seller, thus earning a commission for its services.

The presenting (collecting) bank reviews the documents, making certain that they are in conformity with the collection order. Goods are transported, stored, and insured at the expense and risk of the seller until payment or acceptance occurs.

跟单托收和跟单信用证有两个主要区别：①相关的汇票不是由卖方（出票人）开给银行，而是由买方（受票人）；②卖方银行没有见票即付的义务，而是以代收行或托收行的身份代表卖方收取货款，并收取相应的服务费用。

代收行应审核单证，保证单证与托收委托书的规定一致。在买方付款或承兑前，卖方承担货物装运、存储和投保的费用和风险。

8.12 Documents and Goods Movement in a Documentary Collection 跟单托收下单证和货物的流转

Using this method, the exporter ships the goods and arranges with his bank for the documents (invoices, bills of lading, the insurance policy or certificate and other documents of movement), often together with a bill of exchange, to be dispatched to an appropriate overseas correspondent bank. Depending on the instructions from the exporter and the terms of his contract with the buyer, the documents are only released upon either payment, or acceptance of the bill of exchange, by the importer. The specific transaction steps are as follows (see Figure 8-4).

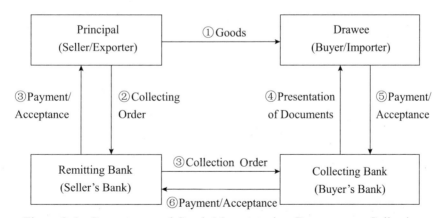

Figure 8-4 Documents and Goods Movement in a Documentary Collection

(1) The exporter ships the goods to the importer as agreed in the sales contract and obtains documents of title from the shipping line.

(2) The exporter submits documents/a draft drawn on the importer to his bank/the remitting bank, and written instructions governing the collection, and document of title (i.e. a complete set of clean, shipped on board bills of lading made out to order and blank endorsed),

and other relevant documents (insurance policy or certificate of CIF).

(3) The remitting bank sends documents, draft, and collection order to the collecting/presenting bank in the importer's country which notifies the importer.

(4) If the instruction is D/P, the importer pays the face amount of the draft plus any charges the importer is responsible for, as stated in the collection order, and the collecting/presenting bank releases the documents. If the instruction are D/A, the collecting/presenting bank will release the documents against acceptance of the draft by the importer.

(5) The collecting bank deducts its fee and sends the importer's payment to the remitting bank for credit to the exporter's account for the face value of the draft minus any fees and charges for which the exporter is responsible.

The above transaction flow indicates that the collection procedure is chronological. The banks in a documentary collection transaction do not act until the preceding steps have been completed. This means that the exporter does not receive payment until his or her bank has received the funds from its correspondent, the overseas collecting bank.

使用这种方法，出口国装运货物并准备银行单证（发票、提单、保险单或证书或者其他单证），这些单证往往连同汇票被寄送到合适的海外通知行。根据出口商指示和与买方签订合同的相关条款，这些单证仅仅是进口商支付或接受汇票的凭证。具体的步骤如下（如图 8-4 所示）。

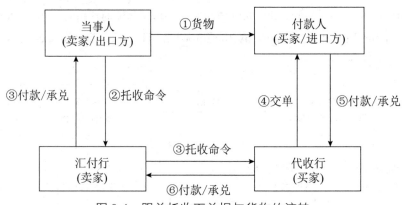

图 8-4　跟单托收下单据与货物的流转

(1) 出口国根据销售合同约定把货物装运给进口商，并且获得船公司的货物装运单证。

(2) 出口商向银行提交以进口国为抬头的汇票、有关托收的书面指示和货物单证（即凭指示和空白背书的一套完整清洁已装船提单），和其他相关的单证 (CIF 保险单或保险凭证）。

(3) 付款行发送单据、汇票和托收单给进口商所在国的托收/承兑行，并通知进口商。

(4) 如果是付款交单，进口商支付汇票面值加上任何其负责支付的费用后托收行/承兑行将放单。如果是承兑交单，托收行/承兑行将在进口商接受汇票后放单。

(5) 代收行扣除其费用并把汇票面值款减去进口商需支付的任何费用的进口商付款打到汇付行出口商账户上。

上述交易流程表明托收过程是按时间顺序排列的。在跟单托收下，前面的步骤已经完成后银行才作为。这意味着出口商只有它所在地的银行收到通知行、托收行的资金才收到付款。

Chapter 9

Special Documents
特殊单证

9.1 Inspection Documents
检验单证

1. Inspection certificate

See Section 6.3.2.

2. Quality certificate (generally issued by the third-party independent testing companies or government agencies)

This document certifies that the products contained in the shipment meet the standards of the importing country. Most countries require that this certification be provided by the exporter and be approved and filed by the appropriate governmental control agency (i.e. the exporting country Department of Consumer Safety) prior to shipment.

3. Phytosanitary certificate (generally issued by the third-party independent testing companies or government agencies)

This document certifies that a shipment of plants or plant products (i.e. seeds, bulbs, flowers, fruits, vegetables, and etc.) is free from pests or disease. This certificate may require on-site inspection during the growing season and is usually provided by the agricultural ministry of the country of export. In some instances, the certificate may be provided by an authorized private company.

4. Fumigation certificate (generally issued by the third-party independent testing companies or government agencies)

This document offers proof that wood-based packing materials, used clothing or packaging (i.e. coffee or cocoa bean bags), and certain other commodities have been fumigated or sterilized to kill any pest. These certificates are issued by private companies authorized to carry out these procedures and include details of the specific process, temperature range, chemicals and concentrations used.

5. Veterinary certificate (generally issued by the third-party independent testing companies or government agencies)

This document certifies that a shipment of live animals or fresh, chilled or frozen meats (and sometimes canned meats) has been inspected for disease.

6. Public health certificate (generally issued by the third-party independent testing companies or government agencies)

This document certifies that a shipment has been inspected for disease.

1. 检验证书

参阅 6.3.2 节。

2. 质量证书（一般由第三方独立检验公司或政府代理机构出具）

此证书证明装运的货物符合进口国标准。大部分国家都要求出口方提供相关政府管理机构(如消费者安全委员会)签署的此证明。

3. 植物检疫证书（一般由第三方独立检验公司或政府代理机构出具）

这个文件证明装运的植物或植物产品(如种子、鳞茎、鲜花、水果、蔬菜等)没有害虫或疾病。一般来说，本证书要求出口国农业部门在作物生长季节进行实地检验。在某些情况下，可能需要提供被授权的私人公司出具的植物检疫证书。

4. 熏蒸证书（一般由第三方独立检验公司或政府代理机构出具）

此证书证明木质包装材料、二手服装或包装(如咖啡或可可豆袋)和其他某些商品都已被烟熏消毒或灭菌。由被授权的私人公司出具此证书，证书内容包括具体细节、温度范围、使用的化学药品和浓度情况。

5. 兽医证明书（一般由第三方独立检验公司或政府代理机构出具）

此证书证明装运的活动物、新鲜肉、冷藏或冷冻肉(有时是罐装肉)已经被检查无疾病。

6. 公共卫生证书（一般由第三方独立检验公司或政府代理机构出具）

此证书证明装运的货物无疾病。

9.2 Insurance
保险

9.2.1 Basic Principles of Insurance
保险的基本原则

(1) Insurable interest: It may pass from party to party during a transaction depending upon the terms of sale.

(2) Utmost good faith: When taking out an insurance policy, the insured must disclose

any "material circumstance" that may influence the judgement of the insurer in establishing a rate (price) for a specific policy.

(3) Indemnity and subrogation: Indemnity means that the insurer will undertake to compensate the insured for any financial loss suffered due to loss or damage. Subrogation is the right of the insurer to collect damages from a negligent third party (i.e. the shipping company or ship's owners), and this right is automatically assigned to the insurer by the insured in the policy.

(1) 保险利益：它取决于销售条款，在交易期间保险利益从一方转到另一方。

(2) 最大诚信原则：当投保时，保险人必须披露"投保物的情况"，这可能影响到保险人对具体某个投保率(价格)的判断。

(3) 赔偿与代位求偿：赔偿是指保险公司将承担被保险人任何由于丢失或损坏造成的投保物的损失。代位求偿是保险人收集来自过失第三方(如船公司或船主)的损失，在保险单里，代位权自动由被保险人分派给保险人。

9.2.2 Types of Insurance
保险种类

1. General Marine Insurance

It is now a general term of insurance for any means of transport. Such coverage is often required when payment is by letter of credit. Different types of policies cover different levels of risks.

Specifically excluded from a Marine Insurance Policy (but often available as supplementary coverage) are losses due to delays, wars, strikes, riots and civil commotions, and unfitness of a vessel, container or conveyance.

Cargo insurance is not available for loss due to misconduct of the insured, ordinary leakage or loss in weight, unsuitable or insufficient packaging, nuclear contamination, and inherent vice (loss due to the inherent nature of the goods such as natural evaporation of water-based products.)

2. Customized Cargo Polices

This coverage may be secured when the nature of the goods excludes their protection under a standard (A, B, C) Marine Insurance Policy. Examples include insurance against product deterioration, refrigeration breakdown, or freezing, insurance for perishable items or time sensitive items, and insurance for equipment that requires special handling.

3. Special Risk Cargo Policies

This coverage is for risk of loss or damage to high-risk cargoes (i.e. computer chips, laptop computers, fine arts, jewelry and antiques). Coverage is also available to high-risk destination and /or for political risk coverage against expropriation, nationalization or confiscation.

4. Open Cargo Policies

These policies are written to cover a number of shipments within a specific time period.

This coverage is also carried by freight forwarders and customs brokers and is made available (for a fee) to their customers for shipments they handle.

5. Export Credit Risk Policies

These policies cover loss due to nonpayment by the importer/buyer. They are often required by the exporter/seller's lender in open account and problematic country of destination transactions. This insurance is often offered by a government or quasi-governmental agency in countries, whose economic and International policy is aligned with the encouragement of exports.

1. 一般海运险

此为一般保险术语，适用于任何交通工具。以信用证作为付款方式时，通常需要投保此险别。不同类型的保险单投保不同的险别。

除外险别（通常可作为附加险别）针对由于延误、战争、罢工、暴乱和内乱、不适用运输工具造成的损失。

货物保险不适用于操作不当、一般渗漏或失重、不恰当或不足包装、核污染、内在缺陷（如水性产品的自然蒸发）造成的损失。

2. 定制的货物保单

在标准海洋保险单下，可投保特定险别使货物免遭损失，如针对产品的变质、制冷故障或冷冻、易腐物品及需要特殊处理的设备的保险。

3. 特殊风险货物保险单

此险别针对高风险货物（如电脑芯片、笔记本电脑、美术品、珠宝、古玩）。此险别也适用于到高风险目的地的货物及/或有政治风险的货物，如货物可能被征用、国有化或者被没收。

4. 预约货物保单

此保险单适用于特定时期大量货物装运的投保。此险别由货运代理人和海关经纪人投保，费用由他们的客户承担。

5. 出口信用保单

此保险单针对由于进口商/买家拖欠付款造成的损失。在往来账户和与有问题的目的国交易时，此保单通常需要由出口商/卖方的贷方提供。本保险适用于鼓励出口的国家政府或国有企业。

9.2.3 Insurance Documents 保险单证

1. Marine Insurance Policy Document (see Sample 6-10)

2. Insurance Certificate

3. Beneficiary Certificate (see Sample 9-3)

4. Customs Bond

A bond is a contractual obligation of an insurance company to insure performance of a principal's obligation as imposed by law or regulation. For example, a US Customs Bond is required by the US Customs Service to ensure payment of all duties associated with an import shipment.

5. The ATE Carnet (Issued by National Chambers of Commerce Affiliated with the Paris-based International Chamber of Commerce (ICC))

This is an international customs document that may be used for the temporary duty-free admission of certain goods into a country (e.g. samples for a trade show, cars for an automobile race, musical instruments for a music concert, and etc.) in lieu of the usual customs documents. Technically, an ATE carnet is a form of insurance or bond. The ATE carnet guarantees that import duties and fees will be paid if the goods are not re-exported within a stated time.

1. 海上保险单（见样单 6-10）

2. 保险凭证

3. 受益人证明（见样单 9-3）

4. 海关担保

担保是保险公司的合同义务，其确保法律或法规规定的委托人义务的实施。例如，美国海关服务部要求海关担保，以确保相关进口货物关税的支付。

5. ATE 通关卡（由设在巴黎的国家商会总部出具）

这是一份国际海关证明，可以用于临时进入某国的免税货物（比如贸易展览品、汽车比赛用的汽车、音乐会乐器等），以代替通常的海关单证。从技术上讲，ATE 通关卡是一张保险单或担保单。在规定的时间内，货物没有复出口的话，它保证支付进口关税和费用。

9.4 Trade Agreement and Trade Preference Documents
贸易协定和贸易优惠单证

1. Certificate of Origin

2. Export/ Import Declaration (see Sample 6-7, Sample 7-2)

The Shipper's Export Declaration(SED) is important because it is the only one of all of the export documents that is filed with the governmental agency. The SED is given to the exporting steamship carrier or air carrier and is filed by them with the Customs Service prior to clearing the port. This document may be prepared by the exporter, or it may be prepared

Chapter 9　Special Documents 特殊单证

by the exporter's agent, the freight forwarder, and the exporter may not see it. Nevertheless, the SED form specifically states that any false statements in the form (which is interpreted to include accidentally false statements as well as intentionally false statements) will subject the exporter to various civil and criminal penalties, including a $10 000 fine and up to five years' imprisonment. Consequently, the exporter has a real interest in making sure that any agent, such as the freight forwarder, prepares the SED correctly and that the information being submitted to the Customs' service is accurate. In that connection, the person preparing the SED is required to certify that he or she has read the instructions set forth in a booklet issued by the Department of Commerce entitled Correct Way to Complete the Shipper's Export Declaration. If the exporter discovers that the Shipper's Export declaration which it or its freight forwarder has prepared is inaccurate, it should file an amended declaration at the same port as the original export.

Exporters or freight forwarders engaging in many shipments are encouraged (and may be required by law or by the transportation carriers) to file electronic SEDs rather than hard copies.

For the SED form, the seller must declare the value of the goods. This is defined to mean the selling price, or if not sold, the cost including the inland freight, insurance, and other charges, to the port of export. It does not include unconditional discounts and commissions. This value declaration is extremely important, because if it varies from the selling price stated in the commercial invoice, consular invoice, special customs invoice, insurance certificate, or, especially, any forms filed by the buyer with the International customs or exchange control authorities, a charge of false statement may arise, subjecting the exporter and/or the International buyer to civil or criminal penalties.

Finally, the SED calls for an export license number or exception symbol, and the Export Control Classification Number (ECCN).

This information relates to the export licensing system applicable in the exported country. The important thing to note at this point is that prior to clearance for shipment from the the exported country, the "exporter" or its agent must declare, under penalty of perjury, that no export license is required, or that the export can be made under a license exception, and the correct license exception symbol must be inserted in the SED, or that a license is required and has been obtained, and the license number issued by the Department of Commerce is stated in the SED. When an individual license is required, there will be an ECCN that also must be inserted in the SED. If this information is not put in the form, the shipment will be detained and will not be permitted to clear. Under the revised regulations, the seller will be responsible for making the license determination unless the buyer has expressly agreed in writing to accept such responsibility and has appointed an agent (such as a freight forwarder) to share such responsibility.

Many exporters are already filing their Shipper's Export Declarations electronically under the Automated Export System. Many carriers are already requiring their customers to file electronically, and filing electronically is mandatory for all items listed on the Commerce Control List. A description of the system, the four options for filing, and Internet filing through the system is contained.

3. The Procedure of Import-export Customs Clearance

Application-Examination and Inspection-Levying Duties-Release.

4. Documents Presented during Customs Declaration

(1) Export Customs Declaration Form.

(2) Commercial Invoice and Packing List.

(3) Shipping Order.

(4) Verification Form of Export Payment of Exchange (see Sample 9-2).

(5) Export Customs Clearance Bill.

(6) Export Licence / Certificate of Quota.

(7) Processing Trade Registration Book.

1. 原产地证书

2. 进出口报关单（见样单6-7、样单7-2）

出口货物报关单很重要，因为它是所有出口单据中唯一一份在国家政府机构备案的单证。出口货物报关单是给出口货运承运人或航空承运人的单据，并于清关前在海关备案。这份单证可能由出口商或出口商的代理、货运人开出，出口商可能看不见它。不过，出口货物报关单特别声明，任何虚假报关单(包括偶然虚假陈述以及故意虚假陈述的内容)，都将使出口商受到出口国民事和刑事处罚，包括10 000美元的罚款和5年徒刑。因此，出口商必须确保任何代理商，如货运人所提交给海关服务部的报关单信息是准确的。为此，提交报关单的人必须声明他或她已经阅读了商务部所签发的、可使托运人正确完成出口货物报关单的小册子说明书。如果出口商发现托运人或者它的货运代理出具的出口报关单不准确的话，应该在同一港口提交一份修改声明。

出口商或货运代理被鼓励提交电子出口货物报关单而不是电子单据。现在出口商或很多从事运输的货运代理被鼓励(法律要求或运输公司要求)提交托运人的出口电子报关单证，而不是纸质单证。

卖方必须在出口货物报关单里申报货物价值。这意味要申报销售价格，如果没有卖出去的话，该价格还包括内地运输成本、保险费以及其他到出口港的费用。它不包括无条件的折扣和回扣。这个价值申报十分重要。因为如果它与商业发票、领事发票、特殊海关发票、保险凭证所述的销售价格不同的话，特别是任何买方提交给海关、外汇管理机构的申请表可能出现的虚假费用陈述，会使出口商和/或外国买家遭受民事或刑事处罚。

最后，出口货物报关单需要填写出口许可证号码、例外号码和出口管理分类码。

这与适用于出口国的出口许可制度有关。在这一点上要注意的重点是,在出运前,发货人或其代理人必须申明,没有出口许可证而出运了需要许可证才能出运的货物的情况,可判伪证罪。当然也有例外,即不需要出口许可证的情况,这时正确的许可证例外号必须填在出口货物报关单上面。如果需要出口许可证并且已经获得了此证,则由商务部签发的许可证的号码必须填在出口货物报关单上面。当需要某个个体执照时,出口管理分类码也必须填在出口货物报关单上面。如果这些信息不在出口货物报关单上面,该货物将被拘留并将不允许清关。根据修订后的规定,除非买方已明确书面同意接受以上这些责任并且已经任命了代理(比如货运代理)承担这样的责任,否则卖方要负责缮制许可证。

现在许多出口商都已通过出口报关单电子自动化系统申报他们的托运人出口声明。许多运输公司已要求客户通过报关单电子自动化系统直接网上申报并提供电子单证,回执要求列出所有商业管制清单上的货物描述、四个选项备案。

3. 进出口清关程序

申报—查验—征税—放行。

4. 办理清关时需提交的单证

(1) 出口报关单。

(2) 商业发票和包装单。

(3) 装货单。

(4) 出口收汇核销单(见样单 9-2)。

(5) 出口清关单。

(6) 出口许可证/配额证。

(7) 加工贸易登记簿。

9.5 Export Drawback 出口退税

Before the export, the drawback is to return the indirect taxes such as the value added tax and the consumption tax, which are levied in the course of production and communication.

Documents presented for drawback (three copies and two documents): The bank presents the form of International exchange settlement, verifying instrument (the drawback copy), export customs declaration form and purchase invoice.

出口前的退税就是退回在生产和流通过程中征收的间接税,比如增值税、消费税。

退税需提交的单据(三份副本和两份单证):银行呈交结汇水单、核销单退税联、出口货物报关单、出口购货发票。

Chapter 10
Electronic Commerce and International Trade Documents
电子商务和国际贸易单证

10.1 E-Commerce and International Trade
电子商务和国际贸易

Electronic commerce, commonly known as e-commerce or e-Commerce, consists of the buying and selling of products or services over electronic systems such as the Internet and other computer networks. The amount of trade conducted electronically has grown extraordinarily since the spread of the Internet. A wide variety of commerce is conducted in this way, spurring and drawing on innovations in electronic funds transfer, supply chain management, Internet marketing, online transaction processing, electronic data interchange(EDI), inventory management systems, and automated data collection systems. Modern electronic commerce typically uses the World Wide Web at least at some point in the transaction's lifecycle, although it can encompass a wider range of technologies such as e-mail as well.

E-Commerce's Influence to International Trade:

(1) E-commerce improves international trade.

(2) The emergence of virtual market changes the environment of international trade.

(3) The emergence of virtual company makes difference of the operating bobby of international trade.

(4) The operation and management of international trade change a lot.

电子商务，通常指通过电子系统买卖产品或服务，如互联网和其他计算机网络。自从互联网普及后，电子贸易的数量飞快增长。电子商务应用于各式各样的商业活动中，促进了电子资金转账、供应链管理、网络营销、在线交易处理、电子数据交换(EDI)、库存管理系统和自动数据采集系统的革新和发展。在交易过程中，现代电子商务一般采用万维网，当然它还包含更广泛的技术，如电子邮件。

电子商务对国际贸易的影响：

(1) 电子商务使国际贸易得到发展。

(2) 虚拟市场的出现改变了国际贸易的环境。

(3) 虚拟公司的出现使国际贸易操作的监管产生差异。

(4) 国际贸易管理和运作改变了很多。

10.2　E-Documents and E-Payment
　　　电子单证与单证付款

1. E-Documents

1) EDI Network

Electronic Data Interchange (EDI) is widely-used technology for the automated exchange of documents between dissimilar applications. It allows value chain partners to exchange purchase orders, invoices, advance ship notices, and other business documents directly from one business system to the other, without human intervention. Proven advantages are fewer errors, lower administrative costs, and faster order-to-cash cycles.

2) eUCP

eUCP is not amendment to UCP, but is a supplement to UCP.

3) Problems in E-Documents

(1) Security.

(2) Reality.

(3) Legal Problem.

2. E-Payment

1) E-Currency

E-currency is precious metal-backed Internet currency. To open an Account, individual "deposits" money with an online e-currency company that then converts the amount into gold bullion. Via the Internet, the account holder can transfer ownership of some or all of that gold into someone else's e-currency account. Ownership can be repeatedly transferred.

2) Development of E-Payment

E-payment has seen a rapid development due to the fast growth of E-commerce, and the market regulation is also underway. Research showed that China's total online payment value would hit RMB60.5 billion Yuan by 2007, maintaining an annual growth rate of 100%. Statistics show that domestic companies specializing in e-payment amounted to nearly 50 by the end of 2005. The rapid innovation of e-payment has gone far beyond the regulation scope and capabilities of relevant laws and regulations. That is the right reason that many policies, laws and regulations concerning E-payment have been successively launched recently.

1. 电子单证

1) 电子数据交换网络

电子数据交换(EDI)是在不同领域广泛应用的文件自动交换技术。它允许贸易伙伴直接从一个业务系统到另外一个业务系统交换采购订单、发票、装船通知和其他商业文件，无须人工干预。它已被证实的优点是错误更少、办公成本更低、处理订单—现金流程更快。

2) 电子跟单信用证统一惯例

电子跟单信用证统一惯例不是跟单信用证统一惯例修订本，而是补充。

3) 电子单证的问题

(1) 安全性。

(2) 真实性。

(3) 合法性问题。

2. 电子支付

1) 电子货币

电子货币是宝贵的、强力后备的网络货币。在网上电子货币公司开户、个体"存款"，然后将这些钱转换成金条。通过互联网，账户持有人可以把部分或全部黄金过户到别人的网银账户。其所有权可以反复转让。

2) 电子支付的发展

目前，利用电子商务业，通过网络直接进行全球范围的收付款，已经成为企业改造传统业务、直接面对全球市场、降低运作成本、增强市场竞争力、提高经济效益、加速发展的最主要方式。

10.3 Electronic Documentation in International Trade 国际贸易中的电子单证

EDI are widely used in international trade documentation. Now, along with the fast development of computer and internet, more and more companies use computers to make out documents.

Future developments in electronic documentation will be diverse. The technology used is shifting from page-based to XML-based documentation, and even further to databases containing indexed documentary units. Multi-agent models are also in use for the development of documentation.

EDI is the computer-to-computer interchange of strictly formatted messages that represent documents other than monetary instruments. EDI implies a sequence of messages between two

Chapter 10　Electronic Commerce and International Trade Documents 电子商务和国际贸易单证

parties, either of whom may serve as originator or recipient. The formatted data representing the documents may be transmitted from originator to recipient via telecommunications or physically transported on electronic storage media.

In EDI, the usual processing of received messages is by computer only. Human Intervention in the processing of a received message is typically intended only for error conditions, for quality review, and for special situations. For example, the transmission of binary or textual data is not EDI as defined here unless the data are treated as one or more data elements of an EDI message and are not normally intended for human interpretation as part of on-line data processing.

EDI 已在国际贸易单证中广泛使用。当前，随着计算机与互联网的快速发展，越来越多的公司开始使用电子计算机来缮制单证。

未来电子单证的发展将多样化。使用的技术将从基于页面的单证扩展到基于 XML(可扩展标示语言) 的单证，甚至是包含索引单证的数据库。同时也在使用智能体模型的单证。

EDI 是严格格式信息在计算机间的交换，这些信息代表的是单证而不是货币工具。EDI 蕴含一系列买卖双方之间的信息。代表单证的格式化数据可通过无线电通信或者电子存储介质由发起者传递给接收者。

就 EDI 而言，通常讯息的接收过程是通过计算机进行处理的。在对接收到的讯息进行处理的过程中，人工干预通常只在接收有误、质量审核和特殊情况下使用。例如，除非数据被视为 EDI 信息的一个或多个数据元素，否则传输的二进制或文本数据并不是在此所定义的 EDI 数据，并且一般都不适合作为在线数据进行处理。

Chapter 11

Practical English of International Business Documents
国际商务单证实用英语

11.1 Practical English Expressions of Documents
实用单证英语表达

11.1.1 Time and Date
时间与日期

1. Key Letter of Credit Dates 主要的信用证日期

Key letter of credit dates include the following dates.

(1) Opening Date: Shipping documents generally may predate the opening date of the letter of credit unless specifically prohibited in the letter of credit.

(2) Latest Ship Date: Shipping documents must be dated on or before this date. It specifies the latest date by which a seller must ship the goods. If the goods are not shipped before the specified date then a discrepancy will occur and the seller may not get paid from the letter of credit.

(3) Latest Date to Present Documents: shipping documents must arrive at the bank before this date, if stated. If not specifically stated the documents must arrive at the negotiating bank at most 21 days after the latest ship date but before the expiration date of the letter of credit.

(4) Expiration Date: Usually the last day to present documents in strict compliance with the terms of the letter of credit. The letter of credit essentially ceases to exist on this date.

主要的信用证日期包括以下的日期。

(1) 开立日期：除非信用证明确禁止，货运单据日期一般早于信用证开立日期。

(2) 最迟装运期：运输单据的日期必须在这个日期或在这个日期之前。它规定在此最迟装运期卖方必须发货。如果货物在指定日期前没有装运而发生争议的话，卖方可能得不到信用证的支付。

(3) 最迟交单期：如果有规定，单据必须在这个日期之前送达银行。如果没有特别规定，单据必须在最迟装运期后21天但必须在信用证有效期之内送达议付银行。

(4) 有效期：严格符合信用证条款，通常是最后一天提交单据。信用证基本上在这一天失效。

2. Ways of Contracting Date of Shipment 装船日期的拟订

There are several ways of specifying the date of shipment in the contract.

合同中有几种规定装运期的方法。

(1) Shipment on or about July 30, 2014. 大约在 2014 年 7 月 30 日装运。

(2) Shipment not later than Aug 18, 2014 or Latest shipment date: Aug.18, 2014. 不晚于 2014 年 8 月 18 日装运或者最迟装运日期是 2014 年 8 月 18 日。

(3) Shipment to be effected during May/June, 2014. 装运期在 2014 年 5/6 月。

4. Other Expressions 其他有关时间的表述

(1) ETD-Estimated time of departure.

(2) ETA-Estimated time of arrival.

(3) Time of loading/unloading.

(4) Time of delivery.

(5) Sailing date.

(6) Date of issue.

(7) Date of inspection.

(8) Date of completion of discharge.

(1) 预定离港期。

(2) 预定到港期。

(3) 装 / 卸货时间。

(4) 交货时间。

(5) 开航时间。

(6) (证书 / 单证的) 签发日期。

(7) 检验日期。

(8) 卸毕日期。

11.1.2　Numbers
数字

1. Numbers of the Copies of Documents 单证副本的数量

(1) In duplicate 一式两份

(2) In triplicate 一式三份

(3) In quadruplicate 一式四份

(4) In quintuplicate 一式五份

(5) In sextuplicate 一式六份

(6) In septuplicate 一式七份

(7) In octuplicate 一式八份

(8) In nonuplicate 一式九份

(9) In decuplicate 一式十份

2. Ways of Indicating the Amount in Bills of Exchange 汇票中表示总额的方式

There are many ways to express the amount in words, let's take the amount USD5 008.30 as an example.

(1) SAY U.S DOLLARS FIVE THOUSAND AND EIGHT CENTS THIRTY ONLY.

(2) SAY U.S DOLLARS FIVE THOUSAND AND EIGHT AND 30/100 ONLY.

(3) SAY U.S DOLLARS FIVE THOUSAND AND EIGHT AND POINT THIRTY ONLY.

有很多方法可以表示金额，下面以 5 008.30 美元为例。

(1) 五千零八美元三十美分。

(2) 五千零八美元和 30/100 美分。

(3) 五千零八点三美元。

11.1.3　Kinds of Packages
　　　　包装种类

(1) Bound with rope externally.

(2) Block covered with poly bag.

(3) Each piece wrapped in a poly bag.

(4) Packed in strong carton.

(5) Full with rolled on tube.

(6) Press packed in iron hooped bale.

(7) With assorted colors/sizes.

(1) 外捆麻绳。

(2) 块装外加塑料袋。

(3) 每件外套一塑料袋。

(4) 用牢固的纸箱装运。

(5) 全幅卷筒。

(6) 机器榨包以铁皮捆扎。

(7) 混色混码。

11.1.4　Relevant Parties Involved
　　　　有关各方当事人

1) L/C Parties Concerned and Its Expressions　信用证有关当事人及其表述

Chapter 11　Practical English of International Business Documents　国际商务单证实用英语

(1) Opener. 开证人。
　　Applicant. 开证人 (申请开证人)。
　　Principal. 开证人 (委托开证人)。
　　Accountee. 开证人。
　　Accreditor. 开证人 (委托开证人)。
　　For account of Messrs. 付 (某人) 账。

(2) beneficiary. 受益人。
　　In favour of... 以 (……) 为受益人。
　　In one's favour. 以……为受益人。
　　Favouring yourselves. 以你本人为受益人。

(3) drawee. 付款人 (或称受票人，指汇票)。
　　To drawn on (or upon)... 以 (某人) 为付款人。
　　To value on... 以 (某人) 为付款人。
　　To issued on... 以 (某人) 为付款人。

(4) drawer. 出票人 /drawee 受票人。

(5) advising bank. 通知行。
　　The notifying bank. 通知行。
　　Advised through...bank. 通过……银行通知。
　　Advised by airmail/cable through...bank. 通过……银行以航空信 / 电通知。

(6) opening bank. 开证行。
　　Issuing bank. 开证行。
　　Establishing bank. 开证行。

(7) Negotiation bank. 议付行。

(8) Paying bank. 付款行。

(9) Reimbursing bank. 偿付行。

(10) Confirming bank. 保兑行。

2) Other Parties in the Business Transactions. 贸易中其他有关当事人。

(1) Payer. 付款人。

(2) Payee. 收款人。

(3) Importer. 进口人。

(4) Exporter. 出口人。

(5) Freight forwarder. 货运代理。

(6) Carrier. 承运人。

(7) Shipper. 托运人。

(8) Consignee. 受货人。

(9) Consignor. 发货人。

(10) Insurer. 保险人。

(11) The insured. 被保险人。

(12) Inspector. 检验员。

(13) Remitter. 寄款人。

(14) Remittee. 收款人。

(15) Collecting bank. 托收行。

(16) Remitting bank. 汇付行。

(17) Principal. 委托人。

(18) Trustor. 信托人。

(19) Acceptor. 承兑人。

(20) Trustee. 被信托人。

(21) Endorser. 背书人。

(22) Endorsee. 被背书人。

11.1.5　Words for Quality, Quantity, Price, Shipment and Payment　质量、数量、价格、装运与支付用语

1. Words for Quality 质量用语

(1) Fair average quality. 大路货 (良好平均品质)。

(2) Representative sample. 代表性样品。

(3) Counter sample. 对等样品。

(4) Sealed sample. 封样。

(5) Duplicate sample. 复样。

(6) Tolerance. 公差。

(7) Specifications. 规格。

(8) Assortment. 花色 (搭配)。

2. Words for Quantity 数量用语

(1) Weight. 重量。

(2) Actual weight. 实际重量。

(3) Short weight. 短重。

(4) A short weight of 5 kilos. 短重 5 千克。

(5) Actual tare. 实际皮重。

(6) Average tare. 平均皮重。

(7) Customary tare. 习惯皮重。

(8) Computed tare. 约定皮重。

(9) Conditioned weight. 公量。

(10) Circa，approximate quantity. "约"量。

3. Words for Price 价格用语

(1) Freight. 运费。

(2) Unit price. 单价。

(3) Total value(amount). 总值。

(4) Landing charges. 卸货费。

(5) Net price. 净价。

(6) Price including commission. 含佣价。

(7) Port dues. 港口税。

4. Words for Shipment 装运词语

(1) Over-shipment. 多装。

(2) Short-shipment. 少装。

(3) Prompt shipment. 即期装运。

(4) Shipment as soon as possible. 尽快装运。

(5) Late shipment. 迟交。

(6) Prompt delivery. 即期交货。

(7) To speed up. 加速。

(8) To effect shipment. 交货，装运。

5. Words for Payment 支付用语

(1) Dishonour. 拒付。

(2) Deferred payment. 延期付款。

(3) Payment by installment. 分期付款。

(4) Payment on terms. 定期付款。

(5) Payment agreement. 支付协定。

(6) Pay order. 支付凭证。

(7) Payment order. 付款通知。

(8) Payment by banker. 银行支付。

11.1.6　Titles of the Frequently Used Documents 常用单证英语名称

(1) Combined transport documents (CTD). 联合运输单据。

(2) Mate's receipt. 大副收据。

(3) Bill of lading (B/L). 提单。

(4) On board B/L. 已装船提单。

(5) Received for shipment B/L. 备运提单。

(6) Direct B/L. 直达提单。

(7) Through B/L. 联运提单。

(8) Straight B/L. 记名提单。

(9) Contract. 合同。

(10) Proforma invoice. 形式发票。

(11) Shipper's letter of instructions (Air). 托运人说明书（空运）。

(12) Ready for dispatch advice. 待运通知。

(13) Dispatch order. 发运单。

(14) Dispatch advice. 发运通知。

(15) Shipping advice. 装船通知。

(16) Loading list. 装货清单。

(17) Insurance policy. 保险单。

11.2 Application of International Trade Documents English
国际商务单证英语应用

11.2.1 Contract
合同

(1) Brief Introduction on Business Contract. 商业合同简介。

(2) Sample of a Contract. 合同样本。

11.2.2 Methods of Payment for International Transactions
国际交易支付方式

(1) Cash in advance. 现金预付。

(2) Letter of credit. 信用证。

(3) Documentary collection. 跟单托收。

(4) Open account or credit. 往来账户。

11.2.3 Trade Documentation
贸易单证

1. Commercial Invoice

The commercial invoice is an invoice/bill for the goods from the seller to the buyer. It is a document that gives a complete description of the trade transaction, i.e. invoice number, full listing of the goods, quantities, shipping date, mode of transport, address of the shipper and buyer and the delivery and payment terms. The buyer requires the invoice to certify ownership and to initiate payment. Some governments use the commercial invoice to determine the true value of the goods when assessing customs duties.

2. Bill of Lading(B/L)

B/Ls are contracts between the owner of the goods(shipper) and the transportation company. It is considered to be a receipt for the goods shipped (given to the seller by the carrier), a contract for delivery (i.e. a contract to deliver the goods as freight to the consignee), and most importantly, a document of title to the goods.

3. Certificate of Origin

Some countries(particularly those subject to lower tariffs and free trade treaties)may require, for entry purposes, a signed statement certifying the origin of the goods being traded. If the buyer requires this document, he should so stipulate in his letter of credit.

4. Inspection Certificate

To add security, some purchasers and countries may require a certificate of inspection attesting to the specifications of the goods shipped, usually performed by a third party.

5. Packing List

A document that lists and itemizes the merchandise contained in each package(box, crate, drum, carton, or container), and indicates the type, number of packages, dimensions, and weight of the container. The packing list is used by customs and transportation companies.

6. Insurance Certificate

A document certifying that goods are insured and stating the type and amount of insurance coverage provided on the goods being shipped. The insurance document is normally issued in a "negotiable form" which means that the party in whose favour the document has been issued (usually the seller but it may be the seller's agent)must endorse it "in blank".

7. Shipper's Export Declaration

The Shipper's Export Declaration is a form prepared by a shipper/exporter indicating the value, weight, destination, and other information about an export shipment. It is basically used to collect trade statistics and to control exports.

8. Phytosanitary(Plant Health) Inspection Certificate

A document certifies that goods have passed inspection (i.e. free from pests and harmful plant diseases) and comply with the International quarantine import regulation.

9. Export License

A document, issued by a government agency in the exporting country, gives authorization to export certain commodities to specified countries.

10. Import License

A document, issued by a government agency in the importing country, gives to import certain commodities.

1. 商业发票

商业发票是卖方把货物转移给买方的发票/账单，是贸易交易对货物进行完整描述的单证，内容包括：发票号、货物清单、数量、装船期、运输方式、托运人和买卖双方的地址及付款条件。买方要求发票应证明货物所有权及付款。一些政府在评估关税时使用商业发票来确定商品的真正价值。

2. 提单

提单是商品所有人(托运人)和运输公司的合同。它是(由承运人给卖方的)装运货物收据，是一份(运费到付)发货合同。最重要的是，它是货物所有权的文件。

3. 原产地证书

以入境为目的，一些国家(特别是那些实行低关税和受到自由贸易条约限制的国家)要求签署声明，证明该交易货物的原产地。如果买方要求这种单证，他应该在信用证中这样规定。

4. 检验证书

为了增加安全性，一些买家及国家可能需要检验合格证明，通常由第三方对装运货物进行检验。

5. 装箱单

它是一份详细列举每一包装下(盒、箱、桶、纸箱或容器)所包含货物的单证，表明商品的种类、包装数量、集装箱尺寸和重量。海关和运输公司都用装箱单。

6. 保险证书

它是一份证明装船的货物已投保，并表明投保的险别和范围的单证。保险单据通常是"可转让形式"的，这意味着利益方(通常是卖方，但可能是卖方的代理人)出具该单证必须空白背书。

7. 托运人的出口货物报关单

托运人的出口货物报关单是由托运人/出口商开立，表明货物价值、重量、目的地和其他有关出口装运信息的单证。它基本上用于贸易统计和控制出口。

8. 植物检疫(植物健康)检验证书

它是一份保证货物已经通过了检验(比如无植物害虫和疾病)并且遵守国际检疫规定的单证。

9. 出口许可证

它是一份由出口国政府机构开立、授权向指定国家出口某些商品的单证。

10. 进口许可证

它是由进口国政府机构出具准予进口某些商品的单证。

11.2.4　Checklist for Reviewing a Letter of Credit
　　　　信用证核对清单

Here are some of the details that you are suggested to check.

(1) Is your company's name spelled correctly and is the address correct?

(2) Does the L/C state it is irrevocable?

(3) Was it necessary for the L/C to be confirmed and, if so, is the confirming bank acceptable?

(4) Is the amount and currency of the L/C correct?

(5) Is the tenor of the draft acceptable?

(6) Is the merchandise described correctly?

(7) Does the Incoterms match your sales contract?

(8) Are the transportation details correct?

(9) Can the shipping date be met?

(10) Are the insurance instructions clear and correct?

(11) Is the expiration date acceptable, and does it expire in your country?

(12) Are the document requirements clear and understandable?

(13) Is the L/C requesting any documents that you weren't expecting? Will this add any additional expense?

(14) Does the L/C contain reimbursement instructions?

(15) Are the banking fees being paid by the correct parties?

(16) Is the L/C subject to the UCP 600?

建议检查以下细节。

(1) 公司名称和地址拼写是否正确？

(2) 信用证是否为不可撤销信用证？

(3) 信用证是否是保兑信用证？如果是，保兑行可以接受吗？

(4) 信用证的数量和货币是否正确？

(5) 汇票的日期可否接受？

(6) 商品描述是否正确？

(7) 买卖销售合同是否符合《国际贸易术语解释通则》？

(8) 运输的细节是否正确？

(9) 装运日期可否接受？

(10) 保险通知是否清晰和正确？

(11) 截止日期是否可接受，是否在你方所在国到期？

(12) 文件是否要求明确和可理解？

(13) 信用证是否要求你出具你不期待的任何单证？这会增加额外的费用吗？

(14) 信用证是否包含索偿指示？

(15) 银行所要求的支付费用是否由正确的当事方来支付？

(16) 信用证是否受《跟单信用证统一惯例》(UCP 600) 的限制？

11.2.5　The Common Discrepancies in Letters of Credit 信用证常见不符点

1. in Relation to Time

credit expired; late shipment; late presentation.

2. in Relation to the Documents, in General

(1) Original documents not marked "original".

(2) Document (s) unsigned.

(3) Documents submitted late to the bank.(Banks will not accept documents presented to them later than 21 days after date of shipment, unless otherwise stipulated).

3. Related to the Invoice

(1) Terms of shipping not clear.

(2) Issued for wrong amount, or for an amount greater than the credit value.

(3) Issued with terms of payment and currency not clearly stated.

(4) Not signed/certified/legalized(when credit calls for signed invoices).

(5) Omits the goods description, as detailed in the credit(different description).

(6) Shipping marks differ from transport documents.

4. Related to the Bill of Lading

(1) Does not indicate the name of the carrier.

(2) Does not clearly define consignee, shipper, or notifying party.

(3) Weights and measurements differ from other documents.

(4) Not signed in accordance with the requirements of UCP 600.

(5) B/L claused("foul" B/L) showing defective goods or packaging, (e.g. "rusty", "leaking drums" etc.).

(6) Goods shipped on deck.

5. Related to Insurance

(1) Certificate presented in lieu of a policy.

(2) Dated after date of shipment(coverage effective after the transport date).

(3) Omission(on its face) of risks covered.

(4) Insured value insufficient.

(5) Absence of endorsement.

(6) Certificate issued under an expired policy.

(7) Not issued in negotiable form.

6. Related to Certificates

(1) Incorrectly titled.

(2) Content not as called for.

(3) Not signed.

7. Telex Advices

(1) Not sent within the time scales laid down in the credit.

(2) Incomplete or incorrect information provided.

8. Miscellaneous Documents

(1) Omit to present certificate of origin as required by the letter of credit.

(2) Omit to sign (or seal by a Chamber of Commerce) certificate of origin.

(3) Packing list not conform to the importing country's requirement.

9. Other Common Discrepancies

(1) Goods shipped by sea instead of by air(or vice versa).

(2) Amount claimed exceeds the credit value.

(3) Partial shipment or transshipment effected when not allowed.

1. 与时间有关的不符点

信用到期、货物迟交、过期交单。

2. 一般与单证有关的不符点

(1) 正本单据不标注"原始"字样。

(2) 单证无签名。

(3) 迟交单给银行 (除非另有规定，银行将不接受晚于装运日期 21 天后的单据)。

3. 与发票有关的不符点

(1) 装运条款不清楚。

(2) 金额有误，或者超过信用总金额。

(3) 开立的付款条件和货币不清楚。

(4) (当信用证要求发票签名时) 无签名 / 证明 / 合法化。

(5) 遗漏信用证中所列出的详细的货物描述 (不同的描述)。

(6) 与运输单据上的唛头不同。

4. 与提单有关的不符点

(1) 无承运人的名称。

(2) 收货人、发货人或通知方不明确。

(3) 重量和尺码与其他单证不同。

(4) 没有根据《跟单信用证统一惯例》(UCP 600) 的要求签署。

(5) 提单 (不清洁提单) 显示货物或包装有缺陷 (如"生锈""桶泄漏"等)。

(6) 货物装于甲板上。

5. 与保险有关的不符点

(1) 保险证明代替保险单。

(2) 保险单日期迟于装运日期(保险在运输日期之后生效)。

(3) 遗漏投保险别。

(4) 保险价值不足。

(5) 缺乏背书。

(6) 保险证明开立过期。

(7) 不是以可转让形式签发保险单。

6. 与证书有关的不符点

(1) 标题不正确。

(2) 无所要求的内容。

(3) 未签名。

7. 与电传有关的不符点

(1) 未在信用证规定时间内发送。

(2) 提供的信息不完整或不正确。

8. 与各类单证有关的不符点

(1) 没有提交信用证要求的原产地证书。

(2) 原产地证书无签名(或由商会盖章)。

(3) 装箱单不符合进口国的要求。

9. 其他常见的不符点

(1) 是海运货物而不是空运货物(或反之亦然)。

(2) 金额超过信用证总金额。

(3) 不允许分批装运或转运却执行了。

Sample
单证样例

Sample 3-1　　　　　　　　　　Sales Contract
样单 3-1　　　　　　　　　　　销售合同

卖方 SELLER:	GUANGDONG FOREIGN TRADE IMP. & EXP. CORP. 15-18/F., 351 TIANHE ROAD GUANGZHOU, CHINA	编号 NO.:	SHDS03027
		日期 DATE:	Apr. 3th, 2021
		地点 SIGNED IN:	SHANGHAI, CHINA
买方 BUYER:	NEO GENERAL TRADING CO., #362 JALAN STREET, TORONTO, CANADA		

买卖双方同意按以下条款达成交易:
This contract is made by and agreed between the BUYER and SELLER, in accordance with the terms and conditions stipulated below.

1. 品名及规格 Commodity & Specification	2. 数量 Quantity	3. 单价及贸易条款 Unit Price & Trade Terms	4. 金额 Amount
		CIFC5 TORONTO	
CHINESE CERAMIC DINNERWARE DS1511 30-Piece Dinnerware and Tea Set DS2201 20-Piece Dinnerware Set DS4504 45-Piece Dinnerware Set DS5120 95-Piece Dinnerware Set	542SETS 800SETS 443SETS 254SETS	USD23.50 USD20.40 USD23.20 USD30.10	USD 12 737.00 USD 16 320.00 USD 10 277.60 USD 7 645.40
Total:	2 039SETS		USD 46 980.00

允许 With	10%	溢短装,由卖方决定 More or less of shipment allowed at the sellers' option	
5. 总值 Total Value		SAY US DOLLARS FORTY SIX THOUSAND NINE HUNDRED AND EIGHTY ONLY.	
6. 包装 Packing		DS2201 IN CARTONS OF 2 SETS EACH AND DS1151, DS4504 AND DS5120 TO BE PACKED IN CARTONS OF 1 SET EACH ONLY. TOTAL: 1 639 CARTONS.	
7. 唛头 Shipping Marks		AT BUYER'S OPTION.	
8. 装运期及运输方式 Time of Shipment & means of Transportation		TO BE EFFECTED BEFORE THE END OF APRIL 2021 WITH PARTIAL SHIPMENT ALLOWED AND TRANSSHIPMENT ALLOWED.	
9. 装运港及目的地 Port of Loading & Destination		FROM: GUANGZHOU, CHINA TO: TORONTO, CANADA	
10. 保险 Insurance		THE SELLER SHALL COVER INSURANCE AGAINST WPA AND CLASH & BREAKAGE & WAR RISKS FOR 110% OF THE TOTAL INVOICE VALUE	

(续表)

11. 付款方式 Terms of Payment	BY IRREVOCABLE SIGHT LETTER OF CREDIT.
12. 备注 Remarks	

The Buyer NEO GENERAL TRADING CO., Y.BAYER	The Seller GUANGDONG FOREIGN TRADE IMP. & EXP. CORP. 张立

Sample 4-1　　　　　Purchase Contract
样单 4-1　　　　　购货合同

合同编号: Contract No.: OA010602	签订日期: Date: June 2nd, 2021	签订地点: Signed at: SHENZHEN, CHINA
1. 买方: The Buyers: SHENZHEN OCDA FOOD CO., LTD. 地址: Address: 7/F, OCDA BLDG, KEYUAN RD., SHENZHEN, CHINA 电话 (Tel): 86-755-2626268　　　　　传真 (Fax): 86-755-2626269		
2. 卖方: The Sellers: ARELLA AND CO., SPA 地址: Address: PLAZA COLLEGIO CAIROLIN. 3 27100 PAVIA, ITALY 电话 (Tel): 81-307-282828　　　　　传真 (Fax): 81-307-282829		
经买卖双方确认根据下列条款订立本合同: The undersigned Sellers and Buyers have confirmed this contract is accordance with the terms and conditions stipulated below:		

3. 商品名称及规格 Name of Commodity & Specification	4. 数量 Quantity	5. 单价 Unit Price	6. 总金额 Amount
CANNED MUSHROOMS 24 TINS×425 GRAMS	1 700CARTONS/FCL	CFRC2% USD7.80/CTN	DAMMAM PORT USD13 260.00 合计: Total: USD13 260.00

7. 总值(大写):
   Total Value (in words): SAY U.S.DOLLARS THIRTEEN THOUSAND TWO HUNDRED AND SIXTY ONLY.
8. 允许溢短 _____ %。
   5% more or less in quantity and value allowed.
9. 成交术语:
   Terms:
   □ FOB　　　☑ CFR　　　□ CIF　　　□ DDU
10. 包装:
    Packing: EXPORT CARTON

(续表)

11. 运输唛头：
    Shipping Mark： N/M
12. 运输起讫：由 _____（装运港）到 _____（目的港）。
    Shipment from PAVIA，ITALY (Port of Shipment) to SHENZHEN，CHINA (Port of Destination).
13. 转运：☐允许 ☑不允许   分批：☐允许 ☑不允许
    Transshipment：   ☐ allowed   ☑ not allowed
    Partial shipment： ☐ allowed   ☑ not allowed
    运输时间：
    Shipment Time: WITHIN 20 DAYS AFTER RECEIPT OF IRREVOCABLE SIGHT L/C.
14. 保险：由 _____ 方按发票金额的 _____% 投保 _____，加保 _____ 从 _____ 到 _____。
    Insurance：to be covered by the SELLER for 110% of the invoice value covering Institute Cargo Clauses(A) 1/1/82 additional Institute War and Strikes Clauses-Cargo 1/1/82 from PAVIA，ITALY to SHENZHEN .
15. 付款条件：
    Terms of Payment：
    ☑ 买方应不迟于 _____ 年 ____ 月 ____ 日前将 100% 货款用即期汇票/电汇支付给卖方。
    The buyers shall pay 100% of the sales proceeds through sight (demand) draft/by T/T remittance to the sellers not later than ____/____.
    ☑ 买方应于 _____ 年 ____ 月 ____ 日前通过 _____ 银行开立以卖方为受益人的 ____ 天不可撤销信用证，有效期至装运后 ____ 天在中国议付，并注明合同号。
    The buyers shall issue an irrevocable L/C at 90 days sight through a BANK in favour of the sellers prior to JUNE 6TH，2021 indicating L/C shall be valid in PAVIA，ITALY through negotiation within 10 days after the shipment effected, the L/C must mention the Contract Number.
    ☐ 付款交单：买方应凭卖方开立给买方的 ____ 期跟单汇票付款，付款时交单。
    Documents against payment (D/P): The buyers shall dully make the payment against documentary draft made out to the buyers at / sight by the sellers.
    ☐ 承兑交单：买方应凭卖方开立给买方的 ____ 期跟单汇票付款，承兑时交单。
    Documents against acceptance (D/A): The buyers shall dully accept the documentary draft made out to the buyers at / days by the sellers.
16. 装运通知：一旦装运完毕，卖方应立即电告买方合同号、品名、已装载数量、发票总金额、毛重、运输工具名称及启运日期等。
    Shipping Advice: The sellers shall immediately, upon the completion of the loading of the goods advise the buyers of the Contract No., names of commodity, loaded quantity, invoice value, gross weight, names of vessel and shipment date by TLX/FAX.
17. 检验与索赔：
    Inspection and Claims：
    (1) 卖方在发货前由 _____ 检验机构对货物的品质、规格和数量进行检验，并出具检验证明。
    The buyer shall have the qualities, specifications, quantities of the goods carefully inspected by the ___/___ Inspection Authority, which shall issues Inspection Certificate before shipment.
    (2) 货物到达目的口岸后，买方可委托当地的商品检验机构对货物进行复验。如果发现货物有损坏、残缺或规格、数量与合同规定不符，买方需于货物到达目的口岸的 _____ 天内凭 _____ 检验机构出具的检验证明书向卖方索赔。
    The buyers have right to have the goods inspected by the local commodity inspection authority

(续表)

after the arrival of the goods at the port of destination. If the goods are found damaged/short/their specifications and quantities not in compliance with that specified in the contract, the buyers shall lodge claims against the sellers based on the Inspection Certificate issued by the Commodity Inspection Authority within ____/____ days after the goods arrival at the destination.

(3) 如买方提出索赔，凡属品质异议需于货物到达目的口岸之日起 _____ 天内提出；凡属数量异议需于货物到达目的口岸之日起 _____ 天内提出。对所装货物所提任何异议应由保险公司、运输公司或邮递机构负责的，卖方不负任何责任。

The claims, if any regarding to the quality of the goods, shall be lodged within ____ days after arrival of the goods at the destination, if any regarding to the quantities of the goods, shall be lodged within ____ days after arrival of the goods at the destination. The sellers shall not take any responsibility if any claims concerning the shipping goods in up to the responsibility of insurance company/transportation company/post office.

18. 不可抗力：

如因人力等不可抗拒的原因造成本合同全部或部分不能履行，卖方概不负责，但卖方应将发生的上述情况及时通知买方。

Force Majeure: The sellers shall not hold any responsibility for partial or total non-performance of this contract due to Force Majeure. But the sellers shall advise the buyers on time of such occurrence.

19. 争议的解决方式：

任何因本合同而发生的或与本合同有关的争议，应提交至中国国际经济贸易仲裁委员会，按该委员会的规则进行仲裁。仲裁裁决是终局的，对双方均有约束力。

Disputes Settlement: All disputes arising out of the contract or in connection with the contract, shall be submitted to the China International Economic and Trade Arbitration Commission for arbitration in accordance with its Rules of Arbitration. The arbitral award is final and binding upon both parties.

20. 法律适用：

本合同的签订地或发生争议时的货物所在地在中华人民共和国境内或被诉人为中国法人的，适用于中华人民共和国法律，除此规定外，适用《联合国国际货物销售合同公约》。

Law Applications: It will be governed by the law of the People's Republic of China under the circumstances that the contract is signed or the goods while the disputes arising are in the People's Republic of China or the defendant is Chinese legal person, otherwise it is governed by United Nations Convention on Contract for the International Sale of Goods.

本合同使用的 FOB、CFR、CIF、DDU 术语源自国际商会 INCOTERMS 2010。

The terms in the contract based on INCOTERMS 2010 of the International Chamber of Commerce.

21. 文字：

本合同中、英文两种文字具有同等法律效力，在文字解释上，若有异议，以中文解释为准。

Versions: This contract is made out in both Chinese and English of which version is equally effective. Conflicts between these two languages arising there from, if any, shall be subject to Chinese version.

22. 附加条款：

本合同上述条款与本附加条款有抵触时，以本附加条款为准。

Additional Clauses: Conflicts between contract clauses here above and this additional clause, if any, it is subject to this additional clause.

23. 本合同共 ____ 份，自双方代表签字/盖章之日起生效。

This contract is in ____ copies, effective since being signed/sealed by both parties.

买方代表人：	卖方代表人：
Representative of the buyers:	Representative of the sellers:
签字	签字
Authorized signature:	Authorized signature:
(SHENZHEN OCDA FOOD CO., LTD. 张立)	(ARELLA AND CO., SPA Y.BAYER)

Sample 4-2　　　Proforma Invoice
样单 4-2　　　形式发票

TO: 　　　　　　　　　　　　　　　**INVOICE NO.**: 2001STD001
NEO GENERAL TRADING CO., 　　　**INVOICE DATE**: Mar. 20th, 2021
P.O. BOX 99552, RIYADH 22766, KSA　**S/C NO.**: NEO2001026
　　　　　　　　　　　　　　　　　S/C DATE: Feb. 28th, 2021
TERM OF PAYMENT: L/C AT SIGHT
PORT TO LOADING: CHINA
PORT OF DESTINATION: DAMMAM PORT, SAUDI ARABIA
TIME OF DELIVERY: Apr. 20th, 2021
INSURANCE: TO BE COVERED BY THE BUYER.
VALIDITY: May. 10th, 2021

Marks and Numbers	Number and kind of package Description of goods	Quantity	Unit Price	Amount
				CFR DAMMAM PORT
ROSE BRAND 178/2001 RIYADH	ABOUT 1 700 CARTONS CANNED MUSHROOMS PIECES & STEMS 24 TINS×425 GRAMS NET WEIGHT (D.W. 227 GRAMS) ROSE BRAND.	1 700 CARTONS	USD7.80	USD13 260.00
	Total:	1 700 CARTONS		USD13 260.00

SAY TOTAL:
U.S. DOLLARS THIRTEEN THOUSAND TWO HUNDRED AND SIXTY ONLY

　BENEFICIARY:
　TIFERT TRADING CO., LTD
　NO.86 ZHUJIANG ROAD, GUANGZHOU, CHINA
　ADVISING BANK:
　BANK OF CHINA GUANGZHOU BRANCH
　HEAD OFFICE 148 ZHONGSHAN SOUTH ROAD GUANGZHOU
　TELEX: 34226/34327 BOCJS CN
　NEGOTIATING BANK:
　BANK OF CHINA TIANJIN BRANCH
　JIEFANGBEI ROAD PEACE ZONE TIANJIN　　　(TIFERT TRADING CO., LTD 张立)
　TELEX: 67356/68523 BOCJS CN

Sample 4-3
样单 4-3

Commercial Invoice
商业发票

To: NEO GENERAL TRADING CO., P.O. BOX 99552, RIYADH 22766, KSA TEL: 00966-1-4659220 FAX: 00966-1-4659213			Invoice No.:	2001SDT001
			Invoice Date:	Apr.16th, 2021
			S/C No.:	NEO2001026
			S/C Date:	Feb.28th, 2021
From:	SHANGHAI, CHINA	**To:**	DAMMAM, KSA	
Letter of Credit No.:	0011LC123756	**Issued By:**	Apr. 16th, 2021	
Marks and Numbers	**Number and kind of package Description of goods**	**Quantity**	**Unit Price**	**Amount**
				CFR DAMMAM PORT
ROSE BRAND 178/2001 RIYADH	ABOUT 1 700 CARTONS CANNED MUSHROOMS PIECES & STEMS 24 TINS×425 GRAMS NET WEIGHT (D.W. 227 GRAMS) ROSE BRAND.	1 700CARTONS	USD7.80	USD13 260.00
TOTAL:		1 700CARTONS		USD13 260.00

SAY TOTAL: U.S. DOLLARS THIRTEEN THOUSAND TWO HUNDRED AND SIXTY ONLY.

A.B.C CORP.
张三

Sample 5-1 Bill of Lading
样单 5-1 提单

Shipper SHANGHAI CHEMICAL IMP. & EXP. CORP. LTD. ROOM 610 NO.27, CHUNGSHAN ROAD E.1. SHANGHAI, 200001 CHINA	BILL OF LADING B/L NO. TO BE USED WITH CHARTER PARTIES Reference NO. SHIPCRAFT TRANSPORT INC.
Consignee TO ORDER	General Agents: SHIPCRAFT A/S P.O Box142
Notify address ABCDIS CO. ASMBERSTRA AT 90 ANTWERPEN	DK-2970 Hoensholm, Denmark Phone: 4-245781 Telex: 37845 Shpcr DK Fax: 4-258745 Agent for Switzerland: MAT TRANSPORT AG ERLENSTRASSES 95 P.O.BOX

Vessel CONIT.JORK V.YCJ009	Port of loading SHANGHAI, CHINA	CH40222 BASEL, Switzerland Phone: 00616866000 Fax: 0616666001
Port of discharge AQABA PORT, JORDAN		

Shipper's description of goods 400 DRUMS NITROCELLULOSE FOR LACQUER	Gross weight 22 000KGS

ORIGINAL

(of which-0-(none) on deck at Shipper's risk; the carrier not being responsible for loss or damage however arising)

Freight payable as per CHARTER-PARTY dated Jan. 20th, 2021 FREIGHT ADVANCE Received on account of freight Time used for loading___days___hours.	SHIPPED at the Port of Loading in apparent good order and condition on board the vessel for carriage to the Port of Discharge or so near thereto as she may safely get the goods specified above. Weight, measure quality, quantity, condition, contents and value unknown. IN WITNESS whereof the Master or Agent of the sid Vessel has signed the number of Bills of Lading indicated below all of this tenor and date.any one of which being accomplish the others shall be void. FOR CONDITIONS OF CARRIAGE SEE OVERLEAF
Freight payable at	Place and date of issued SHANGHAI Jan. 18th, 2021
Number or original Bs/L THREE(3)	Signature

Sample 5-2　Ocean Bill of Lading
样单 5-2　海运提单

Shipper ABC COMPANY NO.128 ZHONGSHAN XILU, SHANDONG		B/L No.

Shipper ABC COMPANY NO.128 ZHONGSHAN XILU, SHANDONG	**SINOTRANS** 中国外运广东公司 **SINOTRANS GUANGDONG COMPANY** **OCEAN BILL OF LADING**
Consignee or order TO ORDER OF UFJ BANK, TOKYO	SHIPPED on board in apparent good order and condition (unless otherwise indicated) the goods or packages specified herein and to be discharged at the mentioned port of discharge or as near thereto as the vessel may safely get and be always afloat.
Notify address XYZ COMPANY 6-2 OHTEMACHI, 1-CHOME, CHIYADA-KU, TOKYO	The weight, measurement, marks and numbers, quality and value, being particulars furnished by the Shipper, are not checked by the Carrier on loading. The Shipper, Consignee and the Holder of this Bill of Lading hereby expressly accept and agree to all printed, written or stamped provisions, exceptions and conditions of this Bill of Lading, including those on the back hereof. IN WITNESS whereof the number of original Bills of Lading stated below have been signed, one of which being accomplished the other(s) to be void.

Pre-carriage by	Port of loading QINGDAO, CHINA
Vessel VICTORY V.666	Port of transshipment
Port of discharge TOKYO, JAPAN	Final destination

Container no. & seal no. or marks and Nos.	Number and kind of package	Description of goods	Gross weight (kgs.)	Measurement (m³)
XYZ TOKYO 04GD002 1-88 CTNS CONTAINER ON. PLU1234567 SEAL NO. 006789 1×20' CY/CY	PACKED IN 88 CTNS. SHIPPEND IN ONE CONTAINER. ON BOARD Jan. 18th, 2021 NAME OF VESSEL: PORTOFLOADING:	HOSPITAL UNIFORM 5 250Pcs VICTORY V.666 QINGDAO, CHINA	1 232.00	4.20

Freight and charges		REGARDING TRANSSHIPMENT INFORMATION PLEASE CONTACT	
Ex. rate	Prepaid at	Freight payable at	Place and date of issue　QINGDAO, CHINA, Jan. 17th, 2021
		3	李好 As Agent

Sample 5-3
样单 5-3

Air Waybill
航空运单

999	999—

Shipper's Name and Address	Shipper's Account Number	Not Negotiable Air Waybill Issued by 中国国际航空公司 AIR CHINA BEIJING CHINA
JIANGSU TEXTILE GARMENT CO., LTD. HUARONG MANSION RM2901 NO.85 GUANJIAQIAO, NANJING 210005, CHINA		Copies 1, 2 and 3 of this Air Waybill are originals and have the same validity.
Consignee's Name and Address	Consignee's Account Number	It is agreed that the goods described herein are accepted for carriage in apparent good order and condition (except as noted) and SUBJECT TO THE CONDITIONS OF CONTRACT ON THE REVERSE HEREOF. ALL GOODS MAY BE CARRIED BY AND OTHER MEANS INCLUDING ROAD OR ANY OTHER CARRIER UNLESS SPECIFIC CONTRARY INSTRUCTIONS ARE GIVEN HEREON BY THE SHIPPER. THE SHIPPER's ATTENTION IS DRAWN TO THE NOTICE CONCERNING CARRIER'S LIMITATION OF LIABILITY. Shipper may increase such limitation of liability by declaring a higher value for carriage and paying a supplemental charge if required.
FASHION FORCE CO., LTD P.O.BOX 8935 NEW TERMINAL, ALTA, VISTA OTTAWA, CANADA		
Issuing Carrier's Agent Name and City		Accounting Information
Agent's IATA Code	Account No.	
Airport of Departure (Addr. of First Carrier) and Requested Routing NANJING, CHINA		FREIGHT PREPAID

To	By First Carrier Routing and Destination	to	by	to	by	Currency USD	CHGS Code	WT/VAL		Other	Declared Value for Carriage	Declared Value for Customs
								PPD X	COLL	PPD X	COLL	

Airport of Destination MONTREAL, CANADA	Flight/Date For carrier Use Only Flight/Date FX0910 APRIL 7, 2015	Amount of Insurance	INSURANCE-If Carrier offers insurance, and such insurance is requested in accordance with the conditions thereof, indicate amount to be insured in figures in box marked "Amount of Insurance."

Handling Information

(For USA only) These commodities licensed by U.S. for ultimate destination ... Diversion contrary to U.S. law is prohibited

No. of Pieces RCP	Gross Weight	Kg lb	Rate Class		Chargeable Weight	Rate Charge	Total	Nature and Quantity of Goods (incl. Dimensions or Volume)
				Commodity Item No.				
1 700 CTNS	19 074.44	K	N		19074.44	20.61	393 124.21	CANNED MUSHROOM PIECES & STEMS 24 TINS×425 GRAMS

Prepaid Weight Charge Collect	Other Charges
393 124.21	
Valuation Charge	AWC: 50.00
Tax	
Total other Charges Due Agent	Shipper certifies that the particulars on the face hereof are correct and that insofar as any part of the consignment contains dangerous goods, such part is properly described by name and is in proper condition for carriage by air according to the applicable Dangerous Goods Regulations.
Total other Charges Due Carrier 50.00	.... Signature of Shipper or his Agent
Total Prepaid 393 124.21	Total Collect	7/APRIL/2021 NANJING JIANGSU TEXTILE GARMENT CO., LTD.
Currency Conversion Rates	CC Charges in Dest. Currency	.... Executed on (date) at(place) Signature of Issuing Carrier or its Agent
For Carrier's Use only at Destination	Charges at Destination	Total Collect Charges	999—

Sample 5-4
样单 5-4

Combined Transport B/L
联合运输提单

Shipper SHANGHAI FOREIGN TRADE IMP. AND EXP. CORP.	PIL **PACIFIC INTERNATIONAL LINES (PTE) LTD** (Incorporated in Singapore) **COMBINED TRANSPORT BILL OF LADING** B/L NO.
Consignee TO ORDER	Received in apparent good order and condition except as otherwise noted the total number of containers or other packages or units enumerated below for transportation from the place of receipt to the place of delivery subject to the terms hereof. One of the signed Bills of Lading must be surrendered duly endorsed in exchange for the goods or delivery order. On presentation of this document (duly) endorsed to the carrier by or on behalf of the holder, the rights and liabilities arising in accordance with the terms hereof shall (without prejudice to any rule of common law or statute rendering them binding on the Merchant) become binding in all respects between the carrier and the holder as though the contract evidenced hereby had been made between them. **SEE TERMS ON ORIGINAL B/L**
Notify Party EAST AGENT COMPANY 126ROOM STREET, ANTERWEIP, BELGIUM	

Vessel and Voyage Number DAFENG E002	Port of Loading NANJING, CHINA	Port of Discharge LONDON, UK
Place of Receipt	Place of Delivery ANTERWEIP, BELGIUM	Number of Original Bs/L 1

PARTICULARS AS DECLARED BY SHIPPER – CARRIER NOT RESPONSIBLE

Container Nos./Seal Nos. Marks and/Numbers	No. of Containers/Packages/ Description of Goods	Gross Weight (Kilos)	Measurement (cu-metres)
CBD LONDON NOS1-200	100CTNS LADIES LYCRA LONG PANT	2 000	6
FREIGHT & CHARGES FREIGHT PREPAID	Number of Containers/Packages (in words) ONE HUNDRED CARTONS ONLY		
	Shipped on Board Date: Oct. 18th, 2021		
	Place and Date of Issue: NANJING, CHINA Oct. 20th, 2021		
	In witness whereof this number of original bills of lading stated above all of the tenor and date one of which being accomplished the others to stand void for PACIFIC INTERNATIONAL LINES (PTE) LTD. as carrier		

Sample 5-5
样单 5-5

Packing List
装箱单

To	NEO GENERAL TRADING CO., P.O. BOX 99552, RIYADH 22766, KSA TEL: 00966-1-4659220 FAX: 00966-1-4659213		Invoice No.	2001SDT001		
			Invoice Date	Apr. 16th, 2021		
			S/C No.	NEO2001026		
			S/C Date	Feb. 28th, 2021		
From	SHANGHAI, CHINA	To		DAMMAM, KSA		
Letter of Credit No.	0011LC123756	Date of Shipment		Apr. 25, 2021		
Marks and Numbers	Number and kind of package/ Description of goods	Quantity	Package	G.W	N.W	Meas.
ROSE BRAND 178/2001 RIYADH	ABOUT 1 700 CARTONS CANNED MUSHROOMS PIECES & STEMS 24 TINS×425 GRAMS NET WEIGHT (D.W. 227GRAMS) ROSE BRAND.	1 700CTNS	1 700CTNS	19 074KGS	17 340KGS	22.80CBM
	TOTAL	1 700CTNS	1 700CTNS	19 074KGS	17 340KGS	22.80CBM
SAY TOTAL	ONE THOUSAND SEVEN HUNDRED CARTONS ONLY.					

A.B.C CO.
张三

Sample 6-1 样单 6-1 Export Licence 出口货物许可证

EXPORT LICENCE THE PEOPLE's REPUBLIC OF CHINA A 类

申领许可证单位　编码 195762654 Exporter 福州毛织品进出口贸易公司	出口许可证编号 Licence No. 2002122433
发货单位 195762654 Consignee 福州毛织品进出口贸易公司	许可证有效期 Validity 2021-12-24
贸易方式 Terms of trade 一般贸易	输往国家（地区） Country of destination 加拿大
合同号 Contract No. ST303	付款方式 Terms of payment 信用证
出运口岸 Port of shipment 福州	运输方式 Means of transport 江海
唛头——包装件数 Marks & numbers/number of packages	无唛头　98 箱
商品名称 Description of commodity 全棉抹布	商品编码 Commodity code 888.666

商品规格、型号 Specification	单位 Unit	数量 Quantity	单价（美元） Unit price	总值（人民币） Amount	总值折（美元） Amount in USD
10"10"	打	16 000	1.31	8 304.00	20 960.00
20"20"	打	6 000	2.51	130 269.00	15 060.00
30"30"	打	11 350	4.73	464 375.25	53 685.50
总计 Total	打	33 350		602 948.25	89 705.50

备注 Supplementary details	发证机关盖章 Issuing authority's stamp 发证日期 Signature date
商务部监制	本证不得涂改，不得转让

Sample 单证样例

Sample 6-2 / 样单 6-2 Entry Application Form for Inspection 入境货物报检单

报检单位(加盖公章):		上海朗明商贸有限公司			*编 号	
报检单位登记号:52304125596 联系人:王明 电话:021-58693215 报检日期:2021年8月12日							
收货人	(中文)	上海朗明商贸有限公司	企业性质(画"√")		☑合资 □合作 □外资	
	(外文)	SHANGHAI LANGMING TRADING CO., LTD.				
发货人	(中文)	东方代理公司				
	(外文)	EAST AGENT COMPANY				
货物名称(中/外文)	H.S.编码	原产国(地区)	数/重量	货物总值	包装种类及数量	
高尔夫球帽 H6-59940BS GOLF CAPS	59019091	日本	1 800打	USD14 580.00	36箱	
运输工具名称、号码			Volendam Voy. 8080		合同号	03TG28711
贸易方式	一般贸易	贸易国别(地区)	日本	提单/运单号	SOCO02596	
到货日期	2021-08-09	启运国家(地区)	日本	许可证/审批号	CT88661125839	
卸货日期	2021-08-13	启运口岸	大阪	入境口岸	上海	
索赔有效期至	两年	经停口岸		目的地	上海	
集装箱规格、数量及号码			20英尺×1			
合同、信用证订立的检验检疫条款或特殊要求				货物存放地点	上海市康元街119号	
				用途	外贸自营内销	
随附单据(画"√"或补填)		标记及号码	*外商投资资产(画"√")		□是□否	
☑合同 ☑发票 ☑提/运单 □兽医卫生证书 □植物检疫证书 □动物检疫证书 □卫生证书 □原产地证书 ☑许可/审批文件	□到货通知 ☑装箱单 □质保书 □理货清单 □磅码单 □验收报告 □ □ □	V.H SHANGHAI C/NO.1-360 MADE IN JAPAN	*检验检疫费		
			总金额(人民币元)		
			计费人		
			收费人		
报检人郑重声明: 1.本人被授权报检。 2.上列填写内容正确属实。 签名:_____王明_____			领取证单		
			日期			
			签名			

注:有"*"号栏由出入境检验检疫机关填写   ◆国家质检总局制

Sample 6-3 Export Application Form for Inspection
样单 6-3 出境货物报检单

报检单位(加盖公章): 　　　　　　　　　　　　　　　*编号 _____
报检单位登记号　　　联系人:张立　电话:13877782512　报检日期:2014年8月12日

发货人	(中文)	江西蓝星有限公司				
	(外文)	JIANGXI LANXING CO., LTD.				
收货人	(中文)	东方代理公司				
	(外文)	EAST AGENT COMPANY				
货物名称(中/外文)		H.S.编码	产地	数/重量	货物总值	包装种类及数量
高尔夫球帽 H6-59940BS GOLF CAPS		59019091	南昌	1 800 打	USD14 580.00	90 箱

运输工具名称、号码	昌海802		贸易方式	一般贸易	货物存放地点	工厂仓库
合同号	03TG28711		信用证号	LTR0505457	用途	外销
发货日期	2014-08-12	输往国家(地区)	日本	许可证/审批号		
启运地	南昌	到达口岸	秋田	生产单位注册号		
集装箱规格、数量及号码	20尺×1					

合同、信用证订立的检验检疫条款或特殊要求	标记及号码	随附单据(画"√"或补填)	
	V.H LAS PLAMS C/NO.	☑合同　□换证凭单 ☑信用证　□厂检单 ☑发票　☑装箱单	□包装性能结果单 □许可/审批文件 □

需要证单名称(画"√"或补填)				*检验检疫费
☑品质证书	__正 __副			总金额 (人民币元)
□重量证书	__正 __副	□植物检疫证书	□	
□数量证书	__正 __副	□熏蒸/消毒证书	□	计费人
□兽医卫生证书	__正 __副	☑出境货物换证凭单	__正 __副	
□健康证书	__正 __副	□	__正 __副	收费人
□卫生证书	__正 __副	□	__正 __副	
□动物卫生证书	__正 __副			

报检人郑重声明:	领取证单
1. 本人被授权报检。 2. 上列填写内容正确属实,货物无伪造或冒用他人的厂名、标志、认证标志,并承担货物质量责任。 签名:____张立____	日期 签名

注:有"*"号栏由出入境检验检疫机关填写　　◆国家出入境检验检疫局制

Sample 6-4
样单 6-4

Shipping Note
出口货物订舱委托书

日期：2015 年 3 月 11 日

1) 发货人 JIANGXI TEXTILES IMP. & EXP. CORPORATION 8/F.JIANGXI TEXTILES MANSION, 168 XIAOBEI ROAD, NANCHANG, CHINA		4) 信用证号码	63211020049		
		5) 开证银行	BNP PARIBAS (CANADA)		
		6) 合同号码	F01LCB05127	7) 成交金额	USD32 640.00
		8) 装运口岸	SHANGHAI	9) 目的港	MONTREAL
2) 收货人 TO ORDER OF BNP PARIBAS (CANADA)		10) 转船运输	ALLOWED	11) 分批装运	NOT ALLOWED
		12) 信用证有效期	2021-04-10	13) 装船期限	2021-03-25
		14) 运费	PREPAID	15) 成交条件	CIF
		16) 公司联系人	李好	17) 电话/传真	044-58818844
3) 通知人 DADAI CORPORATION P.O.BOX 8935 NEW TERMINAL, ALTA, VISTA OTTAWA, CANADA		18) 公司开户行	中国银行	19) 银行账号	58625935148
		20) 特别要求			
21) 标记唛码	22) 货号规格	23) 包装件数	24) 毛重	25) 净重	26) 数量	27) 单价	28) 总价
DADAI F01LCB05127 CTN NO. MONTREAL MADE IN CHINA	LADIES COTTON BLAZER (100% COTTON, 40S×20/140×60)	85 CTNS	19KGS	17KGS	2 550 PCS	USD12.80	USD 32 640.00
	29) 总件数	30) 总毛重	31) 总净重	32) 总尺码	33) 总金额
	85 CARTONS	19KGS	17KGS	21.583 CBM	USD32 640.00

34) 备注

Sample 6-5
样单 6-5

Import Shipping Note
进口订舱委托书

编号：CT8514895　　　　　　　　　　　　　　　　日期：2021 年 12 月 13 日

货　名（英文）	AIR CONDITIONER 空调		
重　量	6 500kgs	尺　码	43m³
合同号	03TG28711	包　装	纸箱
装卸港	大阪	交货期	2021 年 2 月 28 日
装货条款			
发货人名称地址	上海朗明商贸有限公司 上海市天河路 267 号		
发货人电挂	021-58693215		
订妥船名	海鸥 708	预抵港口	上海
备注		委托单位	上海朗明商贸有限公司 王明

①危险品需注明性能，重大物件注明每件重量及尺码；
②装货条款须详细注明。

Sample 6-6
样单 6-6

Shipping Order
托运单

EXOIRTER:　　　　　　　　　　　　　　　No.: YSM1999901
GUANGDONG MACHINERY IMPORT AND　　　DATE: Nov. 11th, 2021
EXPORT CORP.(GROUP)　　　　　　　　　LOADING PORT: GUANGZHOU, CHINA
　　　　　　　　　　　　　　　　　　　　DESTINATION: MELBORNE, AUSTRALIA
　　　　　　　　　　　　　　　　　　　　B/L NO.: MANE962/25

CONSIGNEE:　　　　　　　　　　　　　　NOTIFY:
TO ORDER OF K-MART AUSTRALIA　　　　　K-MART AUSTRALIA LIMITED 800
LIMITED 800 TORONGA VIC 3416 AUSTRALIA　800 TORONGA VIC 3416 AUSTRALIA

SHIPPING MARKS	QUANTITY	DESCRIPTION GOODS	NET WEIGHT	GROSS WEIGHT	MEASUREMENT
KMART CTN NO.1-20	120BAGS	EDGNG KNIFE WITH METAL HANDLE	10 800.00KGS	12 000.00KGS	3.672CBMS
	TOTAL: 120BAGS		10 800.00KGS	12 000.00KGS	3.672CBMS

PARTIAL SHIPMENT: NOT ALLOWED　　　　ORIGINAL B/L: 2
TRANSSHIPMENT: NOT ALLOWED　　　　　COPY B/L: 3
LATEST SHIPMENT DATE: NOV.11TH, 2014　GOODS IN: 大松岗
EXPIRY DATE: DEC.11TH, 2021　　　　　　AMOUNT: USD6 000.00
运费付款方式：FREIGHT PREPAID　　　　L/C NO.: T/T
INVOICE NO.: YSM52165　　　　　　　　CONTRACT NO.: VX562445636
货证情况：
运输方式：江海运输
运输吨：　　　　　运费率：　　　　　　GUANGDONG MACHINERY IMPORT
特殊条款：　　　　　　　　　　　　　　AND EXPORT CORP.(GUOUP)
　　　　　　　　　　　　　　　　　　　　张立

Sample 6-7　CUSTOMS Declaration for Export Commodity
样单 6-7　出口货物报关单

预录入编号：DS9110002　　　　海关编号：

出口口岸 上海浦江海关 (2202)		备案号 ×××	出口日期 2021.03.28	申报日期 2021.03.18
经营单位 南京纺织有限公司 (3201004261)		运输方式 江海 (2)	运输工具名称 SU YUE V.981	提运单号 CSLMJ180180
发货单位 南京纺织有限公司		贸易方式 一般贸易 (0110)	征免性质 一般征税 (101)	结汇方式 信用证 (6)
许可证号 ×××		运抵国 (地区) 加拿大 (501)	指运港 蒙特利尔 (MTR)	境内货源地 南京
批准文号 35/0591540		成交方式 CIF	运费 502/1260/3	保费 502/1250/3	杂费 ×××
合同协议号 F01LCB05127		件数 2 550	包装种类 纸箱	毛重 (千克) 3 015.00	净重 (千克) 2 010.00
集装箱号	CCLU1000752*3(5)	随附单据 INVOICE, PACKING LIST	生产厂家	南京纺织有限公司
标记唛码及备注 FASHION FORCE F01LCB05127 CTN NO. MONTREAL MADE IN CHINA				

项号	商品编号	商品名称、规格型号	数量及单位	最终目的国 (地区)	单价	总价	币制	征免
1	62043200.90	100% 棉女式运动衣 40S×20/140×60	2 550 件	加拿大	12.80	32 640.00	美元	照章
		Total: 2 550 件				32 640.00 美元		

FREIGHT: USD1 000.00
FOB VALUE: USD31 640.00

税费征收情况

税务登记号码：320102134773852

录入员	录入单位	兹声明以上申报无讹并承担法律责任 申报单位 (签章)	海关审单批注及放行日期 (签章)	
			审单	审价
报关员			征税	统计
单位地址	南京中山路 85 号华荣大厦 2901 室		查验	放行
邮编	210005	电话 025-4715004	填制日期 2021-03-18	

Sample 6-8
样单 6-8

Shipping Advice
装船通知

TO: FASHION FORCE CO., LTD P.O.BOX 8935 NEW TERMINAL, ALTA, VISTA OTTAWA, CANADA	ISSUE DATE:	Mar. 21th, 2021
	OUR REF. DATE:	BC954621

Dear Sir or Madam:
We are Pleased to Advice you that the following mentioned goods has been shipped out, full details were shown as follows:

Invoice Number:	NT001FF004
Bill of Lading Number:	COS6314203208
Ocean Vessel:	HUA CHANG V.09981
Port of Loading:	BEIHAI, CHINA
Date of Shipment:	Mar. 20th, 2021
Port of Destination:	MONTREAL, CANADA
Estimated Date of Arrival:	Apr. 25th, 2021
Containers/Seals Number:	MSKU2612114 / 1681316
Description of Goods:	SALES CONDITIONS: CIF MONTREAL/CANADA SALES CONTRACT NO. F01LCB05127 LADIES COTTON BLAZER (100% COTTON, 40S×20/140×60) STYLE NO. PO NO. QTY/PCS USD/PC 46-301A 10337 2 550 12.80
Shipping Marks:	FASHION FORCE F01LCB05127 CTN NO. MONTREAL MADE IN CHINA
Quantity:	201 CARTONS
Gross Weight:	3 015.00KGS
Net Weight:	2 010.00KGS
Total Value:	USD32 640.00

Thank you for your patronage. We look forward to the pleasure of receiving your valuable repeat orders.

Sincerely yours,

GUANGXI TEXTILE GARMENT CO., LTD.
张立

Sample 6-9 / 样单 6-9 — Insurance Application Form 投保单

发票号码	NT001FF004		投保条款和险别	
被保险人	客户抬头 NANJING TANG TEXTILE GARMENT CO., LTD. 过户 FASHION FORCE CO., LTD	(✓)	PICC CLAUSE	
		( )	ICC CLAUSE	
		(✓)	ALL RISKS	
		( )	W.P.A./W.A.	
		( )	F.P.A.	
		(✓)	WAR RISKS	
		( )	S.R.C.C.	
		(✓)	STRIKE	
		( )	ICC CLAUSE A	
		( )	ICC CLAUSE B	
		( )	ICC CLAUSE C	
保险金额	USD (35 904.00) HKD ( ) ( ) ( )	( )	AIR TPT ALL RISKS	
		( )	AIR TPT RISKS	
		( )	O/L TPT ALL RISKS	
启运港	SHANGHAI	( )	O/L TPT RISKS	
目的港	MONTREAL	( )	TRANSSHIPMENT RISKS	
转内陆		( )	W TO W	
开航日期	2021.3.20	( )	T.P.N.D.	
船名航次	HUA CHANG V.09981	( )	F.R.E.C.	
赔款地点	CANADA	( )	R.F.W.D.	
赔付币别	USD	( )	RISKS OF BREAKAGE	
正本份数	1 份正本，1 份副本	( )	I.O.P.	
其他特别条款	COVERING INSTITUTE CIVIL COMMOTIONS CLAUSES.			
以下由保险公司填写				
保单号码		费率		
签单日期		保费		

投保日期： 2021 年 3 月 16 日　　　　投保人签章：

Sample 6-10 / 样单 6-10 — Insurance Policy 保险单

	中保财产保险有限公司 The People's Insurance (Property) Company of China, Ltd.	
发票号码 Invoice No. INV52148		保险单号次 Policy No.

海洋货物运输保险单
MARINE CARGO TRANSPORTATION INSURANCE POLICY

被保险人：
Insured: SHANGHAI FOREIGN TRADE IMP. AND EXP. CORP.

中保财产保险有限公司（以下简称本公司）根据被保险人的要求及其所缴付约定的保险费，按照本保险单承担险别和背面所载条款与下列特别条款承保下列货物运输保险，特签发本保险单。

This policy of insurance witnesses that the People's Insurance (Property) Company of China, Ltd. (hereinafter called "The Company"), at the request of the insured and in consideration of the agreed premium paid by the insured, undertakes to insure the under mentioned goods in transportation subject to the conditions of the policy as per the clauses printed overleaf and other special clauses attached hereon.

保险货物项目 Descriptions of Goods	包装 Packing	单位 Unit	数量 Quantity	保险金额 Amount Insured
LADIES LYCRA LONG PANT	200CTNS		2 400PCS	USD52 800.00

承保险别 Conditions	货物标记 Marks of Goods
COVERING RISKS AS PER "INSTITUTE CARGO CLAUSES (A)", AND INSTITUTE WAR CLAUSES (CARGO)".	CBD LONDON NOS1-200

总保险金额： Total Amount Insured:	U.S.DOLLARS FIFTY TWO THOUSAND EIGHT HUNDRED ONLY.

保费 Premium	As arranged	装载运输工具 Per conveyance S.S.	DAFENG	开航日期 Slg. on or abt.	Oct. 20th, 2021
起运港 From	SHANGHAI, CHINA		目的港 To	LONDON, UK	

所保货物，如发生本保险单项下可能引起索赔的损失或损坏，应立即通知本公司下述代理人查勘。如有索赔，应向本公司提交保险单正本（本保险单共有___份正本）及有关文件。如一份正本已用于索赔，其余正本则自动失效。

In the event of loss or damage which may result in a claim under this policy, immediate notice must be given to the company's agent as mentioned hereunder. Claims, if any, one of the original policy which has been issued in _____ original (s) together with the relevant documents shall be surrendered to the company. If one of the original policy has been accomplished, the others to be void.

赔款偿付地点 Claim payable at	LONDON, UK			
日期 Date	Oct. 20th, 2021	在 at	SHANGHAI, CHINA	
地址 Address				

Sample 6-11 / 样单 6-11

Bill of Exchange 汇票

NO.	T03617	Date:	Oct. 24th, 2021

FOR USD 89 705.50

At ×××××× Sight of THIS SECOND BILL of EXCHANGE

(First of the same tenor and date being unpaid) Pay to BANK OF CHINA GUANGZHOU, BRANCH or order the sum of

SAY US DOLLARS EIGHTY-NINE THOUSAND SEVEN HUNDRED AND FIVE POINT FIVE ONLY.

Drawn under NATIONAL PARIS BANK (CANADA) MONTREAL

L/C NO. TH2003 Dated Oct. 6th, 2021

TO.

NATIONAL PARIS BANK

24 MARSHALL VEDONCASTER MONTREAL CANADA

GUANGZHOU KNITWEAR AND MANUFACTURED
GOODS IMPORT & EXPORT TRADE CORPORATION
张三

BILL OF EXCHANGE (ON COLLECTION)

NO...ST007...**Exchange** for USD15000.00 D/P At ××××××× sight this

First of Exchange (**Second** being unpaid) Pay to the order of The HongKong and ShangHai Banking Corporation, QingDao The sum of U.S.Dollars Fifteen Thousand Only

Value received for Shipment of 100 cartons shoes as per Invoice No.005

To M/S Hamka Trading Co. Ltd.

378 Gold Rd HongKong

China National Metals Corp.
张三

Sample 6-12   Certificate of Origin
样单 6-12   原产地证书

1. Exporter FUJIAN INTERNATIONAL IMPORT & EXPORT CORP. 8TH FLOOR, 200 ZHANQIAN ROAD, FUZHOU, CHINA		Certificate No. **CERTIFICATE OF ORIGIN** **OF** **THE PEOPLE'S REPUBLIC OF CHINA**		
2. Consignee NEO GENERAL TRADING CO., P.O. BOX 99552, RIYADH 22766, KSA TEL: 00966-1-4659220 FAX: 00966-1-4659213				
3. Means of transport and route SHIPMENT FROM SHANGHAI, CHINA TO DAMMAM, KSA BY SEA		5. For certifying authority use only		
4. Country / region of destination SAUDI, ARABIA				
6. Marks and numbers	7. Number and kind of packages; description of goods	8. H.S.Code	9. Quantity	10. Number and date of invoices
ROSE BRAND 178/2001 RIYADH	ABOUT 1 700 CARTONS CANNED MUSHROOMS PIECES & STEMS 24 TINS×425 GRAMS NET WEIGHT (D.W. 227 GRAMS) ROSE BRAND.	2003.1011	1 700CTNS	2001SDT001 Apr. 25th, 2015
SAY TOTAL: ONE THOUSAND SEVEN HUNDRED CARTONS ONLY. **THE NAME OF THE MANUFACTURERS:** XUZHOU SHENGTONG FOODSTUFFS CO., LTD. NO.15 HEPING ROAD, FUZHOU 221009, CHINA TEL: 86-0516-3402323 FAX: 86-0516-3402330 WE HEREBY CERTIFY THAT GOODS EXPORTED ARE WHOLLY OF CHINESE ORIGIN.				
11. Declaration by the exporter The undersigned hereby declares that the above details and statements are correct, that all the goods were produced in China and that they comply with the Rules of Origin of the People's Republic of China. FUZHOU, CHINA APR.25TH, 2015 张三 -- Place and date, signature and stamp of authorized signatory		12. Certification It is hereby certified that the declaration by the exporter is correct. FUZHOU, CHINA APR.25th, 2010 -- Place and date, signature and stamp of certifying authority		

Sample 6-13 Generalized System of Preferences Certificate of Origin
样单 6-13 普惠制原产地证书

1. Goods consigned from (Exporter's business name, address, country) BEIJING TEXTILE GARMENT CO., LTD. HUARONG MANSION RM2901 NO.85 CHANGAN ROAD, BEIJING 100005, CHINA	Reference No. **GENERALIZED SYSTEM OF PREFERENCES CERTIFICATE OF ORIGIN** (**Combined declaration and certificate**) **FORM A**
2. Goods consigned to (Consignee's name, address, country) FASHION FORCE CO., LTD P.O.BOX 8935 NEW TERMINAL, ALTA, VISTA OTTAWA, CANADA	Issued in THE PEOPLE'S REPUBLIC OF CHINA (country) See notes overleaf
3. Means of transport and route (as far as known) SHIPMENT FROM BEIJING, CHINA TO MONTREAL, CANADA BY VESSEL	4. For official use

5. Item number	6. Marks and numbers of packages	7. Number and kind of packages; description of goods	8. Origin criterion (see notes overleaf)	9. Gross weight or other quantity	10. Number and date of invoice
1	FASHION FORCE F01LCB05127 CTN NO. MONTREAL MADE IN CHINA	SALES CONDITIONS: CIF MONTREAL/CANADA SALES CONTRACT NO. F01LCB05127 LADIES COTTON BLAZER (100% COTTON, 40S×20/ 140×60) STYLE NO. PO NO. QTY/PCS USD/PC 46-301A 10337 2 550 12.80	"P"	2 550PCS	NT001FF004 Mar. 20th, 2021
		TOTAL:		2 550PCS	

11. Certification It is hereby certified, on the basis of control carried out, that the declaration by the exporter is correct. BEIJING, CHINA MAR.22ND, 2014	12. Declaration by the exporter The undersigned hereby declares that the above details and statements are correct, that all the goods were produced in **CHINA** (country) and that they comply with the origin requirements specified for those goods in the Generalized System of Preferences for goods exported to (importing country). **CANADA** BEIJING, CHINA MAR.21ST, 2021 张三
Place and date, signature and stamp of certifying authority	Place and date, signature and stamp of authorized signatory

Sample 6-14 / 样单 6-14 — Canada Customs Invoice / 加拿大海关发票

Revenue Canada Customs and Excise	Revenue Canada Douanes et Accise	CANADA CUSTOMS INVOICE FACTURE DES DOUANES CANADIENNES	Page of de
1. Vendor (Name and Address) Vendeur (Nom et adresse) SHANDONG TEXTILE GARMENT CO., LTD. HUARONG MANSION RM2901 NO.85 GUANJIAQIAO, QINGDAO 110005, CHINA		2. Date of Direct Shipment to Canada/Date d' expedition directe vers ie Canade AS PER B/L DATE	
		3. Other References (include Purchasers' Order No.) Autres reterences(inclure ie n de commande de Í acheteur)	
4. Consignee (Name and Address) Destinataire (Nom et adresse) FASHION FORCE CO., LTD P.O.BOX 8935 NEW TERMINAL, ALTA, VISTA OTTAWA, CANADA		5. Purchaser's Name and Address(if other than Consignee)Nom et adresse de Í acheteur(S' ll differe du destinataire) SAME AS CONSIGNEE	
		6. Country of Transshipment/Pays de transbordement	
		7. Country of Origin of Goods pays d' origine des archandises CHINA	IF SHIPMENT INCLUDES GOODS OF DIFFERENT ORIGINS ENTER ORIGINS AGAINST ITEMA IN12 SIL' EXPEDON COMPREND DES MARCHANDISES D' ORIGINES DIFFERENTES PRECISER LEUR PROVENANCE EN12
8. Transportation: Give Mode and Place of Direct Shipment to Canada Transport Preciser mode et point d' expedition directe vercte vers ie canada SHIPMENT FROM SHANGHAI, CHINA TO MONTREAL, CANADA BY VESSEL		9. Conditions of Sale and Terms of Payment (i.e. Consignment Shipment, Leased Goods, etd.) Conditions de vente et modaitites de paiement (P.ex vente, expedition en consignation, location, de marchandises, etc) CIF MONTREAL BY L/C	
		10. Currency of Settlement/Devises du paiement U.S.DOLLAR	

11. No. of Pkgs Nore de colis	12. Specification of Commodities (Kind of Pack-ages, Marks and Numbers, General Decripstion and Characteristics, ie Grade, Quality) Designation des articles (Nature des colis, marques et numeros, description ger erale et caracteristiques, Pex classe, qualite)	13. Quantity Quantite PreciserÍ unite	Selling Price/Prix de vente	
			14. Unit Price Prix unitaire	15. Total
SALES CONDITIONS: CIF MONTREAL/ CANADA SALES CONTRACT NO.F01LCB05127	LADIES COTTON BLAZER (100% COTTON, 40S×20/ 140×60) STYLE NO. PO NO. QTY/PCS USD/PC 46-301A 10337 2550 12.80	2 550PCS	USD12.80	USD32 640.00
201 CTNS	PACKED IN 201 CTNS ONLY			

Sample 单证样例

（续表）

18. if any Of fields 1 to 17 are included on an attached commercial invoice, check this box Si tout renseignement relatlvement aux zones 1 e 17 ligure sur une ou des tactures ommerciaiesci attachees cocher cette case commercial invoice No. 1 N de la factre commerciaie NT001FF004 ☐	16. Total Weight/ Poids Total		17. Invoice Total Total de la facture
	Net 2 010KGS	Gross/Brut 3 015KGS	USD32 640.00
19. Exporter's Name and Address(if other than Vendor) Nom et adresse de Í exportateur(s' ll differe du vendeur) SAME AS VENDOR	20. Originator (Name and Address)/ Expediteur d' origine(Nom et adresse) SHANDONG TEXTILE GARMENT CO., LTD. HUARONG MANSION RM2901 NO.85 GUANJIAQIAO, QINGDAO 110005, CHINA		
21. Departmental Ruling(if applicable)/ Decision du Ministere (S' lly a lieu) N/A	22. If fields 23 to 25 are not applicable, check this box Si ies zones 23 e 25 sont sans objet, cocher cette case ☐		
23. if included in field 7, indicate amount Si compris dans ie total a ia zone 17, preciser （Ⅰ）Transportation charges, expense and insurance from the place of direct shipment to Canada Les frais de transport, depenses et assurancesa partir du point of expedition directe vers is Canada. USD4 590.40 （Ⅱ）Costs for construction, erection and assembly incurred after importation into Canada Les couts de construction, d' erection et d' assemblage, pres imporaation au.Canada N/A （Ⅲ）Export packing Le cout de Í emballage d' exportation N/A	24. If not included in field 17, indicate amount Si non compris dans le total a ie zone 17, Dreciser （Ⅰ）Transportation charges, expense and insurance to the place of direct shipment to Canada Les frais de transport, depenses et assurances Iusqu' au point d' of expedition directd vers ie Canada N/A （Ⅱ）Amounts for commissions other than buying commissions Les commissions autres que celles verses Pour Í achat N/A （Ⅲ）Export packing Le cout de Íemballage d' exportation N/A		25. Check (if applicable) Cochet (s' lly u liso) （Ⅰ）Royalty payments or subsequent proceeds are paid or payable by the purchaser Des redevances ou produits ont ete ou seront Verses par Í acheteur ☐ （Ⅱ）The purchaser has supplied goods or services for use in the production of these goods L' acheteur a fouml des merchandises ou des Services pour ia production des merchandises ☐

Sample 7-1   Import Licence of the People's Republic of China
样单 7-1   中华人民共和国进口货物许可证

1. 我国对外成交单位 编码 Importer 广州明朗商贸有限公司 52304125596			3. 进口许可证编号 License No. CT88661125839		
2. 收货单位 52304125596 Consignee 广州明朗商贸有限公司			4. 许可证有效期 Validity 2021 年 8 月		
5. 贸易方式 Terms of trade 一般贸易			8. 进口国家(地区) Country where consigned 日本		
6. 外汇来源 Terms of foreign exchange 购汇			9. 商品原产地 Country of origin 日本		
7. 到货口岸 Port of destination 广州			10. 商品用途 Use of commodity 外贸自营内销		
11. 唛头——包装件数 Marks & numbers— number of packages			EAST SHANGHAI NOSI-500 MADE IN JAPAN		
12. 商品名称 Description of commodity 空调			商品编码 Commodity No. 84151021		
13. 商品规格、型号 Specification	单位 Unit	14. 数量 Quantity	15. 单价 ( ) Unit Price	16. 总值 ( ) Amount	17. 总值折美元 Amount in USD
制冷量≤4 000 大卡/时分体式空调	台	500	200 美元	100 000 美元	100 000
18. 总计 Total		500			100 000
19. 备注 Supplementary details			20. 发证机关盖章 Issuing authority's stamp 发证日期 Signature date 2021 年 12 月 1 日		

商务部监制   本证不得涂改,不得转让

Sample 7-2 Customs Import Declaration of China
样单 7-2 中华人民共和国海关进口货物报关单

预录入编号：DS9110006　　　　　　　　　　　　　海关编号：

进口口岸 上海浦江海关 (2202)		备案号 ×××	进口日期 2021-04-17	申报日期 2021-04-09
经营单位 5230412559 江苏纺织服装有限公司		运输方式 江海 (2)	运输工具名称 Volendam Voy. 7524	提运单号 782-02458690
收货单位 江苏纺织服装有限公司		贸易方式 一般贸易 (0110)	征免性质 一般征免 (101)	征税比例
许可证号 CT88661182569	起运国 (地区) 加拿大		装货港 蒙特利尔 (MTR)	境内目的地 上海 (2200)
批准文号 0220215	成交方式 CIF(1)	运费 502/1300/3	保费 502/1000/3	杂费 ×××
合同协议号 F01LCB05127	件数 85	包装种类 纸箱	毛重 (千克) 19.00KGS	净重 (千克) 17.00KGS
集装箱号 CLLU1000752*3(5)	随附单据 INVOICE, PACKING LIST		用途 外贸自营内销（1）	

标记唛码及备注
FASHION FORCE
F01LCB05127
CTN NO.
SHANGHAI
MADE IN CANADA

项号	商品编号	商品名称、规格型号	数量及单位	最终目的国 (地区)	单价	总价	币制	征免
1	62043200.90	LADIES COTTON BLAZER 100%COTTON 40S×20/140×60	2 550PCS	中国 (110)	12.80	32 640.00	美元	照章 (1)
		Total: 2 550PCS				USD32 640.00		

税费征收情况

税务登记号码：320102134773852

录入员	录入单位	兹声明以上申报无讹并承担法律责任	海关审单批注及放行日期 (签章)	
			审单	审价
报关员	李平	申报单位 (签章) 江苏纺织服装有限公司	征税	统计
单位地址	南京市管桥 85 号华荣大厦 2901 室		查验	放行
邮编 210005	电话 025-4715004	填制日期 2021-04-09		

Sample 7-3　　　　Shipper's Letter of Instruction
样单 7-3　　　　国际货物托运书

TO:　　　　　　　　　　　　　　　　　　　　　进仓编号：

托运人	江苏长宏物流有限公司				
发货人 SHIPPER	NANJING TEXTILE CO., LTD. HUARONG MANSION RM2901 NO.85 GUANJIAQIAO, NANJING 210005, CHINA				
收货人 CONSIGNEE	FASHION FORCE CO., LTD. P.O.BOX 8935 NEW TERMINAL, ALTA, VISTA OTTAWA, CANADA				
通知人 NOTIFY PARTY	FASHION FORCE CO., LTD. P.O.BOX 8935 NEW TERMINAL, ALTA, VISTA OTTAWA, CANADA				
起运港	SHANGHAI	目的港	MONTREAL	运费	PREPAID
标记唛头 MARKS	件数 NUMBER	中英文品名 DESCRIPTION OF GOODS		毛重（千克） G.W (KGS)	尺码 （立方米） SIZE (M³)
FASHION FORCE F01LCB05127 CTN NO. MONTREAL MADE IN CHINA	85 CARTONS	LADIES COTTON BLAZER 女式棉运动上衣 (100% COTTON, 40S×20/140×60)		19	21.583

1. 货单到达时间：3.17 报关	2. 航班：OZ/3.18	运价：29/KG+50
电　话：84217836 传　真：84217835 联系人：黄汗 地　址：上海市三环路 60 号世贸大厦 2401 室 托运人签字：	★如改配航空公司请提前通知我司 （公章） 制单日期：2014 年 3 月 12 日	

Sample 8-1 Irrevocable Documentary Credit Application
样单 8-1　　　　　　　不可撤销跟单信用证申请

TO: BANK OF CHINA GUANGZHOU BRANCH	Date:
☐ Issued by airmail　　☐ With brief advice by teletransmission ☐ Issued by express delivery ☒ Issued by teletransmission (which shall be the operative instrument)	Credit No. Date and place of expiry　　JULY 30th, 2021 IN CHINA
Applicant GUANGDONG FOREIGN TRADE IMP. & EXP. CORP. 15-18/F., GUANGDONG FOREIGN ECONOMIC AND TRADE BUILDING 351 TIANHE ROAD GUANGZHOU, CHINA	Beneficiary (Full name and address) ROYAL TRADERS LTD. 333 BARRON BLVD., INGLESIDE, ILLINOIS (UNITED STATES)
Advising Bank	Amount USD 570 000.00 SAY U.S.DOLLARS FIVE HUNDRED AND SEVENTY THOUSAND ONLY

Partial shipments ☐ allowed ☒ not allowed	Transshipment ☐ allowed　　☒ not allowed	Credit available with ANY BANK
Loading on board/dispatch/taking in charge at/from NEW YORK not later than　　JULY 15, 2021 for transportation to: GUANGZHOU, CHINA		By ☐ sight payment　☐ acceptance　☒ negotiation ☐ deferred payment at against the documents detailed herein ☒ and beneficiary's draft(s) for　100% of invoice value at ＿＿**** sight drawn on
☒ FOB　　☐ CFR　　☐ CIF ☐ or other terms		

Documents required: (marked with ×)
1. (×) Signed commercial invoice in __3__ copies indicating L/C No. and Contract No.
2. (×) Full set of clean on board Bills of Lading made out to order and blank endorsed, marked "freight [×] to collect / [ ] prepaid [ ] showing freight amount" notifying THE APPLICANT WITH FULL NAME AND ADDRESS .
 (　) Airway bills/cargo receipt/copy of railway bills issued by ＿＿＿＿＿＿ showing "freight [　] to collect/[　] prepaid [　] indicating freight amount" and consigned to ＿＿＿＿＿＿＿＿.
3. (　) Insurance Policy/Certificate in ＿＿ copies for ＿＿% of the invoice value showing claims payable in ＿＿＿＿ in currency of the draft, blank endorsed, covering All Risks, War Risks and ＿＿＿＿＿＿.
4. (×) Packing List/Weight Memo in __3__ copies indicating quantity, gross weights of each package.
5. (　) Certificate of Quantity/Weight in ＿＿＿ copies issued by ＿＿＿＿＿.
6. (　) Certificate of Quality in ＿＿ copies issued by [ ] manufacturer/[ ] public recognized surveyor ＿＿＿＿＿.
7. (×) Certificate of Origin in __2__ copies.
8. (×) Beneficiary's certified copy of fax / telex dispatched to the applicant within __1__ days after shipment advising L/C No., name of vessel, date of shipment, name, quantity, weight and value of goods.
Other documents, if any.
Description of goods:
　　MEN's DENIM UTILITY SHIRT
　　COLOR: MEDDEST SANDBLAS
　　FABRIC CONTENT: 100% COTTON
　　QUANTITY: 2 000 CARTON
　　PRICE TERM: FOB NEW YORK
　　COUNTRY OF ORIGIN AND MANUFACTURERS: UNITED STATES OF AMERICA, VICTORY FACTORY
Additional instructions:
1. (×) All banking charges outside the opening bank are for beneficiary's account.
2. (×) Documents must be presented within __10__ days after date of issuance of the transport documents but within the validity of this credit.
3. (　) Third party as shipper is not acceptable, Short Form/Blank back B/L is not acceptable.
4. (　) Both quantity and credit amount ＿＿＿ % more or less are allowed.
5. (×) All documents must be sent to issuing bank by courier/speed post in one lot.
　　Other terms, if any.

Sample 9-1 Open Cargo Policies
样单 9-1 进口货物运输预约保险合同

合同号	TT080156	2021年12月17日
甲方：	上海朗明商贸有限公司	
乙方：	中国人民保险公司上海分公司	

双方就进口货物的运输预约保险拟订以下条款，以资共同遵守：

一、保险范围

　　甲方从国外进口全部货物，不论运输方式，凡贸易条件规定由买方办理保险的，都属于本合同范围之内。甲方应根据本合同规定，向乙方办理投保手续并支付保险费。

　　乙方对上述保险范围内的货物负有自动承保的责任，在发生本合同规定范围内的损失时，均按本合同的规定，负责赔偿。

二、保险金额

　　保险金额以货物的到岸价格 (CIF) 即货价加运费加保险费为准（运费可用实际运费，亦可由双方协定一个平均运费率计算）。

三、保险险别和费率

　　各种货物需要投保的险别由甲方选定并在投保单中填明。乙方根据不同的险别规定不同的费率，现暂定如下：

货物种类	运输方式	保险险别	保险费率
分体式空调	海运	一切险、战争险	

四、保险责任

　　各种险别的责任范围，以乙方制定的"海洋货物运输保险条款""海洋运输货物战争险条款""海运进口货物国内转运期间保险责任扩展条款""航空运输一切险条款"和其他有关条款的规定为准。

五、投保手续

　　甲方一经掌握货物发运情况，即应向乙方寄送起运通知书，办理投保。通知书一式五份，由保险公司签认后，退回一份。如不办理投保，货物发生损失，乙方不予理赔。

六、保险费

　　乙方按照甲方寄送的起运通知书照前列相应的费率逐笔计收保费，甲方应及时付费。

七、索赔手续和期限

　　本合同所保货物发生保险责任范围内的损失时，乙方应按制定的"关于海运进口保险货物残损检验的赔款给付方法"和"进口货物施救整理费用支付方法"迅速处理。甲方应尽力采取防止货物扩大受损面的措施，对已遭受损失的货物必须积极抢救，尽量减少货物的损失。向乙方办理索赔的有效期限，以保险货物卸离海港之日起满一年终止，如有特殊需要可向乙方提出延长索赔期。

八、合同期限

　　本合同自 2021 年 12 月 17 日起开始生效。

甲方	乙方
上海朗明商贸有限公司	中国人民保险公司上海分公司
王明	张平

Sample 9-2 样单 9-2   Verification Form of Export Payment of Exchange 出口收汇核销单

出口收汇核销单 存根	出口收汇核销单 监制章	出口收汇核销单 监制章
(沪)编号:	(沪)编号:	(沪)编号:
出口单位: 江苏毛织品进出口贸易公司	出口单位: 江苏毛织品进出口贸易公司	出口单位: 江苏毛织品进出口贸易公司
单位编码: 195762654	单位编码: 195762654	单位编码: 195762654
出口币种总价: USD89 705.50	银行签注栏(出口单位盖章): 类别 | 币种金额 | 日期 | 盖章	货物名称: 全棉抹布 | 数量: 367 捆 | 币种总价: USD 89 705.50
收汇方式: L/C		
预计收款日期: 2021 年 10 月 26 日		报关单编号:
报关日期: 2021 年 10 月 18 日	海关签注栏:	
备注:		
此单报关有效期截止到	外汇局签注栏 年 月 日 (盖章)	外汇局签注栏 年 月 日 (盖章)

(未经核销此联不得撕开)

Sample 9-3 样单 9-3   Beneficiary Certificate 受益人证明

GUANGZHOU TEXTILE GARMENT CO., LTD.
HUARONG MANSION RM2901 NO.85 GUANJIAQIAO, GUANGZHOU CHINA

CERTIFICATE

To:	FASHION FORCE CO., LTD P.O.BOX 8935 NEW TERMINAL, ALTA, VISTA OTTAWA, CANADA	Invoice No.:	NT01FF004
		Date:	Mar. 20th, 2021

WE CERTIFY HEREBY THAT ORIGINAL CERTIFICATE OF ORIGIN FORM A, ORIGINAL EXPORT LICENCE, COPY OF COMMERCIAL INVOICE, DETAILED PACKING LISTS AND A COPY OF BILL OF LADING WERE SENT DIRECT TO APPLICANT BY COURIER WITHIN 5 DAYS AFTER SHIPMENT. THE RELATIVE COURIER RECEIPT IS ALSO REQUIRED FOR PRESENTATION.

GUANGZHOU TEXTILE GARMENT CO., LTD.
张三

Sample 9-4
样单 9-4　　　　　　　　贸易进口付汇核销单（代申报单）

印单局代码：320000　　　　　　　　　　　　　　　　　核销单编号：00492425

单位代码 13438589-8	单位名称 北京德鑫贸易公司	所在地外汇局名称 省外
付汇银行名称 中行北京分行	收汇人国别 日本	交易编码 0 1 0 1
收款人是否在保税区： 是□　否☑	交易附言	
对外付汇币种 日元 其中：购汇金额 1 728 600.00 　　　人民币账号	对外付汇总额 1 728 600.00 现汇金额 外汇账号	其他方式金额

付汇性质
☑正常付汇
□不在名录　　　　　□90天以上信用证　　　□90天以上托收　　　□异地付汇
□90天以上到货　　　□转口贸易
备案表编号

预计到货日期 05/12/30	进口批件号 20313768	合同/发票号 DS1032E

结算方式
信用证　90天以内☑　　90天以上□　　承兑日期　/　/　　付汇日期 14/12/12　期限　天
托收　　90天以内□　　90天以上□　　承兑日期　/　/　　付汇日期　/　/　　期限　天

汇款	预付货款 □	货到付汇（凭报关单付汇）□	付汇日期 / /
	报关单号	报关日期　/　/　报关单币种	金额
	报关单号	报关日期　/　/　报关单币种	金额
	报关单号	报关日期　/　/　报关单币种	金额
	报关单号	报关日期　/　/　报关单币种	金额
	报关单号	报关日期　/　/　报关单币种	金额
	（若报关单填写不完，可另附纸）		

其他□　　　　　　　　　付汇日期　/　/

以下由付汇银行填写

申报号码：□□□□□□□□□□□□□□□□□□

业务编号：　　　　审核日期：　/　/　　　（付汇银行签章）

进口单位签章

Key to Assignment
练习题参考答案

Key to Assignment 4.1

COMMERCIAL INVOICE				
TO MESSRS.: EEN CO., VANCOUVER, CANADA				INVOICE NO.: SHE01/7203 DATE: Jan. 28th, 2021 L/C NO.: 044/307587 P.O. NO.: FAB10-20030087/01-02
SHIPPED FROM GUANGZHOU, CHINA TO VANCOUVER, CANADA **VIA HK**				
MARKS & NOS.	DESCRIPTION	QUANTITY	UNIT PRICE	AMOUNT
PO NO. FAB10-20030087/ 01-02 COLOR: INDIGO R/NO.: 1-4, 6-36	GOLDTRON GARMENTS SDN BHD	*2, 920 YARDS*	CIF *Vancouver* USD1.80/YARD	USD5 256.00
100PCT COTTON DENIM-80Z-ROPE DYED INDIGO (CT-121) DOUBLE P/SHRUNK RESIDUAL AHRINKAGE NOT MORE THAN 3-4PCT 82×50/14S×14S-WIDTH: 58/59' AS PER PURCHASE ORDER NO. FAB10-20030087/01-02 CIF Vancouver TOTAL: *US DOLLARS FIVE THOUSAND TWO HUNDRED AND FIFTY-SIX ONLY*				

GUANGDONG HUALIAN TRADING CORPORATION

张三

Key to Assignment 4.2

COMMERCIAL INVOICE	**ORIGINAL**
Exporter: GUANGDONG TEXTILES IMPORT & EXPORT KNITWEARS COMPANY LIMITED TRANSPORT DETAILS: FROM GUANGZHOU, CHINA TO SANTOS, BRAZIL BY VESSEL	DATE: Nov.2nd, 2021 INVOICE NO.: 1103SP023 B/L NO.: SA75214 S/C NO.: DY-039 L/C NO.: KRT2899302

Mark & Numbers	Quantity	Description of goods	Unit price	Amount
N/M	30DOZ/BALE 24BALES	CHILDREN's 65 PERCENT COTTON 35 PERCENT POLYESTER KNITFED JOGGING SUIT	FOB GUANGZHOU USD42.20/DZ	USD30 384.00

TOTAL: US DOLLARS THIRTY THOUSAND THREE HUNDRED AND EIGHTY-FOUR ONLY

TOTAL QUANTITY: 720 DOZ SETS/ TWENTY-FOUR BALES

GUANGDONG TEXTILES IMPORT &
EXPORT KNITWEARS COMPANY LIMITED
王丽丽

Key to Assignment 5.1

Shipper HANJIN ARTS AND CRAFTS I/E CORP. TIANJIN, CHINA		B/L No.	
Consignee or order TO ORDER		中国外运天津公司 SINOTRANS TIANJIN COMPANY **OCEAN BILL OF LADING**	
Notify address SCHLITER.CO.BREMEN 3601AW. HERO ROAD, BREMEN, GERMAN		SHIPPED on board in apparent good order and condition (unless otherwise indicated) the goods or packages specified herein and to be discharged at the mentioned port of discharge or as near thereto as the vessel may safely get and be always afloat.	
Pre-carriage by	Port of loading XINGANG, TIANJIN	The weight, measure, marks and numbers, quality, contents and value, being particulars furnished by the Shipper, are not checked by the Carrier on loading.	
Vessel PAUL RICKERS	Port of transshipment	The Shipper, Consignee and the Holder of this Bill of Lading hereby expressly accept and agree to all printed, written or stamped provisions, exceptions and conditions of this Bill of Lading, including those on the back hereof.	
Port of discharge BREMEN, GERMAN	Final destination BREMEN, GERMAN	IN WITNESS whereof the number of original Bills of Lading stated below have been signed, one of which being accomplished the other(s) to be void.	
Container. seal No. or marks and Nos.	Number and kind of package	Description of goods	Gross weight (kgs.)	Measurement (m³)
BREMEN NO.1—UP 1×20' HQ FCL/FCL CY/CY TGHU7036445/54660	150 CTN IN 15 PALLETS	"WILLOW PRODUCT" ART NO. ISSR-16	4 200	0.04
Freight and charges FREIGHT PREPAID		REGARDING TRANSHIPMENT INFORMATION PLEASE CONTACT	
Ex. rate	Prepaid at	Freight payable at	Place and date of issue TIANJIN Aug. 1st, 2021
	Total prepaid	Number of original Bs/L THREE	Signed for or on behalf of the Master As Agent

Key to Assignment 5.2

	ORIGINAL	
Exporter:		DATE: Nov. 2nd, 2021
GUANGDONG TEXTILES IMPORT &		INVOICE NO.: 1103SP023
EXPORT KNITWEARS COMPANY LIMITED		B/L.NO.: SA75214
TRANSPORT DETAILS:		S/C NO.: DY-039
FROM GUANGZHOU, CHINA TO SANTOS, BRAZIL		L/C NO.: KRT2899302
BY VESSEL		

Marks & No.	Quantity, Description of goods	Net weight	Gross weight	Measurement
N/M	CHILDREN's 65 PERCENT COTTON	@180.00KGS	@195.00KGS	@(100×100×120)
	30DOZ/BALE 35 PERCENT POLYESTER KNITFED			
24BALES	JOGGING SUIT	4 320.00KGS	4 680.00KGS	28.8M³
24BALES		4 320.00KGS	4 680.00KGS	28.8M³

TOTAL QUANTITY: 720 DOZ SETS
TOTAL: TWENTY-FOUR BALES ONLY.

GUANGDONG TEXTILES IMPORT & EXPORT KNITWEARS COMPANY LIMITED
王丽丽

Key to Assignment 5.3

	PACKING LIST	ORIGINAL
Exporter:		DATE: Oct. 28th, 2021
GUANGZHOU ARTS & CRAFTS IMP.		INVOICE NO.: 11KF335
AND EXP.CORP.		B/L NO.: DSA97—1102
628 GUANGZHOU DADAO ZHONG		S/C NO.: 11AJ-KF002A
ROAD, GUANGZHOU, CHINA.		L/C NO.: M20K2710NS4)0032
		DSA11—1102

TRANSPORT DETAILS:
　FROM GUANGZHOU, CHINA TO PUSAN, KOREA W/T HONGKONG
　　BY VESSEL

| 224CTNS | 3 632.00KGS | 4 832.00KGS | 35.84CBMS |

TOTAL QUANTITY: 8 064DOZ
TOTAL: TWO HUNDRED AND TWENTY-FOUR CARTONS

GUANGZHOU ARTS & CRAFTS IMP.AND EXP.CORP
王丽丽

Key to Assignment 5.4

PACKING LIST		ORIGINAL

Exporter:
GUANGZHOU ARTS & CRAFTS
IMP. AND EXP. CORP.
628 GUANGZHOU DADAO ZHONG
ROAD, GUANGZHOU, CHINA.

Date: Oct. 28th, 2021
Invoice No: 2011KF335
B/L No.: *DSA11-1102*
S/C No.: 11AJ-KF002A
L/C No.: M20K2710NS40032

Transport Details: FROM GUANGZHOU, *CHINA* TO PUSAN, *KOREA W/T HONGKONG*
BY VESSEL

Marks & Numbers	Description of goods	Quantity	N.W.	G.W.	Measurement
	ARTIFICIAL FLOWERS				
	ART NO.: AB-*06001* 36DOZ/CTN	*5,184*DOZ/144CTNS	@18.00KGS 2 592.00KGS	@23.00KGS 3 312.00KGS	@ (40×50×80) 23.04CBMS
	ART NO.: AB-07049 36DOZ/CTN	2,880DOZ/80CTNS	@13.00KGS 1 040.00KGS	@19.00KGS 1 520.00KGS	@(40×50×80) 12.80CBMS
	TOTAL QUANTITY: 224CTNS		3 632.00KGS	4 832.00KGS	35.84CBMS

GUANGZHOU ARTS & CRAFTS IMP. & EXP. CORP.
张立

Key to Assignment 6.1

中华人民共和国海关出口货物报关单

预录入编号：BIUY564258　　　　　　　　　　　　海关编号：

出口口岸 青岛 (4200)	备案号 加工贸易手册 B87495612385		出口日期 2021-5-28	申报日期 2021-5-20
经营单位 青岛大地服装有限公司	运输方式 江海运输 (2)		运输工具名称 TSDD/1265F	提单号 TSDD 894521
发货单位 百度有限公司	贸易方式 来料加工 (0214)		征免性质 进料加工 (503)	结汇方式 电汇 (2)
许可证号	运抵国（地区） 韩国 (133)		指运港 釜山 (1480)	境内货源地 青岛 (4200)
批准文号	成交方式 FOB 青岛 (3)	运费 502/6500/3	保费 502/3200/3	杂费 502/300/3
合同协议号 8466127	件数 2 500 件	包装种类 125 箱	毛重（公斤） 3 512	净重（公斤） 3 100
集装箱号 FUTT5499216	随附单据		生产厂家 青岛鑫宏服装厂 (05)	

标记、唛头及备注
无唛

项号	商品编号	商品名称、规格型号	数量及单位	最终目的国（地区）	单价	总价	币制	征免
01	6203.3570	男夹克衫	75 箱 /1 500 件	韩国	10.00	10 000.00	美元	照章 (1)
02	6204.3240	女夹克衫	50 箱 /1 000 件	韩国	12.00	18 000.00	美元	照章 (1)

税费征收情况

录入员　录入单位 张立 青岛大地服装有限公司 报关员 张立 单位地址 邮编：300000　电话：1598526235　填制日期：2021-5-20	兹声明以上申报无讹并承担法律责任 申报单位（签章）	海关审单批注及放行日期（签章）	
		审单	审价
		征税	统计
		查验	放行

Key to Assignment 6.2

```
                        BILL OF EXCHANGE
NO. 546213                           DATE 2021-5-10
DRAWN UNDER  ARAB NATIONAL BANK
EXCHANGE FOR  USD 75 683.00
AT   ×××   DAYS AFTER SIGHT OF THIS FIRST OF EXCHANGE (SECOND OF EXCHANGE BEING
UNPAID)
PAY TO THE ORDER OF   BANK OF CHINA, GUANGZHOU BRANCH
THE SUM OF  US DOLLARS SEVENTY-FIVE THOUSAND SIX HUNDRED AND EIGHTY-THREE ONLY
TO    HONGKONG ABC CO.
      3/F GUANGTEX BUILDING TAIKOKTSUI
      KOWLOON, HONGKONG
                                     GUANGDONG METALS AND MINERALS I/E CORP.
                                                  张三
```

Key to Assignment 6.3

```
凭
Drawn under  FIRST BANGKOK CITY BANK LTD.
信用证              第              号
L/C No.  001-10397-2010
日期
Dated  Jan. 10th, 2021
按息付款
Payable with Interest@                           % per Annum
号码               金额        中国，青岛    年 月 日
No.: WGH5879  Exchange for  USD6 622.00  CHINA, QINGDAO          .
见票                         日后（本汇票之副本未付）
At _____ Sight of This of Exchange (Second of Exchange being Unpaid)
Pay to the Order of  BANK OF CHINA, QINGDAO BRANCH  或 其 指 定 人
付金额
The Sum of SAY  US DOLLARS SIX THOUSAND SIX HUNDRED TWENTY-TWO ONLY
To   NAN HENG INTERNATIONAL TRADING CO.,LTD.
                                           SHANDONG IMP/EXP CORP.
                                                   王丽丽
```

Key to Assignment 6.4

```
凭
Drawn under  ROYAL BANK OF NEW YORK
信用证              第              号
L/C No. 742863(2)         .
日期
Dated  2021-1-10.
按息付款
Payable with Interest@                           % per Annum
号码               金额        中国，江苏    年 月 日
No.: 34567  Exchange for  USD108 000.00  CHANGSHU, CHINA.
见票                         日后（本汇票之副本未付）
At  30 DAYS AFTER  Sight of This of Exchange (Second of Exchange being Unpaid)
Pay to the Order of  BANK OF CHINA, JIANGSU BRANCH  或 其 指 定 人
付金额
The Sum of  US DOLLARS ONE HUNDRED AND EIGHT THOUSAND ONLY
To   ROYAL BANK OF NEW YORK
                                        CHANGSHU ABC LEATHER GOODS CO. LTD.
                                                   张三
```

Key to Assignment 6.5

1. Goods consigned from (Exporters business name, address, country) GUANGDONG DONGFENG IMPORT AND EXPORT CORP. 122 DONGFENG ROAD EAST, GUANGZHOU, *CHINA*	Reference N0.　　　GZ9/12078/631 1 **GENERALIZED SYSTEM OF PREFERENCES CERTIFICATE OF ORIGIN** (Combined declaration and certificate)
2. Goods consigned to (Consignee's name, address, country) ANYEI HONG KONG 14/F., KAISER ESTATE 1, MANYUE STREET, HUNG HOM, SYDNEY, *AUSTRALIA*	**FORM A** Issued in THE PEOPLE's REPUBLIC OF CHINA (COUNTRY) See Notes overleaf
3. Means of transport and route as far as known) FROM GUANGZHOU TO SYDNEY *BY VESSEL*	4. For official use

5. Item number	6. Marks and numbers of packages	7. Number and kind of packages; description of goods	8. Origin Criterion (see Notes overleaf)	9. Gross weight or other quantity	10. Number and date of
1	KMART SYDNEY NO.1-200	*TWO HUNDRED (200) BUNDLES* OF STAINLESS STEEL SPADE HEAD ****************	"P"	2 400PCS	SMI99901 Nov. 11th, 2021

11. Certification 　　It is hereby certified, on the basis of control carried out that the declaration by the exporter is correct. 　　GUANGZHOU NOV.21ST, 2021 Place and date. signature and stamp of certifying authority	12. Declaration by the exporter 　　The undersigned hereby declares that the above details and statements are correct; that all the goods were produced in 　　　　CHINA　 (country) and that they comply with the origin requirements specified for those goods in the Generalized System of Preferences for goods exported to 　　　　AUSTRALIA (importing country) 　(GUANGZHOU NOV.20ST, 2021 张三) 　　Place and date, signature of authorized signatory

Appendix 附录

附录1 国际贸易单证业务中的计算

第一节 成本核算与报价

出口总成本(FOB成本)=(一)+(二)+(三)

(一)采购成本(进货价)(含税价)

税额 = 不含税价 × 税率

不含税价 = 含税价/(1+增值税率)

(二)国内费用

国内仓储、运输、保险、银行、管理……

(三)关税与退税(负)

+关税：一般为零。

-退税额 = 不含税采购成本 × 退税率

　　　　= 含税采购成本 × 退税率/(1+增值税率)

(四)出口运费、出口保险费、佣金(略)

一、出口成本核算

(一)出口换汇成本

出口换汇成本 = 出口总成本(人民币)÷出口外汇净收入(外汇)

若结果低于当时外汇牌价(买入价)，则为盈；反之为亏。

FOB报价 = 出口总成本(人民币)÷换汇成本

【例题】某商品的出口总成本为每公吨2 100元人民币，出口FOB价为300美元，折算率为8.28，求换汇成本及盈亏率。

解：换汇成本 = 2 100÷300 = 7元/美元　　　盈利

(二)出口盈亏率

出口盈亏率 = (出口销售人民币净收入 - 出口总成本)÷出口总成本×100%

出口盈亏率 = (出口销售人民币净收入÷出口总成本 - 1)×100%

　　　　　 = (结算汇率÷换汇成本 - 1)×100%

结果为正数则盈利,反之为亏。

【例题】某公司出口健身椅1 000张,每张17.30美元CIF纽约,总价为17 300美元,其中运费2 160美元,保险费112美元。总进价为人民币113 000元(含增值税),费率定额为10%,出口退税率为9%,当时银行美元买入价为8.28元。求出口商品盈亏率为多少?

解:实际采购成本 = 113 000×(1+13%-9%)/(1+13%) = 104 000(元)

国内费用 = 113 000×10% = 11 300(元)

出口总成本 = 104 000+11 300 = 115 300(元)

出口销售人民币净收入 = (17 300-2 160-112)×8.28 = 124 431.84(元)

出口盈亏率 = (124 431.84-115 300)/115 300×100% = 1.25%

【例题】某公司出口商品5 000箱,每箱净重20千克,毛重22千克,体积0.03立方米,出口总成本每箱人民币999元,外销价每箱120美元CFR纽约。海运运费按W/M计算,每运费吨52美元。试计算该商品的出口盈亏率及换汇成本。(买入价100美元=796元人民币)

解:出口盈亏率 = (出口销售人民币净收入 − 出口总成本) ÷ 出口总成本 × 100%

    = [(120-52×0.03)×7.96-999] ÷ 999×100%

    = -5.6%

换汇成本 = 出口总成本(人民币) ÷ 出口外汇净收入(外汇)

   = 999 ÷ (120-52×0.03)

   = 8.43(元)

(三)出口创汇率

出口创汇率 = 创汇额 ÷ 进口原料CIF外汇支出 × 100%

    = (成品FOB外汇净收入 − 进口原料CIF外汇支出) ÷ 进口原料CIF外汇支出 × 100%

结果为正数则盈利,反之为亏。

二、报价核算

FOBC = (实际采购成本+国内费用)/(1-佣金率-预期利润率-银行手续费率)

CFRC = (实际采购成本+国内费用+出口运费)/(1-佣金率-预期利润率-银行手续费率)

CIFC = (实际采购成本+国内费用+出口运费)/(1-佣金率-投保加成×保险费率-预期利润率-银行手续费率)

实际采购成本 = 含税采购成本×[1-退税率÷(1+增值税率)]

实际采购成本 = 含税采购成本×(1+增值税率-退税率)÷(1+增值税率)

第二节　佣金和折扣

一、佣金

（一）佣金

佣金＝含佣价 × 佣金率

含佣价＝净价/(1－佣金率)

净价＝含佣价 ×(1－佣金率)

注意：除非另有规定，投保金额应以含佣价为计算基数。

【例题】某公司向中国香港客户出口水果罐头 200 箱，每箱 132.6 港币 CIF 香港，客户要求改报 CFR 香港 5% 佣金价，设保险费为 CIF 价的 2%，在保持利润不变的情况下，试求：

① CFRC5 香港价应报多少？

② 出口 200 箱应付给客户多少佣金？

解：① CFR 净价＝CIF 净价－保险费

　　　　　＝132.6－132.6×2%

　　　　　＝129.95(港元)

　　CFRC5＝CFR 净价/(1-5%)

　　　　　＝129.95÷95%＝136.79(港元)

② 应付佣金＝136.79×5%×200＝1 367.9(港元)

（二）佣金额

如"每一件收取佣金 0.2 美元"，则佣金额＝0.2× 件数。

（三）以 FOB 或 FCA 净价为基数计算

佣金额＝FOB 或 FCA 净价 × 佣金率

注意术语换算：

FOB 价＝CFR 价 － 出口运费

FOB 价＝CIF 价 ×(1－保险加成 × 保险费费率)－出口运费

（四）按累计佣金计算

1. 金额累进佣金

按一定时期内推销金额达到的佣金等级计算佣金，如下表所示。

等级	推销额（单位：港元）	佣金率
A	100 万港元及以下	1%
B	100 万港元以上至 200 万港元及以下	2%
C	200 万港元以上至 300 万港元及以下	3%
D	300 万港元以上	4%

年末结算，若实际推销额为 250 万港元，应按 C 级佣金率计算，即为 250×3%＝7.5 万港元。

2. 超额累进佣金

各等级的超额部分，各按适用等级的佣金率计算，然后将各级佣金额累加，求得累进佣金的总额，如下表所示。

等级	推销额（单位：港元）	佣金率
A	100万港元及以下	1%
B	100万港元以上至200万港元及以下	2%
C	200万港元以上至300万港元及以下	3%
D	300万港元以上	4%

年末结算，若实际推销额为250万港元，按累进佣金计算。

A级佣金：100×1%=1(万港元)

B级佣金：(200–100)×2%=2(万港元)

C级佣金：(250–200)×3%=1.5(万港元)

合计佣金：A+B+C=1+2+1.5=4.5(万港元)

（五）佣金的支付

佣金一般是在收到货款后才支付给中间商。为防止误解，应由出口商与中间商在双方建立业务关系之初就加以明确；否则，有的中间商可能于交易达成后，就要求出口商支付佣金，而日后合同能否得到顺利履行，货款能否顺利收到，并无绝对保证。

二、折扣

（一）折扣的规定方法：百分率、折扣的绝对数

（二）折扣的计算与支付方法

$$折扣额 = 原价 \times 折扣率$$

折扣一般在买方支付货款时预先扣除。

除非另有规定，投保金额应以减除折扣后的折实售价为计算基数。

第三节 运费与保险费

一、运费计算

（一）海洋运价（班轮运价、租船运价）

1. 海洋基本运费的计算标准

(1) 重量法：按货物的毛重。"W"，计算单位——吨，小数点后三位。

(2) 体积法："M"，计算单位——m^3，小数点后三位。

(3) 从价法："Ad Val"（"Ad Valorem"）。

(4) 选择法：从高选择。

- W/M：按货物的毛重或体积，以其较高者计收运费(比较时要以公吨和立方米为单位)。一般习惯将重量吨和尺码吨统称为运费吨。

- W or Ad Val：按货物的毛重或货物FOB价值计收运费。

- M or Ad Val：按货物的体积或货物FOB价值计收运费。

- W/M or Ad Val：按货物的毛重或体积或货物FOB价值计收运费。

(5) 综合法。
- W & Ad Val。
- M & Ad Val。
- W/M & Ad Val。

(6) 按件法。

(7) 议价法。

运费的计算公式如下。

运费 = 基本运费率×(1+ 附加费率之和)× 应计费总量

运费 =[基本运费率×(1+ 附加费率之和)+ 各种附加费的金额]× 应计费总量

运费 =[基本运费率×(1+ 附加费率之和)+ 各种附加费的金额]×[1+ 货币贬值附加费]× 应计费总量

【例题】某企业出口柴油机一批，共15箱，总毛重为5.65公吨，总体积为10.676立方米。由青岛装船，经中国香港转船至苏丹港，试计算该企业应付船公司运费多少？

解：(1) 查阅货物分级表：Diesel Engine 10级 W/M。

(2) 查阅中国青岛——中国香港航线费率表：10级货从青岛运至中国香港费率为22美元，中转费13美元。

(3) 查阅中国香港——红海航线费率表：10级货从中国香港到苏丹港费率为95美元。

(4) 查阅附加费率表：苏丹港要收港口拥挤附加费，费率为基本运费的10%。

计算：运费 =(22+13+95+95×10%)×10.676

=139.5×10.676

=1 489.302(美元)

2. 附加费

一般是基本费率运价的若干个百分比，也有按每运费吨计收一定金额确定。附加费包括燃油附加费、货币附加费、港口拥挤费、转船附加费、直航附加费、港口附加费……

【例题】出口到澳大利亚悉尼港某商品100箱，每箱毛重30公斤，体积0.035立方米，运费计算标准为 W/M10级。查10级货直运悉尼港基本运费为200元人民币，加货币附加费35.8%，再加燃油附加费28%、港口拥挤费25%。求总运费。

解：M(0.035 立方米)>W (0.030 公吨)，按 M 计算。

基本运费的币值附加费 =2 005×35.8% =71.6(元)

燃油附加费 =(200+71.6)×28% = 76(元)

港口拥挤费 =(200+71.6)×25% = 67.9(元)

运费合计 =(200+71.6+76+67.9)×0.035×100

=1 454.25(元)

注意件杂货与集装箱货在计收运费时的区别。

(二) 航空运费

$$航空运费 = 运价 \times 计费重量$$

1. 货物实际毛重(千克)或货物体积重量择高者

$$货物体积重量(千克) = 货物体积(m^3)/0.006(m^3/kg)$$

【例题】出口货物100箱,体积16.7m³,总毛重2 300千克,空运,运价为13.58元/千克,求运价。

(1) 求体积重量:16.7÷0.006=2 783.33(千克)

(2) 比较体积重量与实际毛重,择高者:计费重量=2 783.33(千克)。

(3) 运价=2 783.33×13.58=37 797.62(元)

2. 运价(注意级差)

(1) 重量等级;重量分界点;级次越高,费率越低。

(2) 起码运费。

(3) 实际计费重量的运费若超过较高重量分界点的运费,航空公司可同意按较高重量分界点的较低运价收取运费。

二、保险费

Incoterms 2010规定:最低保额=合同价款×110%。

(一) 一般保险费的计算

保险金额=CIF/CIP价×保险加成

保险费=CIF/CIP价×保险加成×保险费率

保险加成=1+保险加成率

【例题】某批出口货物,发票总金额为CIF12 000美元,如果含折扣5%,则投保金额的基数和保险费应为:

投保金额的基数=12 000×(1-5%)=11 400(美元)

保险费=11 400×110%×0.6%=75.24(美元)

(二) 含折扣价保险费的计算

以折后售价为投保基数(除非另有规定)

$$保险费 = CIF/CIP价 \times (1-折扣率) \times 保险加成 \times 保险费率$$

(三) 超成(超出110%的部分)保险费的计算

$$保险费 = CIP/CIF价 \times 超成率 \times 保险费率$$

除非另有规定,超成保险费应由买方负担。

(四) CFR/CPT价与CIF/CIP价互换

$$CIF价 = CFR价 \div (1-保险加成 \times 保险费率)$$

$$CFR价 = CIF价 \times (1-保险加成 \times 保险费率)$$

注意:保险加成=1+保险加成率。

【例题】国内C公司拟从德国进口检测仪100台,每台进口价格130美元FOB汉堡,纸箱包装,每箱装1台,每箱毛重20千克,尺寸为50cm×50cm×54cm。海运费每运费吨基本运费为 96 美元，计费标准 M/W。按 CIF 的 110% 投保，费率为 0.85%；银行贷款年利率为 9%，预计垫款时间为 2 个月。银行费用为进口成交金额的 0.45%；进口关税税率 25%，增值税税率 13%；其他费用还包括领证费 800 元（整批货，下同），报关费 60 元，检验费 200 元，业务费 1 000 元，国内运杂费 840 元，如果 C 公司期望的利润率为 20%（按进口价格计），人民币与美元汇率为 8.01∶1。

(1) 试核算 C 公司在国内销售该仪器的人民币单价。

(2) 如果 C 公司接受国内客户还价 1 950 元/台，那么这次交易 C 公司的利润总额是多少？

(3) 国内客户还价 1 950 元/台，如果 C 公司接受国内客户降价的同时，还要保持 20% 的进口利润，那么这次进口采购成本 (FOB) 应该是多少美元每台？

解：

(1) 采购成本 =130×8.01=1 041.3(元/台)

海运费 =0.5×0.5×0.54×96×8.01=103.8096(元/台)

保险费 =CIF×(1+投保加成率×保险费率)/数量 =1 155.9174×(1+10%)×0.85%/100=10.8078(元/台)

利息 =130×8.01×9%×2/12=15.6195(元/台)

银行费 =130×8.01×0.45%=4.6859(元/台)

关税 =1155.9174×25%=288.9794(元/台)

其他 =(800+60+200+1 000+840)÷100=29(元/台)

利润 =130×8.01×20%=208.26(元/台)

国内销售价格 =(采购成本+费用+利润)×(1+增值税率)

$\quad\quad\quad$ =(1 041.3+103.8096+10.8078+15.6195+4.6859+288.9794+29+208.26)×(1+13%)

$\quad\quad\quad$ =1 923.7823(元/台)

(2) 销售收入 =1 950×100÷1.13=172 566.372(元)

采购成本 =130×8.01×100=104 130(元)

海运费 =0.5×0.5×0.54×96×8.01×100=10 380.96(元)

保费 =[(104 130+10 380.96)÷1−(1+10%)]×1.1×0.85=1 080.7838(元)

贷款利息 =130×8.01×9%×2/12×100=1 561.95(元)

银行费用 =130×8.01×0.45%×100=468.59(元)

进口关税 =115 591.74×25%=28 897.9357(元)

其他费用 =800+60+200+1 000+840=2 900(元)

利润 =销售收入(去税收入)−采购成本−各项费用

$\quad\quad$ =195 000÷1.13−104 130−(10 380.96+1 080.78+1 561.95+468.59+28 897.9357+2 900)

$\quad\quad$ =23 146.156(元)

(3) 采购成本 =FOB×8.01

海运费 =0.5×0.5×0.54×96×8.01=103.8096(元/台)

保险费 =CIF×(1+ 投保加成率)× 保险费率
       =[(FOB×8.01+103.80)÷1-(1+10%)×0.85%]×1.1×0.85%

关税 =[(FOB 价 + 运费)÷1- 保险费率]× 关税税率
     =[(FOB×8.01+103.80)÷(1-0.85%)]×25%

贷款利息 =FOB×8.01×9%×2/12

银行费用 =FOB×8.01×0.45%

其他费用 =(800+60+200+1 000+840)÷100=29(元 / 台)

利润 =FOB×8.01×20%

国内销售价 =1 950(元 / 台)

国内销售价格 =(采购成本 + 费用 + 利润)×(1+ 增值税率)

1 950={FOB×8.01+103.8096+FOB×8.01×9%×2/12+FOB×8.01×0.45%+[(FOB×8.01+103.80)÷1-(1+10%)×0.85%]×1.1×0.85%+(FOB×8.01+103.80)÷(1-0.85%)×25%+29+FOB×8.01×20%}×1.13

解方程得：FOB 价格 =1 017.1351÷8.01 ≈ 123(美元 / 台)

解法二：

国内销售价格 =(采购成本 + 费用 + 利润)×(1+ 增值税率)

→国内销售价格 ÷(1+ 增值税率)=采购成本 + 海运费 + 保险费 + 贷款利息 + 银行费用 + 进口关税 + 其他费用 + 利润

国内销售价格 ÷1.13=CIF 价 + 贷款利息 + 银行费用 + 进口关税 + 其他费用 + 利润

=[(FOB×8.01+103.80)÷1-(1+10%)×0.85%]+FOB×8.01×9%×2/12+(FOB×8.01×0.45%)+(FOB×8.01+103.80)÷(1-0.85%)×25%+29+FOB×8.01×20%

解方程得：FOB 价格 =1 017.1 351÷8.01 ≈ 123(美元 / 台)

第四节　汇率兑换、利息与贴现

一、汇率兑换

(一) 外汇买价和卖价的计算

标价顺序：现汇买入价→现钞买入价→卖出价。

1. 企业将外汇收入卖给银行

$$外汇金额 \times 外汇买入价 = 本币金额$$

2. 企业向银行买入外汇

$$外汇金额 \times 外汇卖出价 = 本币金额$$

(二) 外汇互换的计算

通过人民币牌价间接折算。

二、利息与贴现

(一) 利率 (Interest Rate)

$$利息 = 本金 \times 利率$$

1. 利率的两种表示方法

1) 百分率

年利 = 月利 × 12

月利 = 日利 × 30

年利 = 日利 × 365/360

2) 分、厘、毫

分类	年利	月利	日利
1 分	1/10	1/100	1/1 000
1 厘	1/100	1/1 000	1/10 000
1 毫	1/1 000	1/10 000	1/100 000

(二) 单利和复利

1) 单利

单利 (Simple Interest) 即"利不生利"。

$$利息 = 本金 × 利率 × 期数$$

$$本利和 = 本金 × (1 + 利率 × 期数)$$

2) 复利

复利 (Compound Interest)，即每过一段时期将该利息并入本金，在下段时期重复生利，俗称"利滚利"。

$$利息 = 本金 × [(1 + 利率) × 期数 - 1]$$

$$本利和 = 本金 × (1 + 利率) × 期数$$

三、贴现 (Discount)

$$贴现息 = 票据金额 × 贴现率 × 贴现期$$

$$票据净值 = 票据金额 - 贴现$$

四、增值税

进口商在按国内销售价格向国内客户销售进口商品时，必须按国内销售价格中的货价部分缴纳增值税。

应缴增值税额 = 货价 × 增值税 = [国内销售价格 ÷ (1 + 增值税率)] × 增值税率

实缴增值税额 = 销售增值税额 - 进口代缴增值税额

= [国内销售价格 ÷ (1 + 增值税率)] × 增值税率 - 进口代缴增值税额

进口商在进口报关时海关就已经预先代征了一部分增值税 (进口税费)。

按照《中华人民共和国增值税暂行条例》的规定，进口货物的增值税由海关代征。我国的增值税应税货物全部从价定率计征，其基本税率为 13%，但对于一些关系到国计民生的重要物资，其增值税税率较低为 9%。

下列各类货物增值税税率为 9%：

(1) 粮食等农产品、食用植物油、食用盐；

(2) 自来水、暖气、冷气、热水、煤气、石油液化气、天然气、二甲醚、沼气、居民用煤炭制品；

(3) 图书、报纸、杂志、音像制品、电子出版物；

(4) 饲料、化肥、农药、农机、农膜；

(5) 国务院规定的其他货物。

进口代缴增值税税额计算公式：

$$应纳增值税税额 = 组成计税价格 \times 增值税税率$$

$$组成计税价格 = 关税完税价格 + 关税税额 + 消费税税额$$

【例题】某外贸公司代某手表厂进口瑞士产数控铣床一台，FOB Antwerp SFR223 343，运费 RMB42 240，保险费率 0.3%，填发海关代征税缴款书之日瑞士法郎对人民币外汇市场买卖中间价为 SFR100=RMB387.055。

关税完税价格 =223 343×387.055÷100=864 460.248 65（元）

组成计税价格 =(864 460.248 65+42 240)/(1-0.3%)

=909 428.534 252 8（元）

≈909 429（元）

数控铣床应归入税则税号 8 459.610，税率为 15%，则其应征关税税额 =909 429×15%=136 414.35（元）。

增值税组成计税价格 =909 429+136 414.35=1 045 843.35（元）

【例题】某外贸公司代某手表厂进口瑞士产数控铣床（税则税号 8459.6100，税率为 15%）一台，FOB Antwerp SFR223 343，运费 RMB42 240，保险费率 0.3%（不设投保加成），求应征增值税税额（SFR100=RMB387.055）。

SFR223 343 =223 343×3.87055=RMB864 460.24865

关税完税价格 =(864 460.24865+42 240)÷(1-0.3%)

=909 428.534 252 8

≈909 429（元）

应征关税税额 =909 429×15%

= 136 414.35（元）

增值税组成计税价格 = 909 429+136 414.35= 1 045 843.35（元）

应征增值税税额 =1 045 843×17%= 177 793.31（元）

五、进口税税额

进口税款缴纳形式为人民币。进口货物以外币计价成交的，由海关按照签发税款缴款书之日国家外汇管理部门公布的人民币外汇牌价的买卖中间价折合人民币计征。

完税价格金额计算到元为止，元以下四舍五入。完税税额计算到分为止，分以下四舍五入。

一票货物的关税税额在人民币 10 元以下的免税。

进口关税税额计算公式：

$$进口关税税额 = 完税价格 \times 进口关税税率$$

以 CIF 成交的进口货物,如果申报价格符合规定的"成交价格"条件,则可直接计算出税款。FOB 和 CFR 条件成交的进口货物,在计算税款时应先把进口货物的申报价格折算成 CIF 价,然后再按上述程序计算税款。

【例题】某公司从德国进口钢铁盘条 100 000 千克,其成交价格为 CIF 天津新港 125 000 美元,应征关税税款是多少?

海关填发税款缴款书日的外汇牌价:100 美元 = 857.18 ~ 847.26 人民币元

审核申报价格,符合"成交价格"条件,确定税率根据填发税款缴款书日的外汇牌价,将货价折算为人民币。

100 美元中间价 =(847.26+857.18)/2= 852.22 元人民币

完税价格 =125 000 × 8.5222= 1 065 275(元)

关税税款 =1 065 275 × 15%= 159 791.25(元)

【例题】我国从国外进口一批中厚钢板共计 200 000 千克,成交价格为 FOB 伦敦 2.5 英镑/千克,已知单位运费为 0.1 英镑,保险费率为 0.25%,求应征关税税款是多少?

(海关填发税款缴款书之日的外汇牌价:1 英镑 = 7.0540-7.0681 人民币元;中厚钢板适用于最惠国税率 10%)

完税价格 =[(FOB 价 + 运费) ÷ (1- 保险费率)] × 7.0611

=(2.5+0.1) ÷ (1-0.25) × 200 000 × 7.0611

=3 680 974(元)

进口关税税款 =3 680 974 × 10%=368 097.4(元)

六、消费税税额

1. 消费税的征收对象

根据《中华人民共和国消费税暂行条例》的规定,我国目前仅对 4 类货物征收消费税。

第一类:过度消费会对身体健康、社会秩序、生态环境等方面造成危害的特殊消费品。

第二类:奢侈品等非生活必需品。

第三类:高能耗的高档消费品。

第四类:不可再生和替代的石油类消费品。

2. 消费税的征收方法

消费税的征收方法分为从价征收和从量计征两种。我国消费税采用价内税 (计税价格组成中包括消费税税额) 的计税方法。

组成计税价格 =(关税完税价格 + 关税税额) ÷ (1- 消费税税率)

1) 从价计征的消费税

消费税税额 = 组成计税价格 × 消费税税率

【例题】某公司向海关申报进口一批小轿车,价格为 FOB 横滨 10 000 000 日元,运费为 200 000 日元,保险费率为 5‰(不设投保加成)。该批进口小轿车关税税率为 80%,消费税税率 8%。100 000 日元兑换人民币买卖中间价为 8 500 元。

关税完税价格 =(10 000 000+200 000)/(1-5‰)=10 251 256.28141(元)

10 251 256.28141×8 500÷100 000=871 356.7839196≈871 357(元)

关税税额=871 357×80%=697 085.6(元)

消费税计税价格=(871 357+697 085.6)/(1-8%)=1 704 828.91≈1 704 829(元)

消费税税额=1 704 829×8%=136 386.32(元)

2) 从量计征的消费税

从量计征的消费应税货物有黄酒、啤酒、汽油、柴油4种，实行定额征收。黄酒每吨人民币240元，啤酒每吨人民币220元，汽油每升0.2元，柴油每升0.1元。

从量计征的消费税税额计算公式：

$$应纳税额 = 单位税额 \times 进口数量$$

【例题】某公司进口1 000箱啤酒，每箱24听，每听净重335毫升，价格为CIF US 10 000美元，100美元兑换人民币824元。关税普通税率7.5元/升，消费税税率220元/吨。求消费税税额。

进口啤酒数量=335×1 000×24÷1 000=8 040升=8.137 7(吨)

关税税额=7.5×8 040=60 300(元)

消费税税额=220元×8.1377=1 790.29(元)

3) 进口综合消费税

2021年4月1日前我国对进口高档手表只征收13%的增值税和关税(电力驱动、指针式手表的关税是13.8%，自动上弦的手表关税为13.2%)。无须征收消费税。4月1日后按照20%的税率征收消费税。

以一块CIF为10万元人民币的指针式手表为例。

4月1日消费税调整前为：

进口综合税率=[(1+关税税率)/(1-消费税税率)]×(1+增值税税率)-1

=(1+13.8%)×(1+13%)-1

=28.59%

应交纳进口环节税：10×28.59%=2.859(万元)

4月1日消费税调整后进口综合税率为：[(1+13.8%)/(1-20%)]×(1+13%)-1=24.75%

应交纳进口环节税：10×24.75%=2.4752(万元)

七、进口汽车税

根据我国现行的征税模式，进口汽车产品在到岸后需缴纳关税、消费税、增值税三种税费后才能通关，进口车的实际税率应该是三种税率的综合反映。综合税率的计算公式为

$$综合税率 = (1+关税税率) \times (1+增值税税率)/(1-消费税税率)-1$$

八、海关监管手续费

海关监管手续费是指海关按照《中华人民共和国海关对进口减税、免税和保税货物征收海关监管手续费的办法》的规定，对减税、免税和保税货物实施监督、管理所提供服务征收的手续费。

海关监管手续费按以下标准征收。

(1) 进料加工和来料加工中，属加工装配机电产品复出口的货物，按照海关审定的货物 CIF 价格的 1.5‰ 计征。

(2) 来料加工中引进的先进技术设备，以及加工首饰、裘皮、高档服装、机织毛衣和毛衣片、塑料玩具所进口的料、件，按照海关审定的货物的 CIF 价格的 1‰ 计征。

(3) 进口后保税储存 90 天以上 (含 90 天) 未经加工即转运复出口的货物，按关税完税价格的 1‰ 计征。

(4) 进口免税货物，按照海关审定的货物的 CIF 价格的 3‰ 计征。

(5) 进口减税货物，按照实际减除税赋部分的货物的 CIF 价格的 3‰ 计征。

(6) 其他进口保税货物，按照海关审定的货物的 CIF 价格的 3‰ 计征。

【例题】国内某公司为装配出口机电产品而进口一批料件，CIF 上海 180 000 人民币元，进口后保税储存 100 天后未经加工即转运复出口，问海关应征海关监管手续费多少？

解： 海关规定进口后保税储存 90 天以上 (含 90 天) 未经加工即转运复出口的货物，按关税完税价格的 1‰ 计征海关监管手续费。

该批货物应征海关监管手续费 = 货物 CIF 价格 × 手续费率
$$=180\ 000 \times 1‰$$
$$=180(元)$$

附录 2　信用证结算审单准则

一、按照《跟单信用证统一惯例》的规定审单

《跟单信用证统一惯例》(以下简称《统一惯例》) 是确保在世界范围内将信用证作为可靠支付手段的准则，已被大多数的国家与地区接受和使用。《统一惯例》所体现出来的国际标准银行惯例是各国银行处理结算业务必须遵循的基本准则。我们必须按照《统一惯例》的要求，合理谨慎地审核信用证要求的所有单据，以确定其 (表面上) 是否与信用证条款相符。

二、按照信用证所规定的条件、条款审单

信用证是根据买卖双方的贸易合同而开立的，它一旦为各有关当事人所接受，即成为各有关当事人必须遵守的契约性文件。在信用证结算业务中，各有关当事人必须受其约束，按照信用证所规定的条件、条款，逐条对照，以确定单据是否满足信用证的要求。当信用证的规定与《统一惯例》有抵触时，应遵循信用证优先于《统一惯例》的原则，按照信用证的要求审核单据。这其中又包括表面一致性和内容相符性两条原则。

(1) 遵循表面一致性原则。受益人提交的单据名称及其内容等表面上必须与信用证规定完全一致。例如，某信用证将货物描述为 ATTACHES SANITARY WARE(卫生洁具附件)，而受益人具体的货为 EXPASION BOLT(膨胀螺栓)。虽然如此，有关单据中

货物描述仍必须与信用证的规定相一致。可能有的单据因某种特殊作用如清关报税等需显示具体货名，此时，我们仍必须将信用证所规定的 ATTACHES SANITAIRE 显示在上面，而在其后加注具体货名 EXPASION BOLT。

(2) 遵循内容相符性原则。我们在审单时应注意避免照搬、照抄信用证的原话，只要内容相符即可。例如，信用证的有关人称指向、时态、语态等转到单据上时，即应做相应的调整，以避免不必要的误会。

三、按照银行的经营思想、操作规程审单

国际贸易结算作为银行经营的一项重要业务，在操作过程中，必须按照有关操作规程行事，尤其是向客户融资时，更应明确银行的观点和看法，对单据有关条目的处理做出自己的选择和判断，以体现银行的经营方针和经营作风。

四、按照普遍联系观点，结合上下文内容审单

信用证是一个与商务合同分离的独立文件，其内容是完整的、互相联系的。其中要求的条件、单据等是相辅相成、前后一贯的。审单时必须遵循普遍联系的观点，结合上下文内容进行，避免片面、孤立地看待某一条款。例如，欧盟某国开来一信用证，要求提交的单据中有一项是 CERTIFICATE OF ORIGIN(原产地证书)，而在后文中又要求受益人将正本 GSP CERTIFICATE OF ORIGIN FORM A(普惠制产地证书) 寄交开证申请人。结合上下文内容，我们就能判断出信用证要求向银行提交的是副本 GSP CERTIFICATE OF ORIGIN(普惠制产地证书)，而非一般的原产地证。

五、按照合情、合理、合法的原则审单

所谓合情、合理、合法，是指审单员应根据自己所掌握的国际贸易结算知识，对各种单据的完整性和准确性做出合乎情理的判断。例如，普惠制产地证是施惠国赋予受惠国出口货物减免进口关税的一种优惠凭证，其"收货人"一栏，应填写最终买主。如信用证未作明确规定，我们应根据提单的收货人、通知人及货至目的地对最终买主做出合理的选择。

六、按照商业功能和结算功能相统一的原则审单

单据的商业功能在商务流转及商品买卖过程中的作用是主要的，结算功能是次要的，审单时应着重考虑其商业功能。我们应该了解各类单据的作用及功能，按照其自身的功能及用途审单，避免将不必要的内容强加于单据。

附录 3　集装箱种类和规格

一、集装箱种类

1. 普通集装箱，又称干货集装箱 (dry cargo container)

它以装运件杂货为主，包括文化用品、日用百货、医药、纺织品、工艺品、化工制品、五金交电、电子机械、仪器及机器零件等。这种集装箱占集装箱总数的 70%～80%。

2. 冷冻集装箱 (reefer container)

它分外置式和内置式两种，温度可在 -28℃～26℃之间调整。内置式集装箱在运输过程中可随时启动冷冻机，使集装箱保持指定温度；而外置式集装箱则必须依靠集装箱专用车、船和专用堆场、车站上配备的冷冻机来制冷。这种箱子适合在夏天运输黄油、巧克力、冷冻鱼肉、炼乳、人造奶油等物品。

3. 开顶集装箱 (open top container)

这种集装箱没有箱顶，可用起重机从集装箱上面装卸货物，装运时用防水布覆盖顶部，其水密要求和干货箱一样。开顶集装箱适合于装载体积高大的物体，如玻璃板等。

4. 框架集装箱 (flat rack container)

这种集装箱没有箱顶和两侧，其特点是从集装箱侧面进行装卸。它以超重货物为主要运载对象，也便于装载牲畜以及钢材之类可以免除外包装的裸装货。

5. 牲畜集装箱 (pen container)

这种箱子侧面有金属网，通风条件良好，而且便于喂食，是专为装运牛、马等活动物而制造的特殊集装箱。

6. 罐式集装箱 (tank container)

它又称液体集装箱，是为运输食品、药品、化工品等液体货物而制造的特殊集装箱。其结构是在一个金属框架内固定一个液罐。

7. 平台集装箱 (platform container)

其形状类似铁路平板车，适宜装超重、超长货物，长度可达6米以上，宽4米以上，高4.5米左右，重量可达40公吨，且两个平台集装箱可以连接起来，装80公吨的货，用这种箱子装运汽车极为方便。

8. 通风集装箱 (ventilated container)

其箱壁有通风孔，内壁涂塑料层，适宜装新鲜蔬菜和水果等怕热、怕闷的货物。

9. 保温集装箱 (insulated container)

这种集装箱的箱内有隔热层，箱顶又有能调节角度的进出风口，可利用外界空气和风向来调节箱内温度，紧闭时能在一定时间内不受外界气温影响。其适宜装运对温湿度敏感的货物。

10. 散装货集装箱 (bulk cargo container)

这种集装箱一般在顶部设有2～3个小舱口，以便装货。底部有升降架，可升高成40°的倾斜角，以便卸货。其适宜装粮食、水泥等散货。如要进行植物检疫，还可在箱内熏舱蒸洗。

11. 散装粉状货集装箱 (free flowing bulk material container)

它与散装箱基本相同，但装卸时使用喷管和吸管。

二、集装箱规格

规格	L	W	H	CU ft^3	CU m^3
CONTAINER SPC.	20"	8"	8"6"		

(续表)

规格	L	W	H	CU ft³	CU m³
CONTAINER	19.4" 1/4	7"8" 5/8	7"10"	1 170×1 000	
	5.899m	2.352m	2.386m		33.1×28
CONTAINER SPC.	40"	8"	8"6"		
CONTAINER	39.5" 3/8	7"8" 5/8	7"10"	2 283×2 000	
	12.02m	2.35m	2.38m		67.5×57

附录4 币制符号代码表

币制代码	币制符号	币制名称	币制代码	币制符号	币制名称
110	HKD	港币	300	EUR	欧元
113	IRR	伊朗里亚尔	301	BEF	欧元
116	JPY	日本元	302	DKK	欧元
118	KWD	科威特第纳尔	303	GBP	英镑
121	MOP	澳门元	305	FRF	欧元
122	MYR	马来西亚林吉特	309	NLG	欧元
127	PKR	巴基斯坦卢比	312	ESP	欧元
129	PHP	菲律宾比索	326	NOK	挪威克朗
132	SGD	新加坡元	330	SEK	瑞典克朗
136	THB	泰国铢	331	CHF	瑞士法郎
142	CNY	人民币	332	SUR	俄罗斯卢布
143	TWD	台币	398	ASF	清算瑞士法郎
201	DZD	阿尔及利亚第纳尔			

附录5 报关条件代码表

报关条件	报关证件名称
1	进口许可证(包括商务部、特派员、省级商务厅发证)
4	商务部出口许可证
5	特派员出口许可证
6	省级商务厅出口许可证
7	特定商品进出口登记证明

(续表)

报关条件	报关证件名称
8	商务部禁止出口的商品
9	机电产品进口配额证明
A	进口商检证明
B	出口商检证明
C	动植物检疫放行证
D	医药检验合格证
E	食品进口检验证
F	濒危物种进出口允许证
G	被动出口配额证
H	文物出口证书
I	精神药物进(出)口准许证
J	金银产品出口准许证
K	非军事枪药进(出)口批件
L	无委办无线电设备进关审查批件
M	保密机进口许可证
N	机电产品进口证明
O	机电产品进口登记表
P	进口废物批准证书
R	兽药进口批准证书
S	统一经营的进口商品
T	全国经营管理出口港澳果菜放行证
U	广东经营管理出口港澳果菜放行证
V	有毒化学品进出口放行通知单
W	麻醉药品进出口准许证
X	有毒化学品环境管理放行通知单
Z	音像制品进口管理许可证明
0110	一般贸易
0130	易货贸易
0214	来料加工
0243	来料以产顶进

附录6 贸易方式代码表

贸易方式代码	贸易方式代码简称	贸易方式代码全称
0245	来料料件内销	来料加工料件转内销
0255	来料深加工	来料深加工结转货物
0258	来料余料结转	来料加工余料结转

（续表）

贸易方式代码	贸易方式代码简称	贸易方式代码全称
0265	来料料件复出	来料加工复运出境的原进口料件
0300	来料料件退换	来料加工料件退换
0345	来料成品内销	来料加工成品转内销
0420	加工贸易设备	加工贸易项下外商提供的进口设备
0446	加工设备内销	加工贸易免税进口设备转内销
0456	加工设备结转	加工贸易免税进口设备结转
0466	加工设备退运	加工贸易免税进口设备退运出境
0513	补偿贸易	补偿贸易
0642	进料以产顶进	进料加工成品以产顶进
0644	进料料件内销	进料加工料件转内销
0654	进料深加工	进料深加工结转货物
0657	进料余料结转	进料加工余料结转
0664	进料料件复出	进料加工复运出境的原进口料件
0700	进料料件退换	进料加工料件退换
0715	进料非对口	进料加工（非对口合同）
0744	进料成品内销	进料加工成品转内销
0844	进料边角料内销	进料加工项下边角料转内销
0845	来料边角料内销	来料加工项下边角料内销
0864	进料边角料复出	进料加工项下边角料复出口
0865	来料边角料复出	来料加工项下边角料复出口
1110	对台贸易	对台直接贸易
1139	国轮油物料	中国籍运输工具境内添加的保税油料、物料
1215	保税工厂	保税工厂
1233	保税仓库货物	保税仓库进出境货物
1234	保税区仓储转口	保税区进出境仓储转口货物
1300	修理物品	进出境修理物品
1427	出料加工	出料加工
1500	租赁不满一年	租期不满一年的租赁贸易货物
1523	租赁贸易	租期在一年及以上的租赁贸易货物
1616	寄售代销	寄售、代销贸易
1741	免税品	免税品
1831	外汇商品	免税外汇商品
2025	合资合作设备	合资合作企业作为投资进口的设备物品
2215	三资进料加工	三资企业为履行出口合同进口料件和出口成品
2225	外资设备物品	外资企业作为投资进口的设备物品
2439	常驻机构公用	外国常驻机构进口办公用品
2600	暂时进出货物	暂时进出口货物

(续表)

贸易方式代码	贸易方式代码简称	贸易方式代码全称
2700	展览品	进出境展览品
2939	陈列样品	驻华商业机构不复运出口的进口陈列样品
3010	货样广告品A	有经营权单位进出口的货样广告品
3039	货样广告品B	无经营权单位进出口的货样广告品
3100	无代价抵偿	无代价抵偿货物
3339	其他进口免费	其他进口免费提供货物
3410	承包工程进口	对外承包工程进口物资
3422	对外承包出口	对外承包工程出口物资
3511	援助物资	国家和国际组织无偿援助物资
3611	无偿军援	无偿军援
3612	捐赠物资	华侨、港澳台同胞、外籍华人捐赠物资
3910	有权军事装备	直接军事装备（有经营权）
3939	无权军事装备	直接军事装备（无经营权）
4019	边境小额	边境小额贸易（边民互市贸易除外）
4039	对台小额	对台小额贸易
4200	驻外机构运回	我驻外机构运回旧公用物品
4239	驻外机构购进	我驻外机构境外购买运回国的公务用品
4400	来料成品退换	来料加工成品退换
4539	进口溢误卸	进口溢卸、误卸货物
4561	退运货物	因质量不符、延误交货等原因退运进出境货物
4600	进料成品退换	进料成品退换
9639	海关处理货物	海关变卖处理的超期未报货物、走私违规货物
9700	后续退补税	无原始报关单的后续退、补税
9739	其他贸易	其他贸易
9800	租赁征税	租赁期一年及以上的租赁贸易货物的租金
9839	留赠转卖物品	外交机构转售境内或国际活动留赠放弃特批货
9900	其他	其他

附录7 运输方式代码表

运输方式代码	运输方式名称
0	非保税区
1	监管仓库
2	江海运输
3	铁路运输

(续表)

运输方式代码	运输方式名称
4	汽车运输
5	航空运输
6	邮件运输
7	保税区
8	保税仓库
9	其他运输
Z	出口加工

附录 8　成交方式代码表

代码	名称
1	CIF
2	CFR
3	FOB
4	C&I
5	市场价
6	垫仓

附录 9　各类商品投保险别参考表

商品名称	包装	投保险别名称
土、畜产类，废棉、麻类：	麻布包	平安险或水渍险，附加偷窃提货不着险、淡水雨淋险、污染险、战争险
烟叶	箱装	平安险或水渍险，附加淡水雨淋险、污染险、发霉险、发酵险、战争险
核桃仁、山桃仁	箱装	平安险或水渍险、淡水雨淋险、变潮变热险、发霉险、生虫险、战争险
松子仁、核桃等	袋装	变潮变热险、发霉险、生虫险、战争险。注：5—10月间出运必须利用冷藏设备，保险单上应附贴冷藏条款，负责因冷藏机器损坏所致的损失
苦杏仁、黑白瓜子及其他干果	箱装	平安险或水渍险，附加淡水雨淋险、变潮变热险、战争险
淀粉	袋装	平安险或水渍险、包装破裂险、短量险、淡水雨淋险、受潮受热险、污染险、战争险

（续表）

商品名称	包装	投保险别名称
香料油	桶装	平安险或水渍险、渗漏险、短量险、战争险
木材	无包装	平安险、偷窃提货不着险、战争险
陶瓷器	箱装	平安险或水渍险、偷窃提货不着险、碰损、破碎险、战争险
土纸、神纸	捆扎	平安险或水渍险、淡水雨淋险、污染险、钩损险、战争险
药材	箱装或捆装	平安险或水渍险、淡水雨淋险、受潮受热险、包装破裂险、战争险
袋装成药	箱装	平安险或水渍险、破碎险、渗漏险、战争险
湿肠衣	桶装	平安险或水渍险、渗漏险、短量险、战争险
活家禽		牲畜运输死亡险、战争险
羽毛、鬃类：	箱装	平安险或水渍险、淡水雨淋险、受潮受热险、包装破裂险、战争险
地毯	箱装	平安险或水渍险、偷窃提货不着险、钩损险、污染险、战争险
各种毛皮及毛皮制品		平安险或水渍险、偷窃提货不着险、受潮受热险、钩损险、战争险
纺织、服装类棉布	麻布装	平安险或水渍险、偷窃提货不着险、淡水雨淋险、污染险、战争险
针棉织品	箱装	平安险或水渍险、偷窃提货不着险、淡水雨淋险、污染险、战争险
生丝	包装	平安险或水渍险、偷窃提货不着险、淡水雨淋险、污染险、战争险(包装：加钩损险)
生丝复制品	箱装	平安险或水渍险、偷窃提货不着险、淡水雨淋险、污染险、战争险(包装：加钩损险)
绸缎	包装	平安险或水渍险、偷窃提货不着险、淡水雨淋险、污染险、战争险(包装：加钩损险)
服装	箱装	平安险或水渍险、偷窃提货不着险、淡水雨淋险、污染险、战争险
手工艺品类珠宝、翠钻、木刻、牙刻、料器、陶瓷器、珐琅器等	箱装	平安险或水渍险、偷窃提货不着险、碰损破碎险、战争险，如系邮包寄递应按邮包险投保
泥人、石膏像、宫灯	箱装	平安险或水渍险、偷窃提货不着险、淡水雨淋险、碰损破碎险、战争险
草帽辫、草制品	箱装	平安险或水渍险、偷窃提货不着险、淡水雨淋险、污染险、战争险
台布、枕袋、印花餐巾	箱装	平安险或水渍险、偷窃提货不着险、淡水雨淋险、包装破裂险、战争险
纸制品、绒绢制品、香料及其他手工艺品	箱装	平安险或水渍险、偷窃提货不着险、淡水雨淋险、污染险、战争险

（续表）

商品名称	包装	投保险别名称
茶叶类：		
茶叶	箱装	平安险或水渍险、偷窃提货不着险、淡水雨淋险、污染险、受潮受热险、包装破裂险、变味险、战争险
茶砖	篓装	平安险、战争险
食品类：		
盐黄，蜜黄	木桶装	平安险或水渍险、渗漏险、战争险
鲜蛋	箱装	平安险或水渍险、偷窃提货不着险、淡水雨淋险、污染险、战争险。如使用冷藏设备应附加冷藏条款，负责冷藏机器损坏所致的损失
皮蛋、咸蛋	篓装、坛装	平安险或水渍险、破碎险、战争险
冰冻鲜肉、鱼虾家禽和蛋品等	箱装	平安险或水渍险、偷窃提货不着险、淡水雨淋险、污染险、战争险，附加冷藏条款
新鲜水果	筐、箱装	平安险、偷窃提货不着险、受潮受热险、战争险
新鲜蔬菜	篓装、散装	平安险或水渍险、战争险。注：自然变坏和自然短量均不避免保险责任，应附加易腐货物条款
腌腊食品	各种包装	平安险或水渍险、偷窃提货不着险、淡水雨淋险、战争险
酱油、醋、冬菜	桶装、瓶装、坛装	平安险或水渍险、破碎险、渗漏险、战争险，如装舱面应加保舱面险
酒	坛装、箱装	平安险或水渍险、偷窃提货不着险、破碎险、渗漏险、战争险
各种类罐头	箱装	平安险或水渍险、偷窃提货不着险、包装破裂险、破碎险、战争险
各种果脯、糖果、饼干	箱装	平安险或水渍险、偷窃提货不着险、淡水雨淋险、受潮受热险、战争险
粮油类：		
生仁、生果	袋装	平安险或水渍险、偷窃提货不着险、淡水雨淋险、受潮受热险、短量险、发霉险、生虫险、战争险
大豆、大米、其他豆类	散装	平安险或水渍险、偷窃提货不着险、淡水雨淋险、受潮受热险、短量险、自然险、战争险
大麻籽	袋装、散装	平安险或水渍险、短量险、战争险
甜菜子	袋装	平安险或水渍险、受潮受热险、发霉险、战争险
谷类		平安险或水渍险、受潮受热险、战争险
油类	桶装、散装	平安险或水渍险、短量险、污染险、战争险
桐油	桶装、散装	平安险或水渍险、短量险、污染险、掺杂险(另有散装桐油险)、战争险
食盐	袋装	平安险或水渍险、战争险

（续表）

商品名称	包装	投保险别名称
轻工业品类：	箱装	
窗玻璃、玻璃器皿、热水瓶胆、搪瓷、瓷砖、陶瓷制品		平安险或水渍险、偷窃提货不着险、碰损破碎险、战争险
家用金属制品	箱装	平安险或水渍险、偷窃提货不着险、淡水雨淋险、生锈险、战争险
自行车、缝纫机	箱装	平安险或水渍险、偷窃提货不着险、淡水雨淋险、生锈险、战争险
无线电	箱装	平安险或水渍险、偷窃提货不着险、淡水雨淋险、受潮受热险、碰损破碎险、生锈险、战争险
乐器	箱装	平安险或水渍险、偷窃提货不着险、碰损险、战争险
纸张	卷筒、箱装	平安险或水渍险、淡水雨淋险、污染险、钩损险、战争险
墨水	瓶装外加木箱	平安险或水渍险、偷窃提货不着险、碰碎险、渗漏险、战争险
其他文教用品	箱装	平安险或水渍险、偷窃提货不着险、战争险
五金类：		
小五金	箱装	平安险或水渍险、偷窃提货不着险、淡水雨淋险、生锈险、战争险
大五金	捆装或无包装	平安险或水渍险、偷窃提货不着险、战争险。注：大五金容易生锈，但不影响使用，可不保生锈险，但铝片应加保白锈险 (white rusting)
矿产类：		
滑石粉	袋装	平安险或水渍险、包装破裂险、短量险、战争险
各种矿砂	散装	平安险、短量险、战争险
各种矿砂、矿石	散装	平安险、偷窃提货不着险、战争险
煤	散装	平安险、短量险、自燃险、战争险
化医类：		
粉状化工原料	袋装	平安险或水渍险、偷窃提货不着险、包装破裂险、短量险、淡水雨淋险、受潮受热险、战争险
医疗器械	箱装	平安险或水渍险、偷窃提货不着险、碰损险
液体化工原料	玻璃瓶装，陶瓷器、木、铁桶装	平安险或水渍险、偷窃提货不着险、破碎险、战争险。装舱面时加保舱面险
仪器类：		
各种仪器、仪表、无线电、真空管	箱装	平安险或水渍险、偷窃提货不着险、碰损破碎险、淡水雨淋险、战争险
机械类：		
机械配件	箱装	平安险、偷窃提货不着险、战争险

(续表)

商品名称	包装	投保险别名称
船舶		船舶险、战争险
铁路车辆、其他各种车辆		车辆损失险
汽车	箱装	一切险
	裸装	平安险、偷窃提货不着险、碰损破碎险、战争险

附录10 运输方式代码表

0	1	2	3	4	5	6	7	8	9
非保税区	监管仓库	江海运输	铁路运输	汽车运输	航空运输	邮件运输	保税区	保税仓库	其他运输

附录11 征免税方式代码表

征免税方式代码	征免税方式全称
1	照章征税
2	折半征税
3	全免
4	特案
5	随征免性
6	保证金
7	保函
8	折半补税
9	全额退税

附录12 报关代码表

备案号的标记码

首位代码	备案审批文件	首位代码	备案审批文件
B★	加工贸易手册(来料加工)	RZ	减免税进口货物结转联系函
C★	加工贸易手册(进料加工)	H	出口加工区电子账册
D	加工贸易不作价设备登记手册	J	保税仓库记账式电子账册
E★	加工贸易电子账册	K	保税仓库备案式电子账册

(续表)

首位代码	备案审批文件	首位代码	备案审批文件
F	加工贸易异地报关分册	Y ★	原产地证书
G	加工贸易深加工结转异地报关分册	Z ★	征免税证明
RT	减免税进口货物同意退运证明	RB	减免税货物补税通知

经济区划代码

"1"表示经济特区；

"2"表示经济技术开发区和上海浦东新区、海南洋浦经济开发区两个特殊开放地区；

"3"表示高新技术开发区；

"4"表示保税区；

"9"表示其他。

企业性质代码

"1"表示国有企业，包括外贸专业公司、工贸公司及其他有进出口经营权的国有企业；

"2"表示中外合作企业；

"3"表示中外合资企业；

"4"表示外商独资企业；

"5"表示有进出口经营权的集体企业；

"6"表示有进出口经营权的私营企业；

"8"表示有报关权而无进出口经营权的企业；

"9"表示其他，包括外商企业驻华机构，外国驻华使、领馆和临时有进出口经营权的企业。

贸易方式代码表

贸易方式代码	贸易方式代码简称	贸易方式代码全称
0110 ★	一般贸易	一般贸易
0130	易货贸易	易货贸易
0139	旅游购物商品	用于旅游者5万美元以下的出口小批量订单货
0200	料件放弃	主动放弃交由海关处理的来料或进料加工料件
0214 ★	来料加工	来料加工装配贸易进口料件及加工出口货物
0245	来料料件内销	来料加工料件转内销
0255 ★	来料深加工	来料深加工结转货物
0258	来料余料结转	来料加工余料结转
0265	来料料件复出	来料加工复运出境的原进口料件
0300	来料料件退换	来料加工料件退换
0314	加工专用油	国家贸易企业代理来料加工企业进口柴油
0320	不作价设备	加工贸易外商提供的进口设备
0345	来料成品内销	来料加工成品转内销
0400	成品放弃	主动放弃交由海关处理的来料或进料加工成品

(续表)

贸易方式代码	贸易方式代码简称	贸易方式代码全称
0420	加工贸易设备	加工贸易项下外商提供的进口设备
0444	保区来进料成品	按成品征税的保税区进料加工成品转内销货物
0445	保区来料成品	按成品征税的保税区来料加工成品转内销货物
0446	加工设备内销	加工贸易免税进口设备转内销
0456	加工设备结转	加工贸易免税进口设备结转
0466	加工设备退运	加工贸易免税进口设备退运出境
0500	减免设备结转	用于监管年限内减免设备的结转
0513	补偿贸易	补偿贸易
0544	保区进料料件	按料件征税的保税区进料加工转内销货物
0545	保区来料料件	按料件征税的保税区来料加工转内销货物
0615 ★	进料对口	进料加工(对口合同)
0642	进料以产顶进	进料加工成品以产顶进
0644	进料料件内销	进料加工料件转内销
0654 ★	进料深加工	进料深加工结转货物
0657	进料余料结转	进料加工余料结转
0664	进料料件复出	进料加工复运出境的原进口料件
0700	进料料件退换	进料加工料件退换
0744	进料成品内销	进料加工成品转内销
0815	低值辅料	低值辅料
0844	进料边角料内销	进料加工项下边角料转内销
0845	来料边角料内销	来料加工项下边角料内销
0864	进料边角料复出	进料加工项下边角料复出口
0865	来料边角料复出	来料加工项下边角料复出口
1139	国轮油物料	中国籍运输工具境内添加的保税油料、物料
1200	保税间货物	海关保税场所及保税区域之间往来的货物
1233	保税仓库货物	保税仓库进出境货物
1234	保税区仓储转口	保税区进出境仓储转口货物
1300	修理物品	进出境修理物品
1427	出料加工	出料加工
1500	租赁不满一年	租期不满一年的租赁贸易货物
1523	租赁贸易	租期在一年及以上的租赁贸易货物
1616	寄售代销	寄售、代销贸易
1741	免税品	免税品
1831	外汇商品	免税外汇商品
2025 ★	合资合作设备	合资合作企业作为投资进口设备物品
2225 ★	外资设备物品	外资企业作为投资进口的设备物品

（续表）

贸易方式代码	贸易方式代码简称	贸易方式代码全称
2439	常驻机构公用	常驻机构公用
2600 ★	暂时进出货物	暂时进出口货物
2700	展览品	进出境展览品
2939	陈列样品	驻华商业机构不复运出口的进口陈列样品
3010 ★	货样广告品 A	有经营权单位进出口的货样广告品
3039	货样广告品 B	无经营权单位进出口的货样广告品
3100 ★	无代价抵偿	无代价抵偿货物
3339	其他进口免费	其他进口免费提供货物
3410	承包工程进口	对外承包工程进口物资
3422	对外承包出口	对外承包工程出口物资
3511	援助物资	国家和国际组织无偿援助物资
3612	捐赠物资	华侨、我国港澳台同胞、外籍华人捐赠物资
4019	边境小额	边境小额贸易（边民互市贸易除外）
4039	对台小额	对台小额贸易
4200	驻外机构运回	我驻外机构运回旧公用物品
4239	驻外机构购进	我驻外机构境外购买运回国的公务用品
4400	来料成品退换	来料加工成品退换
4500 ★	直接退运	直接退运
4539	进口溢误卸	进口溢卸、误卸货物
4561 ★	退运货物	因质量不符、延误交货等原因退运进出境货物
4600	进料成品退换	进料成品退换
9639	海关处理货物	海关变卖处理的超期未报货物，走私违规货物
9700	后续退补税	无原始报关单的后续退、补税
9739	其他贸易	其他贸易
9800	租赁征税	租赁期一年及以上的租赁贸易货物的租金
9839	留赠转卖物品	外交机构转售境内或国际活动留赠放弃特批货
9900	其他	其他

征免性质代码表

代码	简称	全称	代码	简称	全称
101 ★	一般征税	一般征税进出口货物	502 ★	来料加工	来料加工装配和补偿贸易进口料件及出口成品
201	无偿援助	无偿援助进出口物资	503 ★	进料加工	进料加工贸易进口料件及出口成品
299 ★	其他法定	其他法定减免税进出口货物	506	边境小额	边境小额贸易进口货物
301	特定区域	特定区域进口自用物资及出口货物	510	港澳 OPA	港澳地区在内地加工的纺织品获证出口

(续表)

代码	简称	全称	代码	简称	全称
307	保税区	保税区进口自用物资	601★	中外合资	中外合资经营企业进出口货物
399	其他地区	其他执行特殊政策地区出口货物	602★	中外合作	中外合作经营企业进出口货物
401★	科教用品	大专院校及科研机构进口科教用品	603★	外资企业	外商独资企业进出口货物
403	技术改造	企业技术改造进口货物	605	勘探开发	勘探开发煤层气
406	重大项目	国家重大项目进口货物	606	海洋石油	勘探、开发海洋石油进口货物
412	基础设施	通信、港口、铁路、公路、机场建设进口设备	608	陆上石油	勘探、开发陆上石油进口货物
413	残疾人	残疾人组织和企业进出口货物	609	贷款项目	利用贷款进口货物
417	远洋渔业	远洋渔业自捕水产品	611	贷款中标	国际金融组织贷款、外国政府贷款中标机电设备零部件
418	国产化	国家定点生产小轿车和摄录机企业进口散件	789★	鼓励项目	国家鼓励发展的内外资项目进口设备
419	整车特征	构成整车特征的汽车零部件进口	799★	自有资金	外商投资额度外利用自有资金进口设备、备件、配件
420	远洋船舶	远洋船舶及设备部件	801	救灾捐赠	救灾捐赠进口物资
421	内销设备	内销远洋船用设备及关键部件	802	扶贫慈善	境外向我境内无偿捐赠用于扶贫慈善的免税进口物资
422	集成电路	集成电路生产企业进口货物	888	航材减免	经核准的航空公司进口维修用航空器材
423	膜晶显	"膜晶显"生产企业进口货物	898	国批减	免国务院特准减免税的进出口货物
499	ITA产品	非全税号信息技术产品	998	内部暂定	享受内部暂定税率的进出口货物
501★	加工设备	加工贸易外商提供的不作价进口设备	999	例外减免	例外减免税进出口货物

监管证件代码表

许可证或批文代码	许可证或批文名称	许可证或批文代码	许可证或批文名称
1★	进口许可证	L	药品进出口准许证
2	两用物项和技术进口许可证	O★	自动进口许可证(新旧机电产品)
3	两用物项和技术出口许可证	P★	固体废物进口许可证
4★	出口许可证	Q	进口药品通关单

(续表)

许可证或批文代码	许可证或批文名称	许可证或批文代码	许可证或批文名称
5	纺织品临时出口许可证	S	进出口农药登记证明
6	旧机电产品禁止进口	T	银行调运现钞进出境许可证
7★	自动进口许可证	W	麻醉药品进出口准许证
8	禁止出口商品	X	有毒化学品环境管理放行通知单
9	禁止进口商品	Y★	原产地证明
A★	入境货物通关单	Z	进口音像制品批准单或节目提取单
B★	出境货物通关单	a	请审查预核签章
D	出/入境货物通关单(毛坯钻石用)	c	内销征税联系单
E★	濒危物种允许出口证明书	e	关税配额外优惠税率进口棉花配额
F★	濒危物种允许进口证明书	s	适用ITA税率的商品用途认定证明
G	两用物项和技术出口许可证(定向)	t	关税配额证明
H	港澳OPA纺织品证明	v★	自动进口许可证(加工贸易)
I	精神药物进(出)口准许证	x	出口许可证(加工贸易)
J	金产品出口证或人总行进口批件	y	出口许可证(边境小额贸易)
K	深加工结转申请表		

用途代码表

用途代码	用途	用途代码	用途
1★	外贸自营内销	7	收保证金
2	特区内销	8	免费提供
3★	其他内销	9	作价提供
4★	企业自用	10	货样、广告品
5★	加工返销	11	其他
6	借用	13	以产顶进

常用货币代码表

货币代码	货币符号	货币名称	货币代码	货币符号	货币名称
110★	HKD	港币	113	IRR	伊朗里亚尔
116★	JPY	日本元	118	KWD	科威特第纳尔
121	MOP	澳门元	122	MYR	马来西亚林吉特
127	PKR	巴基斯坦卢比	129	PHP	菲律宾比索
132	SGD	新加坡元	136	THB	泰国铢
142★	CNY	人民币	143	TWD	台币
201	DZD	阿尔及利亚第纳尔	300★	ECU	欧洲货币单位
301	BEF	比利时法郎	302	DKK	丹麦克朗
303★	GBP	英镑			

(续表)

货币代码	货币符号	货币名称	货币代码	货币符号	货币名称
305	FRF	法国法郎	306	IEP	爱尔兰镑
307	ITL	意大利里拉	309	NLG	荷兰盾
312	ESP	西班牙比塞塔	315	ATS	奥地利先令
318	FIM	芬兰马克	326	NOK	挪威克朗
330	SEK	瑞典克朗	331	CHF	瑞士法郎
332	SUR	俄罗斯卢布	398	ASF	清算瑞士法郎
501	CAD	加拿大元	502 ★	USD	美元
601	AUD	澳大利亚元	609	NZD	新西兰元

结汇方式代码表

结汇方式代码	结汇方式名称	英文缩写	英文名称
1 ★	信汇	M/T	Mail Transfer
2 ★	电汇	T/T	Telegraphic Transfer
3 ★	票汇	D/D	Remittance by Banker's Demand Draft
4 ★	付款交单	D/P	Documents against Payment
5 ★	承兑交单	D/A	Documents against Acceptance
6 ★	信用证	L/C	Letter of Credit
7	先出后结		
8	先结后出		
9	其他		

主要国别/地区/组织代码

代码	中文名称	代码	中文名称
110 ★	中国香港地区	307	意大利
116 ★	日本	331	瑞士
121	中国澳门地区	501	加拿大
132	新加坡	502 ★	美国
133 ★	韩国	601 ★	澳大利亚
142 ★	中国	609	新西兰
303 ★	英国	701	国(地)别不详的
304 ★	德国	702	联合国及机构和国际组织
305 ★	法国	999	中性包装原产国别

附录 13　收结汇方式代码表

收结汇方式代码	收结汇方式名称	收结汇方式英文名称
1	信汇	M/T
2	电汇	T/T

（续表）

收结汇方式代码	收结汇方式名称	收结汇方式英文名称
3	票汇	D/D
4	付款交单	D/P
5	承兑交单	D/A
6	信用证	L/C
7	先出后结	
8	先结后出	
9	其他	other

Resources
参考文献

I. On-line resources
常用资源

1. 中华人民共和国商务部网站。
2. 中华人民共和国海关总署网站。
3. 阿里巴巴网站。
4. 中国企业在线。
5. 中华大黄页。
6. 中国出口商品网。
7. World Trade Organization 官方网站。
8. Business Guide to the Web。
9. 中国展览网站。
10. 中国国际展览中心集团公司网站。
11. 中国展览交易网。
12. 南京世格软件有限公司网站。
13. 中国反倾销反补贴保障措施网上图书馆。
14. Find Law International Trade Law Sources。
15. 中国法律在线。
16. 中华人民共和国对外经济法律法规汇编。
17. 中国国际货运代理协会网站。
18. 东方海外货柜航运有限公司网站 (OCCL)。
19. A.P.MOLLER-MAERSK GROUP 马士基集团网站。
20. P & O NEDLLOYD 铁行渣华网站。
21. 中国国家税务总局网站。

II. Books
参考书目

1. 谢娟娟. 国际贸易单证实务与操作 [M]. 北京：清华大学出版社，2007.
2. 郑淑媛，邹建华. 实用进出口单证 [M]. 北京：电子工业出版社，2005.
3. 耿伟. 出口贸易单证实务 [M]. 北京：首都经济贸易大学出版社，2003.
4. 余世明. 国际商务单证 [M]. 广州：暨南大学出版社，2001.
5. 周瑞琪，王小鸥，徐月芳. 国际贸易实务 [M]. 北京：对外经济贸易大学出版社，2008.
6. 姚大伟. 国际贸易单证实务 [M]. 北京：中国对外经济贸易出版社，2002.
7. 刘启萍，周树玲. 外贸英文制单 [M]. 北京：对外经济贸易大学出版社，2006.
8. 黎孝先. 国际贸易实务 [M]. 北京：对外经济贸易大学出版社，2007.
9. 郑淑媛，邹建华. 外贸单证模拟实训 [M]. 海口：南海出版公司，2003.
10. 全国国际商务单证专业培训考试办公室. 国际商务单证理论与实务 [M]. 北京：中国商务出版社，2008.
11. 易露霞. 国际贸易实务双语教程 [M]. 2 版. 北京：清华大学出版社，2010.
12. [美] 布朗奇. 国际贸易实务 [M]. 5 版. 孔雁，译. 北京：清华大学出版社，2008.
13. Edward G. Hinkelman. International Trade Documentation [M]. 3rd edition. Novato：World Trade Press，2008.
14. Thomas E. Johnson. Export/Import Procedures and Documentation [M]. 4th edition. New York：Ama. com，2002.

III. Forms Software

南京世格外贸制单软件。